THE ART OF THEFT

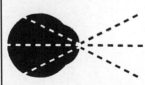

This Large Print Book carries the
Seal of Approval of N.A.V.H.

THE ART OF THEFT

SHERRY THOMAS

THORNDIKE PRESS
A part of Gale, a Cengage Company

Farmington Hills, Mich • San Francisco • New York • Waterville, Maine
Meriden, Conn • Mason, Ohio • Chicago

LIBRARY OF CONGRESS CIP DATA ON FILE.
CATALOGUING IN PUBLICATION FOR THIS BOOK
IS AVAILABLE FROM THE LIBRARY OF CONGRESS

ISBN-13: 978-1-4328-7183-3 (hardcover alk. paper)

Published in 2019 by arrangement with Berkley, an imprint of Penguin Publishing Group, a division of Penguin Random House, LLC

Printed in Mexico
1 2 3 4 5 6 7 23 22 21 20 19

To Janine Ballard,
who makes all my books better

ONE

Miss Olivia Holmes often found other women intimidating: the beautiful ones, the fashionable ones, the well-connected ones. And if they were all three at once, then she was certain to feel like a lowly grouse that had somehow wandered into an ostentation of peacocks.

The woman in front of her was handsome, rather than beautiful. She could not possibly be well-connected. And her attire would have bored Charlotte, Livia's frippery-loving sister, to sleep; even Livia, who leaned toward the austere in her tastes, thought her guest's visiting gown could use *something:* a brighter color, a more tactile texture, even a few folds and tucks to enliven the monotonous wintry blue of her skirt.

Yet Livia had never been as intimidated by a woman as she was now.

"Milk? Sugar?" she croaked. "And would

7

you care for some Madeira cake, Mrs. Openshaw?"

Mrs. Openshaw was otherwise known as Mrs. Marbleton, who was otherwise known as the late Mrs. Moriarty. And she wasn't really dead.

She inclined her head. "Thank you, Miss Holmes. Madeira cake would be delightful."

"Excellent choice," enthused Lady Holmes. "My housekeeper makes an exceptional Madeira cake."

The Holmes family used to have a cook who made good cakes, when she'd been given the proper allowance for ingredients. But that cook had left their service several years ago, and the current cook was at best an indifferent baker. And the family hadn't employed a housekeeper, who presided over a stillroom of her own, in decades — certainly never in Livia's memory.

Livia would not have bragged about any cakes from the Holmes kitchen, not when their quality, or lack thereof, could be ascertained with a single bite. But her mother was a woman of scant foresight, for whom the pleasure of boasting in this moment always outweighed the embarrassment of eating her words in the next.

Their caller, who had already dined once

8

in their household and had followed with an afternoon call, wisely set down the plate of Madeira cake Livia handed her.

Lady Holmes launched into a monologue on the importance of her family in the surrounding area (lies and exaggerations), and the advantageous match her eldest daughter had made (Livia wouldn't touch Mr. Cumberland, Henrietta's husband, with a ten-foot pole).

Then again, that might be why Livia herself approached spinsterhood at an alarming speed: There were too many men she wouldn't touch with a ten-foot pole — and she was invisible to all the rest.

Except one.

When he'd unexpectedly walked into her house five days ago, she'd been so astounded — and enraptured — that she hadn't immediately noticed that he wasn't alone.

With him had come his parents.

Her pleasure had — well, not soured exactly, but been marred by enough tension and discomfort that she'd spent the rest of the evening on edge, unable to enjoy herself. Charlotte, in telling Livia about this young man, had been frank about the dangers of his existence — a hunted family, without a fixed abode or a trusted wider community, always on the move and never safe for long.

Livia, to her credit, had not imbued that life with any romance or excitement. She'd been deeply concerned, but even in her deepest concern she had not foreseen that —

"And what are your plans for this winter, Miss Holmes?"

Livia started. When had Mrs. Marbleton silenced Lady Holmes and taken charge of the conversation? She must have done so with sufficient skill, since Lady Holmes still gazed upon her with an intense and almost fearful hope.

That naked aspiration mortified Livia. But for her own purposes, Livia counted on Lady Holmes's zeal for at least one more married daughter.

"I do very much enjoy a country Christmas," said Livia in answer to Mrs. Marbleton's question, not that she'd ever known any other kind of Christmas. "And you, ma'am, have you anything in mind for you and your family?"

This was a question she'd intended to ask anyway.

Mrs. Marbleton studied her for a minute. "I have been thinking," she said with a certain deliberateness, "of the South of France. Winter is not the most charming

10

season on this sceptred isle. The Côte d'Azur, on the other hand, has a sunny, temperate disposition even in December."

Livia yearned to visit the South of France. She didn't need to feign wistfulness as she replied, "Oh, how lovely that sounds. I can already imagine the aquamarine waters of the Mediterranean."

"We might also spend only a day or two on the coast, and the rest of our time inland," mused Mrs. Marbleton. "In Aix-en-Provence, perhaps. Or in a little hilltop village in the Alpes-Maritimes. Sitting by a roaring fire, sipping local wine, and savoring peasant stews, while looking down toward the distant sea."

Livia felt a pang of homesickness for a life she had never known. She reminded herself that she must not forget that the Marbletons had been on the run or in hiding for at least two decades. That as alluring as Mrs. Marbleton made the experience sound, it couldn't have been all sybaritic contentment. That even as they wined and dined and wallowed in the panoramic views, their pleasures were veined with fear and their lives riddled with instability.

"I daresay I don't have the courage to try French peasant fare. I'd be afraid of a frog in every pot," said Lady Holmes, laughing

11

too loudly at her own joke.

Mrs. Marbleton did not respond to that. "And you, Miss Holmes, how would you fare in the French countryside?"

"Oh, I'll be all right, ma'am. I don't pay too much mind to my suppers. If there is sunshine I can walk beneath, and a good book to read in peace and quiet, then I'll be happy."

This earned her another considering look from Mrs. Marbleton.

Not an approving look, but at least not a contemptuous one. Mrs. Marbleton had her mind quite made up about Lady Holmes, but she didn't seem to have an equally decided view concerning Livia. Yet.

Livia didn't know what to make of it.

The door opened then, and her father and the Marbleton men came in — Sir Henry had taken the gentlemen to his study to inspect his latest acquisition of Cuban cigars, an extravagance the family could ill afford.

The senior Mr. Marbleton walked with a slight limp. Whether as a result of natural grace or sheer willpower, his strides gave the impression of near nimbleness, as if the ground he traversed were uneven, rather than his gait. And unlike Sir Henry, who put on a heartiness that seemed to say, *Look how well pleased I am with myself. Could anything be amiss in my life?,* Mr. Crispin Marbleton did not bother to convey any great conviviality. But in his soft-spoken words and his occasional smiles, especially those directed at his wife and his son, Livia thought she glimpsed a warmth that he reserved for his inner circle.

The younger Mr. Marbleton exuded far greater liveliness. It really was a shame that he'd led such a peripatetic life, never staying in one place for long: Livia could easily see him as a favorite among any gathering of young people, one whose good cheer and easy demeanor made his company sought after by both gentlemen and ladies.

She looked into her teacup.

She had longed to see him again, but she hadn't been ready to meet his parents. Even his sister had been on hand, he'd told her, sitting in the servants' hall disguised as their groom, visiting with the house's meager staff.

They barely knew each other. They'd had three conversations months ago, during the Season, while he pretended to be someone else. Since then, he'd sent her a few small tokens of his regard, but had not appeared before her again until the dinner five nights

13

ago, as she sat expecting Sir Henry's newest business associate and his family.

Thank goodness her parents still had no idea what was going on, still thought of young Mr. Openshaw as an excellent but unlikely prospect for Livia. Everyone else, however, knew the true purpose of the visits: Stephen Marbleton was serious enough about Livia that his parents had no choice but to meet — and judge — her in person.

Too soon. Too soon. When she didn't even know whether she wished to maintain her affection for him or to let it wither away in his continued absence — the wiser choice, given that the life he led was not one she would have chosen for herself.

The parlor filled with small talk, carried on capably by Stephen Marbleton. But soon Lady Holmes inquired, with no preamble and even less subtlety, whether young Mr. Openshaw would care for a stroll in the garden, accompanied by her daughter. Stephen Marbleton responded with just the right amount of enthusiasm to please, but not embarrass, Livia.

But as they exited the house, properly coated and gloved against the damp, chilly day, her heart palpitated with apprehension.

No, with dread.

What if he should offer her the choice to leave behind her current existence, which she hated, for something that would not resemble anything she'd ever known?

She didn't know whether she dared to commit herself to Mr. Marbleton. She didn't know whether marriage would suit her — her sister Charlotte wasn't the only Holmes girl with deeply skeptical views on matrimony. And above all else, she didn't know — though she had an unhappy suspicion — whether a trying marriage wouldn't turn her into an exact replica of her disappointing mother.

Livia glanced back at the house. Through the rain-streaked window of the parlor her mother was just visible, gesticulating with too much force. Lady Holmes could be vain, petty, and coarse, sometimes all at once. Yet Livia still saw, on the rare occasion, the echo of the girl Lady Holmes must have been, once upon a time. Before she fell in love with Sir Henry Holmes, before she learned to her lasting bitterness that Sir Henry had never reciprocated her sentiments — and had courted her only to spite his former fiancée, Lady Amelia Drummond, by marrying another on the day originally intended for their wedding.

And the ghost of *that* girl reminded Livia

uncomfortably of herself: She too possessed a fierce pride, alongside a bottomless need for affection and a desire to give that warred constantly with the fear of rejection.

Trapped in a miserable marriage, far away from family and friends, having for companions only a philandering husband and a quartet of difficult children, Lady Holmes had succumbed to all the worst tendencies of her character and hardened into an utterly unlovely woman.

Livia stepped on the garden path. The uneven gravel poked into the thinning soles of her Wellington boots — a sensation of jabbing discomfort, much like her awareness of the unlovelier elements in her own character. She could hold a grudge — oh, how she could hold a grudge. She was angry at the world and mistrustful of people. She wanted too much — wealth, fame, wild acclaim, not to mention abject groveling from everyone who had ever slighted her, however unintentionally.

Could the young man next to her, strolling lightly on the leaf-strewn garden path, know all that? Or was he under the illusion that she was someone whose gratitude at being rescued would ensure that she would remain a happy, pliant partner for the rest of her life?

"I think we fear the same thing," he said softly. "That you would choose me — and someday regret your choice."

She halted midstep. Their eyes met; his were clear, but with a trace of melancholy. For a fraction of a moment it hurt that he had fears — that his feelings for her hadn't inspired an invulnerable courage, blind to all obstacles. And then relief inundated her, so much so that her heart beat wildly and her fingertips tingled, as if they were recovering sensation after being chilled to the bone.

"I mistrust myself," she said, resuming her progress. "I'm not happy here, and there's a chance I'll bring that unhappiness with me wherever I go. I'd be concerned to be asked to make a home for anyone."

"Some people are like desert plants, needing only a bit of condensate and perhaps a rainstorm every few years. The rest of us require decent soil and a reasonable climate. It is no fault of yours not to have thrived at the edge of a desert. Your eldest sister married a stupid man at the earliest opportunity to get away. Your younger sister chose to shed her respectability rather than to remain under your father's thumb."

Charlotte would have preferred to overthrow their father's control while *keeping* that respectability, but Livia understood his argument. "They are women of strength. I would label Henrietta a brute, but brutes know what they want and they care not what impediments stand in their path. And while Charlotte is no brute, she is both ruthless and resilient.

"More than anything else I envy her that resilience. She goes around if she cannot go through — and a cup of tea and a slice of cake seem to be all she needs to keep herself even-keeled. But I will work myself into a state. I will teeter between desperate hope and black despair. And I fear that I will not bend but simply break, should life become too heavy to bear."

He sighed. The sound conveyed no impatience, only a deep wistfulness. "You are telling me that before you can be sure of your affections, you must be sure of yourself."

And she was so very unsure of herself.

"I will gladly attribute some of the blame to Charlotte. She has always viewed romantic love as highly perishable."

"I hold a slightly more optimistic view of romantic love. I see it not as doomed to spoilage but as prone to change. Yes, it can dwindle to nothing. Or harden into bitterness and enmity. But it can also ripen like a fine vintage, becoming something with extraordinary depth and maturity."

He spoke with confidence and conviction. Briefly her gloved hand came to rest against the topmost button of her bodice. How did it feel to hold such lovely, uplifting views — was it like having been born with wings? His views did not change her own, but she rued that her own beliefs were nowhere near as luminous.

The garden path turned — she'd been waiting for this moment, when they would be temporarily hidden from view by an arbor. She gave him a letter. "Will you drop this in the post for my sister?"

He stowed the missive inside his coat. "Of course."

His cheeks were pink with cold. He wore a beard as he had in summer, when they first met, but this beard was much shorter, the accumulation of a fortnight at most. She wondered how it would feel against her palm — and was astonished both at the direction of her thoughts and that she had lived to be twenty-seven and never had a thought like that before.

He gazed at her intently. She realized she was doing the same, sustaining an unblinking stare that made her forget everything. Hurriedly she resumed walking. A few more seconds and her mother — or worse, his — would wonder what they were doing behind the arbor.

"Will you really go to the South of France?" she asked, her voice holding steady but her pace much too fast, as if she were trying to get away from a scene of misdeed.

This was the Openshaws' farewell visit, the last time she would see him in goodness knew how long.

"I very much doubt it. Nor are we likely to spend Christmas together. Calling on others as a family — that isn't what we normally do. It has made my sister highly uneasy. She wants us to leave Britain, disperse, and disappear for a good long while."

"Oh!"

"She tries, but she doesn't yet dictate everything we do." He smiled. "I will try to remain in the country as long as possible. And I will write — long letters on everything under the sun."

He had never written before. The idea of those letters, of their compact weight in the envelope, of the decadent, luxuriant sprawl of lines, of the intimacy and escape they promised — she yearned for them.

For this substitute of his companionship.

But how long would he persist?

"Speaking of letters, Mr. Marbleton," she said, "I must tell you something about the one I asked you to post for me. It involves you and your family — and it involves fraud."

"I told Mamma I'd make her a book of pressed pansies," said Lucinda, Lord Ingram's daughter, a budding botanist who loved to potter about in gardens and hothouses.

They were in the orangery at Stern Hollow, his country estate, and she was inspecting a trough of pansies with a serious, critical eye that belied her tender years. He looked her over carefully — nowadays he was always looking his children over carefully, alert to the least signs of unhappiness. But Lucinda was a sturdy soul. And even Carlisle, shyer and more sensitive, hadn't moped too much.

Through the orangery's glass walls, he could see Carlisle by the duck pond, holding on to Miss Yarmouth's hand. The governess held a loaf of bread in her other hand and offered it frequently to Carlisle so he could tear off a piece to toss to the waterfowl.

Not long ago he'd been afraid of the honking and sometimes aggressive ducks. Lord

21

Ingram was heartened to see the boy calmly shooing off one particularly large goose when it came too close. Miss Yarmouth smiled and spoke to him, no doubt with words of praise and encouragement.

Perhaps on her own Miss Yarmouth could be too dreamy and impractical, but her gentle, undemanding presence cushioned the children against the blow of their mother's departure.

As if sensing his gaze, Miss Yarmouth glanced toward the orangery. She probably wasn't able to see him past the bank of potted orange and lemons trees lining the glass walls. But nevertheless, as if feeling abashed, she tucked a strand of hair behind her ear and, after a moment of hesitation, turned back to Carlisle.

Lord Ingram frowned. He didn't care to flatter himself, but of late, there had been something in Miss Yarmouth's demeanor to suggest that she felt more for him than the obligation owed an employer.

The lot of a governess was trying enough — she was neither a servant in the strict sense of the word nor a member of the family. To add sentiments to the mix . . .

At least he had the comfort of knowing that he'd never given her any encouragement. Indeed, never spent a moment longer with her than strictly necessary.

"Maybe not these ones," said Lucinda. "I don't think Mamma likes orange."

And these pansies were very orange.

"Does Mamma like pansies?" he asked.

He'd thought her tastes leaned more toward roses and orchids, elegant, stately flowers.

"I like pansies. Mamma said that I should do what I like — for her. So I told her I'd collect pansies and make really pretty pressed flowers. And that every time I see a pansy, I'd think of her."

He crouched down beside her and traced a thumb down her cheek. "That is thoroughly lovely of you."

"Yes," she agreed without any self-consciousness. "And when she sees how many pressed pansies I've made, she'll know I've thought so, so much about her."

A shard of pain pierced deep in his chest. This was not the life he had imagined for her when he'd first held her, tiny and swaddled, in his arms. "I'm sure Mamma will be deeply moved. And she'll treasure every one of the pressed pansies."

"I'm going to make so many that even if she loses some, she'll still have lots."

She didn't sound sad, but determined and matter-of-fact about her absent mother. But what would happen if she were to learn about the divorce? His petition had been logged with the Probate, Divorce and Admiralty Division of the High Court, but the case was unlikely to be heard before the Hilary sitting in January. Or maybe not until the Easter sitting, he was beginning to hope.

When the divorce was granted, he would need to tell his children the truth. But increasingly he worried that they might learn it first from someone other than him. His sister-in-law, the Duchess of Wycliffe, had invited his children to Eastleigh Park for Christmas, and he had accepted: The little cousins adored one another, and he couldn't deny such joy to Lucinda and Carlisle, despite the rumors they might hear, visiting an estate as large as Eastleigh Park.

The door of the orangery opened. Carlisle took a few steps inside, still holding on to Miss Yarmouth's hand. When he saw Lord Ingram he let go and rushed to him. "Papa, look at this feather I found."

"Look at it indeed." The feather was almost a foot long, perfectly clean, perfectly white, each barb neat and orderly. "A most handsome find."

"Can I give it to Mamma?"

Lord Ingram was acutely aware of Miss

Yarmouth's presence. He would much prefer never to speak of his wife again in front of an outsider, but he couldn't very well order the children's governess to absent herself every time her charges brought up their mother. "Of course you may. Do you have a place to put it?"

"On my nightstand."

More pain punctured his heart. Carlisle's nightstand was becoming crowded with small objects that he wished to pass on to his mother.

Lucinda looked up from her pansies. "Can we go to London, Papa? Mamma might be in London."

He blinked and almost demanded to know where his daughter had got that idea from. Then he remembered that last time they'd been taken to London, they had, much to their surprise and delight, met their mother.

Lady Ingram had been about to go on the run again, not from the Crown, which had promised to no longer pursue her for past misdeeds against its agents, but from Moriarty, a shadowy figure of power she had openly accused of serious crimes. Lord Ingram did not know where she had gone, but he doubted that she was waiting in London to see her children.

Carlisle's eyes lit. "Can we, Papa? Can we

please?"

Once again he was intensely aware of Miss Yarmouth. Thank God she wasn't looking at him with pity, but it was almost as bad that she regarded him in admiration.

"I don't think Mamma is in London. She has gone abroad, far away."

"But if she came back, she'd be in London first," said Lucinda, most reasonably.

"And I can give her this feather!" said Carlisle, waving the feather in the air.

"If you'd like, my lord, I can take the children back to the house," said Miss Yarmouth diffidently, trying to help.

"Thank you, but that won't be necessary, Miss Yarmouth. I am going to take them to Story Cottage. You may see to your other duties."

"Yes, my lord." Her reply sounded reluctant, but she went.

"Are you children ready for a nice long walk?"

They were. They were sturdy walkers who didn't mind a little cold. And they loved Story Cottage, which he had rehabilitated from a derelict hut to something out of the pages of a fairy tale, a tiny, immaculate house in the midst of a tiny, immaculate garden.

They stopped by the manor for a supply

of foodstuffs, then set out for the long hike to Story Cottage, at the other end of the estate. Halfway there, Lucinda asked, "So when are we going to London?"

He hadn't thought she'd forgotten, not this child. "Tomorrow."

The children exclaimed, "Tomorrow?"

"Yes, tomorrow. We are anyway expected at your aunt and uncle's place in a few days. And London is on our way. So we might as well stay a short while in London, until it's time to head to Eastleigh Park."

The children jumped up and down and hugged him tight. He buried his face in Carlisle's downy hair and did not remind them that their mother would not be there. In time they would learn that seeing her again would be an infrequent and improbable event.

And he had reasons of his own for wanting to be in London.

The next day, Miss Charlotte Holmes, who made her living as oracle to her fictional brother Sherlock, was regretting the fact that she was a far more inept oracle where her real-life sister Bernadine was concerned.

Sir Henry and Lady Holmes had four daughters. Bernadine, the second eldest, had been born closed off to the world. She was not mad or violent, but she could not look after herself, nor be made presentable in public. And because of that, her existence had been all but erased.

Charlotte, who had run away from home this past summer, had concocted a ruse and removed Bernadine from their parents' home as soon as she'd saved up enough funds from helping clients as Sherlock Holmes, consulting detective. Her small enterprise flourished thanks to Mrs. Watson, her partner and benefactress.

Charlotte also lodged with Mrs. Watson, and Bernadine seemed to like the room that had been prepared for her — it contained an entire rack of gears and spools on rods, and she loved nothing more than spinning objects. But she still wasn't feeding herself, and Charlotte could not get her to eat more than half of a small bowl of porridge.

She tried to tempt Bernadine with a slice of cake. Charlotte very much wanted to consume it herself. But alas, she must refrain from such blatant gourmandise only an hour after lunch. And even more unfortunately, this moist, buttery morsel with the gravitational pull of a major planet — to Charlotte, at least — somehow managed to repel Bernadine, who spun another spool and turned her face resolutely away.

Charlotte exhaled — and wished that she had Bernadine's distaste for cake. Not always, of course, but for brief and intense spells that made it easier to give up extra servings in times of impending Maximum Tolerable Chins.

Charlotte preferred to indulge herself perennially. Alas, her love of cake and other sweet confections sometimes conflicted with her vanity: at around 1.5 chins the shape of her face changed. But Maximum Tolerable Chins wasn't merely a matter of features; it was also the point at which her garments became restricting. And beyond that, uncomfortably tight.

She had a great many uses for her money and didn't have room in her budget for outgrowing her entire wardrobe.

Charlotte tried one last time to offer the cake to Bernadine. This final overture was also rejected.

"She's got a mind of her own, our Miss Holmes," said Rosie Banning, one of Mrs. Watson's servants, who'd been sitting with Bernadine. "Don't you think, Miss Charlotte?"

Bernadine was the eldest unmarried Miss Holmes. Since her arrival in this house, her sister had been addressed as Miss Charlotte, as befitting a younger daughter.

"A very firm mind of her own," answered Charlotte.

But the rest of the world was not privileged to know what was in, or on, Bernadine's mind. Even Charlotte could only guess ineffectually. She watched for a while as her sister tirelessly spun spool after spool. Then she took out a notebook and shook open a newspaper.

Ever since summer, she'd kept a careful track of the small notices in the papers. Moriarty's organization had disseminated keys to ciphers via small notices. She and Livia had sent coded messages to each other. She had also communicated with the Marbleton family in this manner.

But at the moment she was waiting for news from a different quarter. The small notices were thick as ants and about as legible. But she'd been at it for so long that she could spot the new ones right away, even among the dozens and dozens of coded personal messages.

There was nothing from Mr. Myron Finch, her half brother, whom she'd last seen at the end of the Season. She'd received two small-notice messages from him, one in early September, the other roughly four weeks later.

The two were identical. After decoding,

30

both read, *Dear Caesar, how fares Rome? Here in Italy all is well. 3 N N.*

The mention of Italy meant that he was in Britain. The number indicated the level of danger he was in: 3 out of 10 was the best one could hope for, if one had betrayed Moriarty. The first N signaled that he was north of London, in relative position. The second N meant that no, the message would not be followed by a more detailed letter, which Charlotte would call for at the General Post Office under a previously agreed upon alias.

But now two months had passed by without any news and Charlotte was beginning to feel uneasy about his chances. Had he been captured by Moriarty, which would indeed account for his silence? Or was it far more likely that he was on a fifty-day voyage from London to Adelaide via the continental United States, which would also explain his lack of communication?

As she was about to set aside the newspaper, a knock came on the door. It was Mr. Mears, Mrs. Watson's butler, with the latest correspondence that he had retrieved from Sherlock Holmes's private box at the General Post Office.

Charlotte and Mrs. Watson had been absent from London recently. Before they left, they had advertised Sherlock Holmes's sabbatical in the papers. During their time away, they unexpectedly handled a case at Stern Hollow, Lord Ingram's country estate. Miss Redmayne, Mrs. Watson's niece, rushed back from Paris, where she was studying medicine, to help with the investigation. And Mrs. Watson, who had seen Miss Redmayne only briefly, had wished to spend some more time with her. Soon after she helped Charlotte move Bernadine to London, she'd taken off for Paris.

Charlotte had also not been in a great hurry to resume her work: Bernadine had been moved around a great deal in a short time, and Charlotte wanted to make sure that her sister was properly settled down before she took on any tasks that might require her attention elsewhere.

So they had not made it known to the public that Sherlock Holmes was back. Therefore not many letters came for the consulting detective. But today there were a few, and she was glad to see them: She could postpone, for a little more time, the reply she owed Lord Ingram.

There should be nothing difficult about writing to him — they'd corresponded since they were children. The nature of that correspondence had changed upon his marriage, the wide-ranging, sometimes digressive discussions of their youth narrowing to concrete and immediate subjects. He wrote about his archeological digs, his children, and his other responsibilities. She gave accounts of the gatherings she attended, her minor chemical experiments, and occasionally, very occasionally, Bernadine's unhappy bowels.

Both their lives had changed dramatically in the past six months. Yet now that their correspondence had resumed, he still stuck to the same topics. She supposed she could easily tell him about her cases, Madame Gascoigne's latest foray into fine pastry, and occasionally, very occasionally, Bernadine's still tormented bowels.

But she didn't want to. And she didn't want to with a force that surprised her.

With a flick of her wrist, she sliced open the letters that had come for Sherlock Holmes.

Half were early Christmas cards, wishing the great detective and his very helpful sister the joys of the season. Two more were clearly pranks, composed by those who didn't have enough cunning or experience to make a convincing go of it.

The last letter in the stack came on stationery from the Langham Hotel.

Dear Mr. Holmes,

It has come to my attention that you are someone to whom one could appeal, if one needed important objects retrieved.

I should very much like such a retrieval. May I call on you at your earliest convenience?

Yours,

A Traveler from Distant Lands

She read the letter again, then she picked up the newspaper she'd just discarded. If she was correct in her assumptions, then this was a woman in need.

And Charlotte Holmes could use the distraction of a woman in need.

TWO

The woman in need was indeed a traveler from distant lands. It was obvious that she hailed from the Indian subcontinent — and she was exceptionally lovely.

Well, *lovely* was a lazy description. Her features were clean and sharp, her eyes large and dramatic. But more than beauty she possessed magnetism, a commanding presence that mesmerized without ever needing to be something as commonplace as pretty.

Lifting one elegant hand, she adjusted the diaphanous shawl draped around her hair. The shawl, which matched her dark green tunic and trousers, was a translucent green, embroidered with golden flowers and leaves. The hair it covered contained a few traces of grey. But her face was very nearly unlined; only her hand, with its faintly crepe-like skin, gave away her age.

"I am very sorry to hear of Mr. Holmes's misfortune," she said, her voice soft and cultured, her accent as subtle as the fragrance of a rose petal.

But Charlotte heard her disappointment.

From the moment she had walked into the parlor at 18 Upper Baker Street, and had seen that she would be received by Charlotte and Charlotte alone, that disappointment had been palpable. She'd politely listened to Charlotte's usual explanation of Sherlock Holmes's incapacity. But whereas other clients became anxious, wondering whether the consulting detective would still be able to help them, what Charlotte read on this woman's face was an absolute certainty that she had wasted her time.

"Despite his handicap," Charlotte pressed on, "my brother has helped a number of clients, many of whom are happy to provide testimonials for the services they have received. Would you like a list of names to whom you may apply for such reassurances?"

A vertical crease appeared at the center of the woman's forehead. "That will not be necessary. I thank you for your time, Miss Holmes, but I do not believe that your brother is the right person for the task I have in mind."

"I'm sorry to hear that. Are you sure, ma'am, that there is nothing we can do to convince you otherwise?"

The woman looked as if she were on the verge of another emphatic *no.* But then she glanced toward the closed door of the bedroom. "Frankly, Miss Holmes, I am not even convinced that there is indeed someone in that room."

Different clients reacted differently to news of Sherlock Holmes's incapacity, but this was the first time anyone had openly called into question the fundamental conceit of Charlotte's masquerade.

Charlotte raised a brow. Her client's tone was not adversarial — in fact, her voice remained as soft as a shower of feathers. But there was no mistaking the challenge in her claim.

"Madam, I cannot satisfy your wish in that regard. My brother cannot speak due to his injuries, and you must forgive me for not allowing clients to intrude on his privacy. So my word will have to suffice on this matter — my word, that is, and a demonstration of Sherlock's mental acuity."

"And how will this demonstration proceed, given all Mr. Holmes's infirmities?"

Despite her disinclination to use Sherlock Holmes's services, there was still a note of curiosity in her voice.

"We have built a camera obscura between

37

those two rooms, so he has observed your image as projected on his walls. And he can communicate by touch via a modified Morse code." Charlotte rose from her chair. "I will be a very short while. And when I return, I will relay my brother's deductions and you can judge to what extent he is correct."

She stayed inside for three minutes. During that time, her client did not move, nor did she take either tea or cake.

"Thank you for your patience, madam," said Charlotte, upon her return. "Or perhaps I should say, Your Highness."

The woman had not been relaxed in her demeanor — no one who came to these premises for help was. But now she tensed, and Charlotte was put into mind of an eagle about to take flight. But to flee or to hunt?

"Not every Indian woman in London is a maharani, Miss Holmes." Her voice was still soft, as soft as a velvet glove around a hand that had just drawn a sword.

"Indeed not. The last one I came across was an indigent widow of a British soldier, trying to gather enough funds to go home. But you wrote from the Langham and expressly labeled yourself *a Traveler from Distant Lands.*

"Upon seeing your note my brother recalled reading in the papers that a princely delegation from India had landed in the Langham last week. After he said that, I found another article concerning said delegation's reception at Windsor Castle two days ago, in which it was mentioned that Her Majesty the queen was particularly gracious to the Maharani of Ajmer, holding a conversation with the latter lasting nearly three quarters of an hour."

The maharani's face shuttered. She now regarded Charlotte as if she, too, had drawn her weapons.

Charlotte reached for her teacup. "Madam, clients do not choose to consult Sherlock Holmes if they can seek help closer to home. As an establishment of last resort, we take our role seriously and would never needlessly expose anyone's difficulties."

"Needlessly?" murmured the maharani. "So if you believe it needed, you will set aside this veneer of confidentiality."

"Indeed. We have done so twice. The first time to prevent the possibility of further physical harm to a client; the second time when we found out that a client had come to us under fraudulent pretenses — and that there were lives at stake. Given the circumstances and the stakes, we are at ease with the choices we have made."

The maharani was silent.

"You may or may not wish to confide in us. But if you are being blackmailed and hope to extract the incriminating evidence rather than continue to dance to the tune of your extortionist, we will be happy to offer our assistance."

The maharani, too, reached for her teacup. She stirred its contents delicately, then set it down again. "As I do not intend to further pursue Mr. Holmes's assistance, I will make no comments on his deductions. I wish him the best of luck and health. You, too, Miss Holmes."

This had not happened before, that a client would leave a meeting without engaging Sherlock Holmes's services. But Charlotte had not expected a different outcome. "In that case, let me ring for Mr. Hudson to show you out. And you need not worry about the consultation fee, madam. Consider it waived."

"No need on either account," said the maharani, rising. "I will show myself out and pay the consultation fee."

Charlotte also rose. "Good day, madam."

"Good day, Miss Holmes." A trace of a smile briefly animated her lips. "And I must say, I have seen no evidence that it was this brother of yours and not you yourself, Miss

40

Holmes, who made these so-called deductions."

Charlotte inclined her head. "If I am so good as to pass for the great consulting detective, then you, madam, are no worse off for having seen only me."

In her luxuriantly appointed town coach, Mrs. Watson sighed, supremely pleased with her Parisian interlude.

Penelope's friends had crowded around her. They had told her about their lives, sought her advice on matters ranging from fashion to professional choices, and invited her and Penelope to future summer holidays in Biarritz and winter idylls on the Côte d'Azur.

Not to mention . . .

Mrs. Watson grinned to herself, remembering the lavish compliments from the brother of one of Penelope's classmates — and the parting note another classmate's youngish aunt had pressed into her hand.

But now that was behind her. And she was glad to drive through the rain-soaked streets of London, toward her lovely and comfortable home, toward further adventures of Watson and Holmes.

Yes, she thought. She *had* made the right choices in life, to have arrived at this point.

Even if some of those choices had been deeply painful . . .

The coach stopped before her house, and Mr. Mears was on the pavement almost instantly, to open the carriage door himself.

"Welcome back, ma'am. How was Miss Redmayne?"

She smiled in sincere pleasure. "More grown-up every time I see her — and more wonderful. How are you, my dear Mr. Mears?"

Before Mr. Mears could answer, a raspy voice exclaimed, "Why, Mrs. Watson! I heard you visited Paris!"

The voice belonged to Mrs. Watson's neighbor Mrs. Raleigh, an elderly widow whose husband had done rather well as a captain of merchant ships. Mrs. Raleigh was, in other words, a thoroughly respectable woman, unlike Mrs. Watson, whose respectability was more than a little suspect.

"Indeed, I have only just returned from the City of Light. How do you do, Mrs. Raleigh?"

Mrs. Watson made sure that she never misrepresented herself to other women, especially those on the other side of the respectability divide. Therefore Mrs. Raleigh had never invited Mrs. Watson to call on her at home. And once, when her widower brother had visited and beamed too eagerly at Mrs. Watson, she'd yanked him away so hard the two siblings had nearly fallen in a heap.

But on her own Mrs. Raleigh was a little bolder and enjoyed speaking to Mrs. Watson on the pavement, in broad daylight, secure in the knowledge that if anyone saw her conversing with a former actress, she could always blame the actress for being too familiar.

Mrs. Watson had never minded. Especially in those years when she had been a widow raising a child and her life consisted of very little excitement, it had amused her to be a source of frisson to the Mrs. Raleighs of the world, an adventure in and of herself.

They chatted about this and that while Mr. Mears and Mr. Lawson, her groom and coachman, unloaded her luggage. Then Mr. Lawson drove off and Mrs. Watson was about to take leave of Mrs. Raleigh when a passing carriage slowed — then stopped altogether a little farther down.

This in itself wasn't worthy of notice. They were near an entrance to Regent's Park, and those living too far to come on foot were often dropped off for their daily constitutional. But no one alit.

Mrs. Watson let Mrs. Raleigh finish speaking then excused herself. As soon as she was inside her house she slipped to the dining room, which was on the ground floor, facing the park. The carriage remained in place for at least a quarter of an hour before it finally left.

No passenger had ever come out, and none had climbed in.

Her mood lost some of its buoyancy. Her house had been under watch before, the surveillance conducted by minions of Moriarty.

At the end of the Stern Hollow investigation, that name, hitherto known to few and spoken only in whispers, was abruptly thrust into the bright glare of publicity. Given that development, and given Moriarty's general preference for operating in the shadows, Mrs. Watson had rather thought that they'd go a while without dealing with those minions again.

The front door opened once more, startling her, but it was only Miss Charlotte Holmes walking in, clad in a rather somber tailor-made jacket-and-skirt set.

"My dear!" This was the longest time they'd spent apart since they first met during the summer. "Have you been well?"

They exchanged their latest news as they walked upstairs to the afternoon parlor.

Rather than bringing up the carriage that had stayed in place too long, Mrs. Watson rang for tea. She didn't want to spoil the warm mood with the specter of Moriarty. Instead she presented Miss Charlotte with a limited selection of miniature confections that she and Penelope had chosen together.

"I hope you may still take one or two of these *mignardises.*"

Miss Charlotte considered the matter: The approach of Maximum Tolerable Chins was, in this household at least, treated with all the gravity of an outbreak of war. "I suppose, if I eliminate all puddings from my other meals, I may take one of these a day at tea."

Mrs. Watson exhaled, resting her palm against her heart.

"And perhaps we can resume our *canne de combat* practice. We might yet stave off Maximum Tolerable Chins, if you put me through my paces, ma'am."

Mrs. Watson chortled. Miss Charlotte was not otherwise the most eager participant in vigorous activities. Maximum Tolerable Chins might be doing her a favor, forcing her to exercise more.

They spoke of Paris. Mrs. Watson glowed again, describing the farewell banquet Penelope and her friends put on the day

45

before her departure. Part of her felt ridiculous, at her age, to take such pleasure in being popular. But a different part told her she was too old to feel shame in such harmless enjoyments: If she liked being popular then she liked being popular; what was there to berate herself about?

After a while she yawned and begged Miss Charlotte's indulgence. "Oh, dear, I don't know why traveling makes me so tired. You would think that I should be fresh as a daisy from having sat from Paris to London."

"I might have been there at London Bridge Wharf, ma'am, to welcome you back. But I had a prospective client."

"Oh, have you already advertised Sherlock Holmes's return?"

Miss Charlotte gave a firm shake of her head. "This was someone who didn't know that Sherlock Holmes is still officially on sabbatical. But her need seemed great so I agreed to see her."

Mrs. Watson exhaled in relief — she didn't think Miss Charlotte would have announced Sherlock Holmes's availability without consulting her. "I'm sure you managed to solve her problem."

"I didn't. The lady chose not to use our services."

"She — *what*?" Mrs. Watson couldn't help

the sudden rise of her voice. How could anyone, having met the marvel that was Miss Charlotte Holmes, make such a decision?

"She seemed to be in need more of a cat burglar than a consulting detective. And once she learned that the consulting detective was bedridden, she made up her mind very easily," said Miss Charlotte, sounding not only unsurprised but unaffected.

"I find myself speechless," muttered Mrs. Watson, who was nowhere near as unaffected. She felt personally insulted, in fact. Personally rebuffed.

"It had to happen at some point. And between you and me, ma'am, I am relieved not to be attempting cat burglary."

Mrs. Watson was going to ask for the identity of this foolish woman, but when Miss Charlotte reached for a *religieuse,* a choux pastry concoction, Mrs. Watson understood that her young friend was done with the subject.

And somehow, Mrs. Watson already knew the topic Miss Charlotte would broach next, even before the latter spoke. Despite the lively fire in the grate, the room suddenly felt colder.

With a sigh Miss Charlotte set the *religieuse* down again and turned her large, limpid eyes to Mrs. Watson. "By the way, ma'am, why were you looking out of the window of the dining room earlier?"

Charlotte was in Bernadine's room again when Mr. Mears came with a message. "Miss Charlotte, there is a gentleman to see you. He says his name is Wiggins."

Charlotte knew the name and had expected to hear from the gentleman, though perhaps not in person. "Please show him to the afternoon parlor."

Wiggins turned out to be a rather shabby-looking man with thinning hair and droopy whiskers — a rather good disguise. Charlotte offered him a seat. They chatted sedately about the weather — cold, dreary drizzles in London, and similar conditions where he'd just been — until the arrival of the tea tray.

Once they were alone again, Charlotte said, "You have concluded your visit with my family, Mr. Marbleton."

He had laid down a letter on the occasion table next to his chair. On the envelope was Mrs. Watson's address, written in Livia's hand.

"The rest of my family have already dispersed to Dover and Southampton, on their way out of the country."

He looked unusually grave as he spoke.

Charlotte nodded. "I thought that your family would wish to see for themselves the woman who has become unexpectedly significant to you. I take it my sister was ambivalent about meeting them."

"And they were just as ambivalent about meeting her — through no fault of hers, of course." He sighed. "I would have preferred not to have said anything to anyone for a while, but as I've told you, we cannot have secrets in our family."

Because they were hunted by Moriarty and any secrets could doom all of them.

He looked at her. "Were Miss Olivia any less unhappy where she is, I would have made myself scarce. And please don't mistake me — I do not dream of rescuing any damsel from her benighted existence."

She understood what he meant: only because her own life was so narrow and uninspiring could Livia possibly overlook the inherent danger and instability in his. "I must warn you, Mr. Marbleton. Earlier today Mrs. Watson saw a carriage stopped across the street with no one getting in or out. Perhaps this isn't the best time for you to be here."

He frowned. "Is that so? I circled the area for some time before I rang the bell. It

49

didn't seem to me that there was anyone watching either this house or 18 Upper Baker Street."

"I trust that you would recognize surveillance when you see it," said Charlotte simply.

All the same, why did he risk this visit at all?

The next minute, she scoffed at her imperceptiveness. He risked it because he wished to speak of Livia. It would not make for an enjoyable conversation with his disapproving family. Charlotte, too, believed it would be better for their feelings to dwindle into nothing, but at least she could not possibly object to hearing the latest news about her sister.

So she let him have that, the pleasure and necessity of discoursing on his beloved to a pair of sympathetic ears. Eagerly he related their meetings: The first at the Holmes house, the second when the "Openshaws" reciprocated the dinner invitation at their hotel in a nearby town, the third out on a walk, during which — bliss! — Miss Olivia agreed to let him be the first to read her Sherlock Holmes story, and the last at the Marbletons' farewell visit.

As complicated as his personal circumstances made things, his happiness was

50

uncluttered, the joy he radiated as pure and simple as that of a boy who had just met the puppy that was going to turn his childhood magical.

When Lord Ingram had been forced to admit his sentiments toward Charlotte, it had happened under police questioning. The heaviness of the occasion had been oppressive, the reluctance of his confession unleavened by any flutter of gladness.

Perhaps that was the reason their brief stint as lovers had been so easy and lighthearted, relatively speaking. He had made it clear that the liaison would take place only for reasons of strategy and safety. And since they both knew there would be no future, they had allowed themselves to enjoy the present.

An addictive pleasure, as it turned out.

She studied the glow upon Mr. Marbleton's face, his agreeable features made doubly so by the sincerity and elation of first love. Did he not realize how unlikely it was for his budding romance to blossom any further? Did he not understand that to seek permanent ties would be to place his own needs far, far above Livia's?

But that glow faded. He fell silent. When he looked at Charlotte again, it was with a gentle but deep-seated melancholy. "She

51

was relieved that I didn't propose to her."

"Good. I should think less of you if you did."

"So would I." He sighed, then smiled beatifically. "But let's speak of happier things. I, for one, am delighted that I will see Miss Olivia again within days."

"Oh, are you not also departing these shores?"

"Yes, yes, but I have convinced my family to let me remain here a little longer. Which" — he lifted the letter from Livia and proffered it with theatrical flair — "brings me to the purpose of my call. Miss Olivia Holmes, I have come to realize, has a devious mind. And rather breathtaking audacity."

Livia had long struggled with the sense of worthlessness that their parents had, carelessly or intentionally, instilled in her. Charlotte, on the other hand, never doubted that she could be both bold and clever — she needed only to see past her own doubts. "What does she have in mind?"

"She would very much like for you forge a letter, purportedly from my mother — Mrs. Openshaw, that is — inviting her to spend Christmas with the Openshaw family," declared Mr. Marbleton, clearly relishing every word. "She reasons that Sir Henry and Lady Holmes, the latter especially, are desperate enough to marry her off that they would seize any opportunity to thrust her into the company of an eligible young man.

"Given that the Holmeses and the Openshaws haven't known one another very long, Lady Holmes would have accompanied Miss Olivia — under different circumstances. I understand that an attractive widow recently took up residence in the village and that Lady Holmes is intent that no friendship should develop between Sir Henry and this newcomer. Therefore there is no moment like the present for Miss Livia to make a bid for temporary freedom."

Charlotte nodded. Lady Holmes tended to be riled by the presence of good-looking, experienced women nearby, because her husband almost invariably sniffed at their skirts — and sometimes managed to get under those skirts. Another woman, faced with Sir Henry's incurable wondering eye, would have resigned herself to the inevitable and concentrated her efforts on her one remaining eligible daughter. But Lady Holmes was ruled by her reactions, and she reacted with far more rancor and bile to her husband's disrespect than anything Livia had or hadn't done.

"I already spoke to my family," continued Mr. Marbleton, "and they are amenable,

53

since Miss Olivia's goal is to spend time not with us, but with you. She believes that once you have dispatched the letter, you can send Mrs. Watson in disguise to retrieve her from home, as a chaperone from Mrs. Openshaw. And she hopes that once she leaves home, she will be able to stay with you until mid-January."

Charlotte smiled. "This is an excellent plan. And has every chance of success."

"I am counting on it."

"Does your family know that she is the reason you're delaying your departure from Britain?"

"Of course. No secrets, remember? I even begged my mother to write the letter herself, but she refused."

"Hardly surprising."

After all, their goal was to dissuade him from this courtship, not to make it easier for him to see Livia.

He grinned, undaunted. He was young, his family — with their kind but firm op-position — had left the country, and he was about to see the object of his affections again. He would probably still grin even if he stepped out of Mrs. Watson's house and was drenched by the splash from a speeding carriage. "Anyway, Miss Olivia has passed along a short note that my mother wrote to

Lady Holmes. She also composed the missive that she wants you to copy."

Charlotte at last opened the envelope. There was a letter from Livia, confirming what Mr. Marbleton had said. There was the handwriting sample. And there was the text to be forged.

She handed the last to Mr. Marbleton. "Does the tone strike you as sufficiently similar to your mother's?"

Mr. Marbleton glanced down. "Ah, I see what you mean. It lacks a certain imperiousness. May I make some changes?"

She showed him to the desk at the window, where he proceeded to redraft the note, deleting any words or phrases that conveyed any measure of deference.

"Is my sister overawed by Mrs. Marbleton?" Charlotte asked mildly.

Livia had always been easily intimidated by authoritative women — perhaps from having lived in the shadow of their high-handed eldest sister, Henrietta. But Henrietta was nothing and no one next to Mrs. Marbleton.

"At the present, yes." Mr. Marbleton thought for a moment. "But if I have to worry about her getting along with anyone in the family, it would be my sister."

"She did say to me that she didn't think

Miss Olivia would last a week in the kind of life you lead."

"That would be an exaggeration. We've had many uneventful weeks."

And the rest? Charlotte thought but didn't ask.

"Frances means well, but she can be overbearing at times." He shook his head. "But Miss Olivia need not worry about Frances. Now that she's left the country, chances are slim that they will see each other again, let alone —"

He shrugged.

Let alone become related?

She changed the subject. This was something Livia had taught her. *When you don't know what to say, or if you aren't sure you won't say something wrong, start a different topic.* "When did you and your family call on mine to take your leave?"

"Yesterday evening." He seemed glad to move away from the impossibility of any real future with Livia.

"In that case it wouldn't seem overly hasty for a letter purportedly from Mrs. Openshaw to reach my parents tomorrow, on the evening post."

As if Mrs. Openshaw, waking up on her second morning in London, had the idea drop into her head and decided to give in to her impulse.

"Excellent!" enthused Mr. Marbleton. "Will you perform the forgery yourself?"

The front bell rang. They both looked up, Mr. Marbleton with a trace of alarm in his eyes. Charlotte rose and moved to the parlor's door and listened as Mr. Mears spoke to the caller below.

Then she returned to her seat, took a deep breath, and said, "No, Mr. Marbleton, I will not forge the letter myself."

Even before Mr. Mears announced him, Lord Ingram's gaze already fell on Holmes.

She looked up, and Lord Ingram could almost swear that she smiled at him with her eyes. His heart skipped a beat. But the next moment her expression assumed the same slight aloofness she had worn years ago as she regarded the artifacts he had unearthed from the ruins of a Roman villa on his uncle's property — as if they were mere curiosities, and not precious keys to a long-lost era.

She rose. "My lord, how do you do?"

"Miss Charlotte."

The man in the blue padded chair across from hers also rose. Lord Ingram regarded him for a moment. "Ah. Mr. Marbleton, is it not?"

They had never met, but Lord Ingram had seen Stephen Marbleton, both in person, if rather briefly, and in a number of photographs. In his current disguise Mr. Marbleton didn't look very much like himself, but Lord Ingram couldn't think of that many men who would call on Holmes not at 18 Upper Baker Street, but at Mrs. Watson's house.

The two men shook hands. Lord Ingram thanked Mr. Marbleton for the help he had given Holmes, when she was working to clear Lord Ingram's name.

"You are most welcome. But as Miss Charlotte would tell you, my motives were somewhat impure."

"I have learned not to disdain impure motives," said Lord Ingram. "Impure motives can still be excellent and admirable."

Mr. Marbleton laughed. "Thank you, my lord. I came to give a message to Miss Charlotte. Having done so, I will see myself out."

"Not so fast, Mr. Marbleton," said Mrs. Watson, walking in. "Nobody leaves my house without a good chat with me."

Mr. Marbleton exclaimed with pleasure. "My dear Mrs. Watson! Of course I shall not leave now that you are here."

Mrs. Watson radiated such warmth and goodwill, it was difficult not to exclaim with pleasure in her company: One felt seen and understood. Whereas in Holmes's company, one felt seen through and analyzed.

More tea was brought in, along with a plate of French *mignardises,* for which Mr. Marbleton happily found room in his stomach. Holmes, who abstained, gave him a look of wistful envy.

Mr. Marbleton, alternating between bites of a mille-feuille and an even prettier confection Lord Ingram couldn't name, told Mrs. Watson of the reason for his visit.

The last time Lord Ingram had met Holmes, before she, Mrs. Watson, and Miss Bernadine had quit the cottage near his estate in Derbyshire, she'd told him about the hesitant courtship between her sister and the man who was very possibly Moriarty's son. But it astonished him no less to hear that there had been a formal visit — albeit under false pretenses — from the Marbletons to the Holmeses.

Presently Mr. Marbleton came to the conclusion to his recital. "Miss Charlotte said she wouldn't be doing the forgery herself. And then you came, my lord."

"Lord Ingram is a far superior counterfeiter of handwriting," said Holmes. "When he is here, I need not expose my mediocrity."

"No wonder you were delighted to see me," said Lord Ingram, hoping he didn't sound openly disappointed. In anyone else, such a subtle smile might mean nothing. But on Holmes, that almost qualified for a surge of happiness.

All because she needed a forger and he happened to walk in?

"Miss Holmes, do please show Lord Ingram to the study, so that he may start on the letter," said Mrs. Watson. "And you, Mr. Marbleton, let's hear all about your visits to Miss Olivia Holmes in far greater detail."

Mr. Marbleton, given the opportunity to expound upon his courtship, looked like a child about to go on his first journey to the seaside. The look Holmes cast him was half-sympathy, half-resignation.

She rose and led Lord Ingram to a room in the house that he'd never visited — the late Dr. Watson's study, judging by the presence on the shelves of *Gray's Anatomy, British Pharmacopoeia,* treatises on tropical diseases, and at least a dozen years' worth of *The Lancet* in bound volumes.

She lit the wall sconces. The light made her hair a richer gold. That hair, shorn for her role as Sherrinford Holmes when she'd investigated the case at Stern Hollow, was still short, barely reaching her nape and just beginning to curl. "Would you mind if I stayed here? Mr. Marbleton might enjoy the recitation of his courtship more without my dampening presence."

His heart skidded. She could wait anywhere in the house, if her goal was merely not to be in the afternoon parlor while Mr. Marbleton waxed poetic about his beloved. So . . . she *was* happy to see him then?

"By all means," he said.

A large desk had been set against a wall. Next to the desk, a chair stood facing away from the wall. She sat down in this chair. He took the chair before the desk, several feet of diagonal distance separating them.

He spread open the handwriting sample.

What were the height and width of the individual letters? Were the words packed together or strung long and loose? Did they have the bearing of proud soldiers, or were they hunched over like beggars trying to escape the attention of patrolling bobbies?

These were the questions he should be asking himself. Instead, all his attention was on Holmes. She had set one arm on the periphery of the desk, the camel-and-red plaid fabric of her dress a burst of colors at the edge of his vision. He stared harder at the handwriting sample, trying not to recall the warmth and pliancy of her skin.

Or her laughter at his rare ribald comments.

The door of the study stood open. Through it wafted Mr. Marbleton and Mrs. Watson's animated conversation from down the hall. But he thought he heard her breaths more clearly, and the slide of her hair against the high collar of her dress as she turned her face toward the window.

It took what seemed forever before he could lift a pen from the stand, and twice as long before he warmed up with some lines and squiggles across the page.

"The imitation doesn't need to be top-notch," she said. "My mother wouldn't think to check it against other instances of Mrs. Marbleton's writing in her possession, even if she remembered where she keeps them."

He nodded, pulled out his multipurpose pocketknife, and used the three-inch-long ruler to measure the heights of the a's, e's, and o's, the typical length of the ascenders and descenders, and the width of the gaps Mrs. Marbleton left between words and between letters of the same word.

The size and spacing of a person's handwriting were as characteristic of it as the specific look of each individual letter. Even if his work here wasn't required to be top-notch, it still needed to be good.

Incorporating the measurements, he drew faint lines on a piece of paper as guides to practice writing letters that resembled Mrs. Marbleton's. They had used to do this, he and Holmes, she sitting somewhere in the vicinity while he worked. But that hadn't happened in years; not since he'd met Lady Ingram, at the very least.

The familiarity of it was both comforting and unsettling.

At the end of their brief "affair" — it still shocked him that they'd been lovers — she'd asked him whether, in some indeterminate future, they and those they loved couldn't together go on a long trip abroad. He had answered emphatically in the affirmative.

Yes, I would like that.

But to what, exactly, had he said yes? And what was he to do with her — and himself — between now and that golden but distant tomorrow?

He hadn't the slightest idea. And for once, he suspected that she didn't either.

Holmes being Holmes, she remained silent and still until he'd made three copies of the letter. He pushed them across the desk to her. "What do you think?"

She examined all three, studied the sample, then examined his imitations again. "She also used a feigned script, did she not?"

"A good thing." The slight hesitancy of Mrs. Marbleton's script was echoed in his, making it a better facsimile than he'd have otherwise been able to achieve, given the short notice.

"I think this is the best," Holmes said, tapping at his third attempt.

"I agree, but we'll leave the final choice to Mr. Marbleton."

He returned the pen to its stand, put the blotting paper in the wastebasket, and began to tidy the loose papers on the desk.

"What brought you to London, Ash?" she asked suddenly.

He stilled, then arranged the papers into a neat stack.

You.

"The children wanted to come. London was where they last saw their mother — and they harbor hopes of seeing her again."

She didn't say anything.

He had wanted marriage, children, and an upstanding life. He still had the children, thank God, but a man who had salvaged his greatest treasures from the smoldering ruins of his home remained in the middle of smoldering ruins.

Down the hall, Mr. Marbleton and Mrs. Watson at last fell silent. Were they — or Mrs. Watson, at least — wondering whether too much time had passed since he and Holmes had left together?

Holmes rose. "Let's go and show these to Mr. Marbleton."

They did, walking into the afternoon parlor as Mrs. Watson was pouring a fresh cup of tea for Mr. Marbleton.

"Back so soon?" said Mrs. Watson, sounding almost disappointed. "I thought it would take you much longer."

Ah, what could he have been thinking? Of course Mrs. Watson would wish to sequester him with Holmes for as long as possible.

Mr. Marbleton made his selection from the forged letters — the same one Lord Ingram and Holmes had favored.

"Will you also address an envelope for us, my lord?" asked Holmes. "Once we have that we can post the letter for it to arrive tomorrow evening at my parents' house."

"And when do you expect to hear back?" asked Mr. Marbleton.

"The day after that. Or two days later, at the very most. At which point, Mrs. Watson, will you kindly go and fetch my sister?"

Lord Ingram expected an immediate assent from Mrs. Watson. Instead the latter was silent for a few beats, then said, smiling widely, "My dear Miss Charlotte, I believe I have a better idea."

THREE

Livia had done her calculations. If Mr. Marbleton, upon arriving in London yesterday, immediately posted her letter, it would have reached Charlotte by evening. And if Charlotte worked fast and had a letter ready to post this morning, then it might arrive late today.

How much time her parents would take to debate the matter was unpredictable. Lady Holmes might react by being either deliriously thrilled or extremely suspicious. And Sir Henry would contradict his wife's wishes, out of sheer habit and ill humor.

Of course they wouldn't consult *Livia* on the matter, but would argue between themselves and list each other's inadequacies, long, long catalogues compiled from thirtysome years of resentful partnership.

All of which meant that, even if Livia expected that their desire to marry her off would eventually prevail over other concerns, she could not begin packing. Not yet. No matter how much she wished to.

She glanced out of the window of the breakfast parlor. A fog roiled, thick and all-encompassing. The doorbell rang. She started. It was a quarter after nine, a bit early for callers.

She heard footsteps going upstairs to inform her parents. After two minutes, a maid came into the breakfast parlor. "Miss, a Mrs. Collins here to see you. She says she's Mrs. Openshaw's companion and has a message from her."

Livia stood up so fast she almost knocked over her chair. "Show her to the drawing room."

The woman in widow's weeds who walked into the drawing room was extremely respectable-looking, with salt-and-pepper hair and the somewhat papery skin of a well-preserved sixty-year-old.

"You must be Miss Holmes," she said, her accent cultured, as befitting someone who had spent significant time in the household of a duke.

Mrs. Watson.

Still, it took Livia a moment to be completely sure she was looking at the same person. Mrs. Watson, as herself, a beautiful woman of a certain age, would have been of great interest to Sir Henry. Mrs. Watson, in this role, received only a cursory glance as the latter walked in, immediately dismissed as both too old and too prim.

Lady Holmes arrived looking hastily put together — she, like Livia, rose later and later as winter deepened. Her expression conveyed both the annoyance of having been yanked from bed and a burning curiosity as to why Mrs. Openshaw, of all people, had sent a messenger. Her own companion, no less.

Mrs. Watson started talking. Livia could not hear anything except the thudding of her heart. This was not the first time Mrs. Watson had come before her parents. Mere weeks ago, she had been sent by Lord Ingram to accompany Livia on a rail journey to Stern Hollow. To be sure, Sir Henry and Lady Holmes had barely paid her any mind that day. And to be sure, she'd been a rather broad woman then, with glasses and a thick Yorkshire accent.

Still, it terrified Livia that they might realize she was the same woman.

But they didn't. And they did not take long to accede to Mrs. Openshaw's wish to squire their daughter around France, once their initial openmouthed astonishment that anyone would single Livia out for such lavish attention had faded somewhat. Mrs. Watson accompanied Livia to her room, where they packed in record time. And before she knew it, they were sitting in a rail compartment, giggling.

The trip flew by as Livia poured out all her problems to Mrs. Watson. She arrived in London beautifully cocooned in sympathy and understanding, with hope in her heart for the first time that something good might yet come of her association with Mr. Marbleton.

Her courage faltered a little when she saw Charlotte. Oh, it was still wonderful — so very wonderful — to hold Charlotte in her arms. Still wonderful to hear the calm, measured cadence of her speech. And still wonderful to be fed plates upon plates of sandwiches and French pastry; her appetite, usually weak, now roared like a furnace, and everything tasted as scrumptious as mother's milk must to a newborn.

But she couldn't help a twinge — or many — of her conscience.

Earlier she'd been either too worried about whether she would manage her escape or too busy unburdening herself to Mrs. Watson, but now that she was here, she remembered very well that Charlotte was not in favor of any development between herself and Mr. Marbleton.

She would hardly have been pleased to learn that he and his family had visited their own.

When the two sisters were alone at last in the room that had been prepared for Livia, with a lively fire, fresh notebooks on the writing desk, and narcissus bulbs blooming in a glass vase, their fragrance sweet and heady, Livia asked tentatively, "I hope you don't mind that I involved Mr. Marbleton in my scheme. Really, I meant only for him to post my letter so that it would reach you faster."

It had thrilled her to learn that he'd taken the trouble to call in person to deliver her request. But Charlotte couldn't have been as glad to see him.

"It was difficult to begrudge Mr. Marbleton his happiness at having been involved in this task," answered Charlotte. "He was glowing. Incandescent."

Livia's cheeks warmed. It was beyond her comprehension that anyone could be delighted by *her,* but it made her feel . . . glowing. Incandescent, even. "But you must still disapprove."

"I do not approve or disapprove, Livia — it isn't my place to do so. I have concerns about the practicality of this arrangement

71

and whether you will see suitable returns for your investment of time and sentiment."

Livia sighed. "I wish I knew what to do."

Charlotte was quiet for some time, staring into the fire. And then she said, "So do we all, Livia. So do we all."

It was efficient to travel back-to-back: All Mrs. Watson needed to do the day before was to pick up her still-packed satchel, which had everything she needed for an overnight stay, and head to the railway station.

But with all that back-and-forth, she was truly tired now. In her room, with her corset cast aside, she closed the curtains and slid under the soft weight of her feather duvet. Ah, nothing like the rest that came after a job well done.

She had barely closed her eyes when an urgent knock came at her door. "Ma'am? Ma'am?"

Mr. Mears? But he never disturbed her in her hours of repose. Had she slept so long that it was already time for dinner? Her eyelids seemed firmly glued together. Only with great effort was she able to peel them apart. The small clock on her nightstand indicated that only twenty minutes had passed since she laid down.

"Yes?" she croaked.

"Her Highness the Maharani of Ajmer wishes to see you, ma'am."

Mrs. Watson bolted upright. No, she must have heard wrong. The Maharani of Ajmer had not come to call. How did she even know where Mrs. Watson lived? And why would she, after all these years?

"Ma'am, are you at home to her?"

Mrs. Watson leaped off her bed, nearly knocking her shoulder into a bedpost, and shoved her arms into the sleeves of her dressing gown. She was still tying the sash when she opened the door. "Are you *sure* it's her?"

Mr. Mears looked only a little less stunned than she felt. "It's her," he said in a whisper.

When she didn't say anything else — she couldn't — he asked quietly, "Shall I say that you are not at home?"

She grimaced. "No, no, please show her to the morning parlor."

Mr. Mears hesitated. "Yes, ma'am."

Mrs. Watson grimaced again. "But before you do that, first send the Bannings to me."

In her daily life, Mrs. Watson was perfectly capable of seeing to her own toilette. But this was not daily life. She was a woman of more than half a century, roused abruptly

73

from a heavy slumber, her face pillow-creased, her hair askew, and she needed to look her very best since her wedding day.

Which, of course, took longer than she expected, as she agonized over a choice of dresses.

"Ma'am, you look good in all of them!" said Polly Banning.

Yes, she knew that. But which one made her appear closest to her twenty-five-year-old self?

A look in the mirror disabused her of such aspirations. The lines around her eyes, the slackness in her lower cheeks, the deep grooves extending down from the sides of her nose — no frock, however comely, could strip half a lifetime from her face.

She exhaled, thanked her maids, and marched down to meet her past.

But her footsteps slowed as she neared the morning parlor. What if — what if she walked in and it was as if nothing had happened and no time at all had passed? What if they rushed into each other's arms? What if they held on tight and sobbed incoherent apologies?

Would that be so terrible?

She bit her lower lip and pushed open the door.

The afternoon parlor was the cozy, com-

74

fortable spot where she took tea and met her friends. The morning parlor, in contrast, was where she'd received Miss Charlotte, the first time the latter came to call. It was what would be deemed a proper drawing room, its walls covered by dark blue silk with tracings of silver. A large landscape surmounted the fireplace. And portraits of her late husband's ancestors — all conveniently dead before he decided he wished to marry a former music hall performer — declared that this was the sort of home where residents had ancestors who had the means and the leisure to commemorate themselves in oil on canvas.

Generations of respectability, in other words.

She'd always enjoyed the irony. But suddenly she wondered whether the maharani thought the portraits pretentious. She might even believe that Mrs. Watson had acquired them wholesale somewhere.

Mrs. Watson walked in, scarcely able to feel the floor beneath her feet. Her caller stood with her back to the room, looking at the street below. She was dressed in a white, long-sleeved blouse cut close to the body, a white floor-sweeping skirt, and a diaphanous long white shawl that seemed to wrap all the way around her, draping her as if in a nimbus of mist.

Mrs. Watson's heart pounded wildly. From the back, the maharani looked exactly the same. Exactly.

The woman turned around. Mrs. Watson blinked. Had the maharani sent a terribly severe-looking aunt in her place?

The next moment she recognized those remarkable eyes. But it was as if the same bouquet of flowers was now encased in a block of ice, in which case, it was not the bouquet one noticed, but the ice.

There would be no embrace, no tears of either joy or sorrow.

Mrs. Watson steeled herself and curtsied. "Your Highness."

The maharani inclined her stately head.

Mr. Mears brought in the tea tray and left. The two women remained standing. How imposing the maharani appeared — and how statue-like. Whereas the young woman Mrs. Watson remembered had been all softness and mobility, her eyes deep wells rather than shuttered windows.

"May I offer you a seat, Your Highness?" said Mrs. Watson.

The maharani sat down. Her motion, too, had a glacial grandeur. "I apologize for not first sending a note. The truth is I had no idea where you resided or whether you were even in London. I happened to pass before this house yesterday and see you enter."

Mrs. Watson hoped she didn't look too taken aback. "Were you in the carriage that stopped across the street for a while?"

"Yes, I was. You noticed?"

"I — chanced to look out of the window."

"And here I thought I was being unobtrusive."

Was that a note of irony in the maharani's voice? Mrs. Watson busied herself pouring tea and making offerings of French delicacies. Mr. Marbleton had finished the treats she'd brought back from Paris, but Madame Gascoigne, her cook, had made both madeleines and macarons in honor of Miss Olivia's visit.

"A very tempting selection," murmured the maharani. "Have you developed a taste for French baking?"

"It is rather that I have living with me a young woman who has a taste for all baking."

"Your . . . niece?"

How did she know about Penelope? Had she taken the trouble to find out, or was it merely something she'd overheard?

"Not at the moment. My niece is studying medicine in Paris."

"How time passes," murmured the maharani. "I thought her a child still."

"So do I, but she is nevertheless old enough to live in a different country and pursue a demanding curriculum." Despite her nerves, Mrs. Watson smiled a little at the thought of dear Penelope. "Your children, how are they?"

A shadow crossed the maharani's face, but she said calmly, "They are well. And I now have four grandchildren."

"Many congratulations," murmured Mrs. Watson, shaking her head a little. "Has it really been so long?"

Yes, long enough for her to have spent seven years as the late Duke of Wycliffe's mistress, borne his child, her darling Penelope, and then married another man and become his widow. Long enough that they had once drunk tea from cups commemorating twenty-five years of the queen's reign and now the Golden Jubilee was only months away.

The maharani stirred her tea. "Yes, it has been that long. My son rules on his own now."

Mrs. Watson thought she heard an unhappy note. Because her regency had ended and she was no longer in charge? Once upon a time Mrs. Watson would have asked outright. But now she could only approach

78

the question obliquely.

"You must be less busy now. Have you enjoyed your hours of well-deserved leisure?"

The maharani didn't answer, but asked, "What about you, Mrs. Watson? Are you also less busy these days, with your niece away?"

"I was for a while. But since then I've found some new occupations and the days are again going by rather fast."

The maharani smiled slightly. "That is fortunate indeed."

Their conversation went on, polite and stilted, until the maharani took her leave, accompanied out by a deferential Mr. Mears.

From the window Mrs. Watson watched as she climbed into her carriage. The carriage rolled away. Still Mrs. Watson remained, staring at the spot where the carriage had turned and disappeared from view.

It wasn't until someone cleared her throat that Mrs. Watson realized that Miss Charlotte had come into the morning parlor — and that she herself had never left her place at the window, even though her caller had departed half an hour ago.

"I understand the Maharani of Ajmer

called on you, ma'am," said Miss Holmes.

Mrs. Watson took a seat and made herself smile. "Yes, she did. She's an old friend. Remember when I thought someone might be watching the house? That was her. She happened to be driving by and saw me. We hadn't seen each other for many years and had completely lost touch. But she must have taken that coincidence to be a sign and decided to pay me a formal call."

Miss Holmes nodded.

In the silence that followed, Mrs. Watson felt obliged to add, "We met so long ago that I was still on the stage. She was in London at the queen's personal invitation. I think Her Majesty has very great sympathy for young women who lose their husbands, except between the maharani and the late maharaja, it had been less a loverly rapport than one of student and teacher."

Miss Holmes was quiet for some more time. Then she said, "It was not chance that brought you together again, ma'am. Or at least not blind chance. When the maharani saw you, she had just left Upper Baker Street, where she consulted Sherlock Holmes."

Mrs. Watson sat up straight. The woman who didn't engage Sherlock Holmes's services, the one who needed a cat burglar rather than an armchair detective?

"That was *her*? But why would *she* need a thief?"

"I take it then she didn't confide in you," Miss Holmes said calmly. "Did she give a purpose for her visit to London?"

"A diplomatic mission that she decided to take part in. I assumed it was because she had become accustomed to the work of ruling and her current idleness did not suit her."

"I see," said Miss Holmes.

"Do you — do you think she needs a brooch found or something of the sort?" asked Mrs. Watson.

They'd had such cases before, with clients who had lost items in their own homes. She rather desperately wanted this to be the case, that the maharani had misplaced her small kingdom's crown jewels and must discover their whereabouts.

"That is possible."

Mrs. Watson's heart sank. "But you don't think so?"

"No. I think her problem is much thornier than that."

Mrs. Watson gripped the arms of her chair. "What should we do?"

Miss Holmes's gaze was level. "Once I learned that she called here and is known to you, I was duty bound to inform you of her visit to Sherlock Holmes. But we are not obliged to do anything else. In fact, she specifically did not want help from Sherlock Holmes. Nor from you yourself — or she would have said something about it."

"But her problem —" Mrs. Watson heard herself cry.

"We cannot solve all problems under the sun," said Miss Holmes. "Only those that are entrusted to us."

Mrs. Watson nodded and forced herself to smile again. "You are right. Of course you are right."

Miss Holmes looked at her a moment, then returned the nod and left.

Seated at the desk in the study of his town house, Lord Ingram frowned. Messages had come from Mrs. Watson's house. The thank-you letter penned by Miss Olivia Holmes was wholehearted and effusive. The accompanying note from her younger sister, on the other hand, said next to nothing. Lord Ingram stared at it. How should he interpret this apparent coolness on Holmes's part?

She'd long been open in her desire to take him as her lover. Now that it had happened, were two forays to his bed enough? Were his days of being propositioned by Holmes over?

And what would he do if that was the case?

A knock came on the door, startling him. He put away Holmes's note. "Come in."

The door opened to reveal Miss Yarmouth, the children's governess.

He rose. "Is something the matter, Miss Yarmouth?"

It was not scandalously late, but late enough that the other servants had retired after dinner. And Miss Yarmouth was not in the habit of seeking him out at this time of the night.

She closed the door, something else she was not in the habit of doing. She had her reputation to consider, and on previous occasions when they'd spoken in this room, she'd always made sure to leave the door ajar, so that no one could possibly misconstrue the platonic and professional nature of their exchanges.

"My lord, may I have a word?"

He indicated the farthest chair from his desk. "Please, have a seat."

She did, her hands laced together in her lap. He had only one desk lamp on in the study and could not be entirely sure but — did she have on a new dress? Something that did not immediately declare her to be a governess?

He waited.

She shifted. "My lord, I'm not sure how to begin."

"Does it concern the children?"

"No. I mean, yes, it does, perhaps somewhat. But I — I wouldn't say it's about the children, precisely."

"Then what is it about?"

Whatever it was, he already knew he wasn't going to like it.

Miss Yarmouth looked down at the carpet. "I — I have a cousin I grew up with. Eight years ago, she emigrated to Australia. She wanted me to go with her then but I was too afraid to leave the country. She's done very well there for herself and is very enviably settled with a well-to-do husband and a large house."

He didn't say anything.

She hesitated. "And Mrs. Culver — my cousin, that is — has once again invited me to join her in Sydney. She says that there are many eligible men in the area and it's far easier for a woman like me to achieve matrimony there than in England."

She was neither old — about Holmes's age — nor unsightly, though hers was a nondescript prettiness that did not promise to last long. Had she come from a wealthier family, she might have achieved marriage by now. But she did not have that safety net of pound sterling and instead had to support herself by working. And life as a governess was not exactly rife with opportunities for meeting eligible men.

Lady Ingram had wanted to educate her children early, at three, rather than five. As a result, neither Lucinda nor Carlisle could remember life without Miss Yarmouth. She had been a constant in their lives, one that was needed more than ever in the absence of their mother.

He had already increased her wages after the events of Stern Hollow, but he did not hesitate to say, "Is there a figure that would tempt you to stay, Miss Yarmouth? Please name it."

She bit her lower lip, but when she answered, her voice was resolute. "You have always been a generous employer, my lord. But at this point in my life, having a home and a family of my own is more important than greater wages."

"I understand," he said mechanically.

"I — I don't wish to go either. I adore Miss Lucinda and Master Carlisle — they are such lovely children. But I'm not getting any younger."

"I understand," he said again, and wondered whether there was anything he could do to cushion his children from this blow.

"Unless, that is, my lord, you wish to —"

She looked up now, her eyes imploring. He stared back at her, half in incomprehension, half in . . . all too much comprehension.

Dear God, Holmes would probably have seen where this was going while Miss Yarmouth was still on the other side of the door.

Miss Yarmouth blushed furiously, but now that she'd started, her courage seemed to rise. "I know you are still married, sir. But your petition for divorce is certain to be granted. And if you'll please listen to me . . ."

"I am listening."

"I've heard what people say about you and Miss Charlotte Holmes. That you love and admire her, but can't marry her because she is no longer respectable and you must think of the children."

That had never been the reason he wouldn't marry Holmes, but he wasn't about to explain himself to Miss Yarmouth, who in any case went on without waiting for corrections. "But *I* am respectable. And the children already know me. And since you must find another mother for them, you know they will accept me. You know that their welfare is of tremendous importance to me.

"And I hope that during my years of service, you have gained some insight into my character, my lord. I am loyal, you know that. I will never betray you. And I understand that our arrangement will be one of convenience — that your heart belongs elsewhere. I will never be jealous or unpleasant. I will make this a harmonious, happy home."

Or at least that was what he thought he heard. His ears rang. And he had the sensation that he was, in fact, standing on a stage, in the middle of a play, with his partner in the scene suddenly sprouting lines she'd made up on the spot, and him having no idea what he ought to do. Or if there was anything he could do at all.

"Miss Yarmouth —"

She leaped up. "No, my lord, you mustn't think it necessary to give me an answer right away. In fact, I beg you not to. I beg you to instead take some time to think about it. Good night, my lord."

And then she was gone, leaving the door wide open in the wake of her hasty departure.

Mrs. Watson spent the evening hiding in her

room, barely touching the plate of supper Mr. Mears had brought for her. More than once she heard Miss Olivia whispering outside to her sister. She didn't need to be Sherlock Holmes to guess that Miss Olivia feared she'd exhausted herself fetching the young woman from her parents — and she felt horribly guilty for making Miss Olivia think that way.

But not enough to leave her room, put on a smile, and pretend that everything was all right.

By eleven o'clock she could stand it no more. She shrugged into her dressing gown and headed for Miss Charlotte's room. The door opened just as she raised her hand to knock.

"Please come in," said Miss Charlotte.

Miss Charlotte's mind was an orderly place; her private space, less so. Personal letters stood on their sides on the mantel, held in place by a pair of pillar candles as thick as Mrs. Watson's upper arm. The walls were papered by drawings of *canne de combat* stances. Books she'd borrowed from Mrs. Watson's collection sat on the desk and also in stacks on the floor.

Miss Charlotte lifted a pile of newspapers from her spare chair and swung a kettle into the fireplace. Mrs. Watson closed the door and, with rather heavy steps, crossed the room to take the seat Miss Charlotte had just cleared.

"I do apologize, Miss Charlotte, for intruding on you so late."

"No apologies necessary," said her young friend, putting out a plate of madeleines. "As you can see, I was expecting a visit."

Mrs. Watson laughed, both embarrassed and relieved. "I can see that indeed."

Miss Charlotte waited for her to continue.

"You were correct, my dear, in your advice that Sherlock Holmes cannot take on everyone's problems. Still, I can't help but feel that I must help the maharani, now that I know she is in need. And of course by that I mean I shall need you to participate in this mad endeavor of mine, because I can't imagine attempting it without you."

Miss Charlotte extended the plate of madeleines toward Mrs. Watson. When Mrs. Watson declined, she rose and exiled the plate to her vanity table. When she returned, she asked, "So you will go to Her Highness and tell her that you learned of her problem because you are in fact one of the animating forces behind Sherlock Holmes, consulting detective?"

Mrs. Watson nodded.

"She was already somewhat suspicious

about the existence of Sherlock Holmes. After learning of your involvement in the inner workings of our enterprise, she may very well come to the correct conclusion that Sherlock Holmes doesn't exist."

"She will not be the only one who knows. Three of the four Ashburton brothers do. Inspector Treadles does. As do the Marbletons."

"But their knowledge has either been unavoidable or gleaned on their own. We have never simply walked up to someone and confessed the matter. What makes you willing to set that precedent, ma'am?"

Mrs. Watson took a deep breath. "Would it shock you to know that we were once in love?"

Miss Charlotte's expression remained perfectly unaffected. "No."

Of course not. Mrs. Watson bit the inside of her cheek: The next confession was more difficult. "I hope you will also not be surprised that I was a mercenary soul back then."

"If by mercenary you mean that you demanded to be paid your worth, then yes, I can see that."

"I mean that I was serious about how much money I could extract from my nubile years. I adored the theater; I was a decent singer, a decent dancer, and a decent actress. But I never had it in me for theatrical greatness, to give the kind of performances that would live forever in an audience's memory.

"So from the beginning I was clear-eyed about my chances and my true goals: I wanted roles that would distinguish me from the other girls long enough to get me noticed by rich men in private boxes, men who might be looking for their next mistress.

"I had only so many exploitable years and I was determined not to waste a single day. Which meant that even though I had an occasional flirtation with a woman, I didn't cultivate them, since my time was much more profitably spent on men.

"But then I met the maharani and . . . it was love at first sight." She sighed. "Perhaps if I hadn't been so mercenary, if I'd had some real affairs by that point, I wouldn't have been so swept off my feet. But I hadn't. I was pretty enough and sought after enough that I had a choice of protectors and I never had to settle for one I didn't like. Still, all of them were business arrangements. Until I experienced what the French called the *coup de foudre* — with her."

Before she quite realized it, she'd laid a hand on her own cheek, as if she were once

91

again that young woman whose face flamed with the intensity of her own feelings. She dropped that hand rather hastily.

"You cannot imagine — even I can barely imagine, nowadays — how consumed I was. I wanted to look at her all day, listen to her all day, and hold her all day. From a blasé sophisticate I became a lovestruck cliché overnight.

"Inconceivably, she returned my feelings. She, a queen, and me, not only a commoner but a woman of very questionable morals. We spent every possible moment together and couldn't wait for doors to close before hurtling into each other's arms.

"But the day came for her to return to India. I was heartbroken, of course, but I'd always known that we were on stolen time. That she must go back to her life and me mine. And then she did the impossible: She asked me to leave with her.

"She had thought of everything. To others I would be an employee, her children's instructor in Western etiquette. But in private I would become a member of her immediate family, as well as her closest companion and confidante . . ."

She could still feel the maharani's hands gripping her forearms, and see the light burning in her eyes. *Come with me. We have*

92

our entire lives ahead of us. Let's spend them together. Let's grow old together.

The kettle trilled, yanking her out of her reverie. "What she offered me, in reality, was marriage," she said slowly, the words heavy on her tongue.

Miss Charlotte brought the hot water to the desk, made tea, and said, coolly, "The inner workings of which were never to be divulged."

Mrs. Watson shook her head. "She had a difficult enough task ruling in her son's stead. The last thing I wanted was to make her the subject of malicious rumors."

"Which meant you would have had no recourse whatsoever, should things have gone awry. I have little interest in matrimony myself, but being a man's wife does confer certain rights and powers upon a woman. And even his official mistress enjoys a number of benefits, not the least of which being the recognition of her position."

"Oh, that I knew well."

By that point in her life, she'd served as several gentlemen's official mistress.

"Then you don't need me to point out that an arrangement with a protector has certain protocols that both sides observe. And that when it's done properly, the mistress can expect economic gains, if nothing else. I assume your maharani did not offer you anything of the sort?"

"She offered me love and devotion. I don't believe it ever occurred to her to sully that with monetary compensation. And I don't blame her in the least for it. We women have always been taught that our love is the most valuable thing we can give."

"That's because sometimes a woman has nothing to give except her body and her affections. But a queen who can afford an etiquette tutor for her children should have offered more."

"And who would have told her that?"

Miss Charlotte looked at her directly. "*You,* ma'am."

Mrs. Watson laughed, even as tears stung her eyes. "I know. I know. Ridiculous, wasn't it? I'd negotiated ruthlessly with gentlemen and their solicitors for what I would receive from them. But with her, I never once broached the subject of money. I couldn't bear the possibility of disillusioning her. And I never wanted to cheapen our love with demands of pounds and rupees.

"So I could either leap headlong into this future in which I had love and no other guarantees. Or I could remain where I was, contract every penny I was to receive for my time and affections — and have no love."

She plunged her fingers into her hair. "In the end I told her no. I did not tell her the truth — only that I couldn't leave my entire life behind. I hated myself afterward. Without meaning to, I'd punished her for not being a man, for not being able to marry me or give me the stature of an official mistress."

Miss Charlotte shook her head. "You'd worked hard to be independent, ma'am. Had you left with her then, you'd have been dependent on her the rest of your life. Not to mention, you would have had to give up thoughts of children. Did you wish for children?"

"I did. I often wish I had more children."

She'd never acknowledged that Penelope was her child, but then again, judging by Miss Charlotte's utter lack of surprise, she'd known that from the very beginning.

"Then that would have been yet another sacrifice you would have had to make. It was not wrong for you to think of your own future, while considering someone else's happiness."

Mrs. Watson rubbed her palm across her forehead. "I know I was not wrong, per se. I know that if Penelope came to me with a similar dilemma today I would counsel her to think very carefully of her own needs and

95

wants. All the same, I broke the maharani's heart. I was the proverbial greedy woman for whom love was not enough."

"In the world we live in, women for whom love is enough often suffer for that belief."

Miss Charlotte was so unmoved that Mrs. Watson's heart sank. To be sure, a part of her was fiercely glad to have Miss Charlotte defend her long-ago choices so staunchly and unapologetically. But she'd said all the same things to herself and she was still here, begging Miss Charlotte to reconsider.

Perhaps her despair showed. Miss Charlotte regarded her for a moment. And though her face did not deviate from its usual custard-smooth blankness, something about her expression seemed to soften.

"I shall continue to hold the firm belief that you acted with both sense and honor in the dissolution of your affair with the maharani. But I accept that in your own estimation, you owe her a debt that must be repaid — and I will bow to your choice and join you in that endeavor."

"My dear!" Mrs. Watson sprang up, gripped Miss Charlotte's hands in her own, and laid them over her heart. "Thank you. I cannot thank you enough!"

"You need not thank me, ma'am — please do not forget that I owe you much more than you have ever owed anyone."

Mrs. Watson dropped Miss Charlotte's hands and pulled up to her full height, intending to educate her partner on how much *she* had benefitted from their association.

But Miss Charlotte was not yet finished. "I only hope that you will not regret your choice of gallantry. After all, you are no housebreaker and my sole attempt at burglary ended with me fleeing the scene so fast I almost left my shoes behind."

Miss Charlotte smiled a little at her own anecdote but her smile faded fast. "I fear we will be out of our depth in this matter. I fear that everything we learn about the maharani's problem will make it worse. And I fear that hers will, in the end, turn out to be the sort of problem that swallows anyone who dares to approach it."

Mrs. Watson shivered, forgetting what she meant to say.

"Ah, your tea has grown cold," said Miss Charlotte, as if she hadn't just warned Mrs. Watson of possibly mortal danger. "Shall I make us another pot?"

FOUR

The maharani's hotel suite was essentially a compact town house, with its own street entrance. Inside, it was decorated in the style that seemed to please hotel managers everywhere: an unobjectionable palette, solidly built furniture, and paintings that depicted scenes from classical antiquity.

Mrs. Watson stood in the parlor, next to a pot of blooming narcissus, its fragrance delicate yet heady. She remembered her lover's refusal to burn incense. *To us incense is as unremarkable as lavender water is for the English. But here, shorn of its natural surroundings, it becomes exotic. And I don't care to be thought of as exotic.*

The maharani appeared, looking outwardly composed. But Mrs. Watson sensed her surprise and puzzlement.

And, perhaps, a trace of excitement?

Mrs. Watson's heart skipped a beat.

"Please take a seat, Mrs. Watson," said the

maharani. "Shall I ring for some tea?"

"I have already ordered tea. If you will be so kind as to have your staff open the door to the hotel."

The town house also had an entrance from inside the hotel.

The maharani's brow furrowed, but she did as Mrs. Watson asked. Soon her maid returned with a hotel porter bearing a large tea tray — and Miss Charlotte, in a powder blue visiting gown trimmed with enough lace to edge a fishpond.

The maharani stared at her.

When all the servants had left, closing the door behind themselves, Miss Charlotte said, "You were correct, Your Highness, in detecting something suspect about the arrangement chez Sherlock Holmes. There is no Sherlock Holmes. There is only me, using my skills to help clients who come to see my 'brother.' And Mrs. Watson is my partner in this enterprise."

"When Miss Charlotte Holmes learned that you had called on me, she felt duty-bound to disclose that you had also visited Sherlock Holmes," said Mrs. Watson. "Perhaps it is delusional for me to think I can be of any aid to you, but I must offer my help. If you have gone so far as to seek Sherlock Holmes's ear, Your Highness, your need must be very great indeed."

The maharani said nothing.

Mrs. Watson tried to read her expression. Was she at all gladdened that Mrs. Watson had reached out? That she didn't want the maharani to be alone at a time like this? But that once-mobile face had become as expressive as a wall.

Mrs. Watson took a deep breath and went on, "Miss Charlotte told me of your misgivings concerning the confidentiality of your visit. I'm sure you are not pleased that not one but two people are now privy to it. But please keep in mind that we, too, worry about confidentiality. The truth of Sherlock Holmes is something we have never admitted to anyone not associated with our services. I hope you will take that as a token of our sincerity."

The maharani stirred her tea. "I will not waste anyone's time by saying that I am not in need, but I declined to engage Sherlock Holmes's services for a reason. I do not need murders solved; nor do I need mysterious noises in my attic explained."

"Then why did you approach Sherlock Holmes, Your Highness?" asked Miss Charlotte.

"To see whether he had other skills. When it turned out he was bedridden, that eliminated his usefulness."

"He doesn't exist," Miss Charlotte said.

"And *your* skills, Miss Charlotte, while impressive, are still of no use to me."

"I understand that you need to retrieve something that is, I assume, tightly secured."

"I don't imagine you have much experience in that regard."

Miss Charlotte was perfectly composed. "But I do. I have rifled through my father's study many times."

The maharani laughed humorlessly. "Oh, you have?"

"The principle of the matter isn't very different. One learns to find and use those hours when the house is relatively empty. One learns to quickly locate the relevant and interesting items. One even learns to get around locks and seals that a man thinks sufficient to guard his secrets from members of his family."

"Your point being?" The maharani was beginning to sound impatient.

"That Your Highness shouldn't underestimate what sneaking around her own house can teach a woman."

Miss Charlotte extracted an ivory-inlaid case from her reticule and set it on the tea table.

The maharani's expression instantly

changed. "Where — where did you get this?"

"From here, obviously."

"But how?"

"It is so much more impressive if you don't know the details, Your Highness."

Her Highness gave Miss Charlotte a look.

Miss Charlotte took a sip of her tea. "Very well. First we booked the suite of rooms next to yours. There is a connecting door between these two with no locks but a dead bolt on either side. You yourself might not have paid attention, but this morning a hotel maid came after the initial cleaning had been done and asked to be let in to get an item she left behind in the dining room."

"And the dining room is where the connecting door is."

"Correct."

The maharani glanced around the parlor. "But still, there were people here."

"Not for the entire day. After you left, someone informed your staff that there might be a gas leak — not at this esteemed establishment, naturally, but next door. Nevertheless, it was prudent for the guests to clear out for a while so that everything could be checked. Would everyone care to pile into this hackney that has already been engaged to take them to the British Museum, where the entrance is free of charge? And here's even some money for the return trip."

The maharani's lips thinned.

"I hope you will not blame your staff," Miss Charlotte went on. "After all, what reason did they have not to believe what they were told? Not to mention that they made sure the door was properly locked on their way out. But we, of course, had access to the connecting door that had been unbarred from both sides. And since the suites are laid out in an identical manner, we already knew where the safe was to be found."

"And the safe was that easy to open?" The maharani's gaze strayed to the small painting that concealed the wall safe.

Miss Charlotte's gaze, on the other hand, was affixed to the Victoria sandwich on the tea table. "Easy? I wouldn't say so. But neither was it especially difficult. It was locked with a key and not a combination, which made my task much less tedious."

The maharani raised a brow. "*Your* task?"

"This past summer we needed the services of a lock picker. Time was short so we used someone we knew. But afterward I decided to acquire those skills myself — if we needed a lock picker once, who was to say we wouldn't need one again?

"So you are right, Your Highness, in that I have very little experience retrieving anything that has been highly secured," said Miss Charlotte without any trace of smugness to her voice. "But when retrieving things that have been barely secured, I seem to do all right. Now is there anything, however secured, that Mrs. Watson and I may retrieve for you?"

The maharani fell silent again.

Miss Charlotte was often and spectacularly silent. But her silence was that of the woods and hills, a natural absence of speech. The maharani's, on the other hand, made Mrs. Watson think of the walled forts of Jaipur, a silence that watched and hid.

She had not used to be like this. The woman Mrs. Watson had loved had been keen to share her thoughts. And Mrs. Watson had marveled at the range of topics she'd read and studied about, and at the depth and accuracy of her knowledge.

Then again, she'd been a young widow who had just come into power of her own as the regent, and the world had been her oyster, her admirer, and her willing sycophant. Today she was a middle-aged woman who'd had to relinquish power — and seek help from an English stranger.

How much of her reluctance was an unwillingness to accept that help? How much because she didn't want to let Mrs. Watson see any more of her reduced circumstances?

"Very well," she said at last. "At this point, it can't hurt to have Sherlock Holmes look into the matter."

"Thank you for trusting us," said Mrs. Watson quickly. Perhaps too quickly.

"There are some letters of mine that I do not wish to come before unfriendly eyes. Earlier I was assured they were kept safe and out of the way, but recently I was informed that due to a certain unforeseen turn of events, they have arrived as part of a shipment of artwork at Château Vaudrieu."

Now that she had decided on a course of action, her tone became brisk, uninflected. But Mrs. Watson's fingertips dug into the padded arms of her chair: The woman who could have been her lifelong companion was being blackmailed.

"Have you ever heard of the place?" asked the maharani.

Mrs. Watson made an effort to exhale. "I seem to have some faint recollection that it plays host to an extravagant annual affair."

"A yuletide masquerade ball to which the

flower of French society flocks, where champagne flows like a river, caviar is strewn like bread crumbs, and fifty million francs' worth of jewelry dangle from the most beautiful women of Paris," said Miss Charlotte. "I read about it a few years ago in a magazine."

"You have a good memory, young lady," said the maharani, though the look she flicked Miss Charlotte's way contained not so much admiration as wariness. "Château Vaudrieu is tightly built and well secured. But for the ball, the gates are thrown open, and the opulence of the occasion is said to be legendary.

"That opulence, however, has a purpose. The ball is, in fact, also the night of a significant private art sale. So it is not just a gathering of Parisian Society, but also that of art connoisseurs from around the world, as well as agents for English manufacturers, American millionaires, and Persian princes — anyone looking to add to their social cachet by amassing a collection of pedigreed art.

"Everything sells — or at least that has been the case for years. I expect my secrets will remain safe until the night of the ball. But after that . . . I'm told that my letters are in the back of a Van Dyck painting. A new owner might very well want a new frame. And the moment the canvas leaves the old frame, my secrets will be exposed to the world."

Mrs. Watson wondered about the contents of the letters — and the identity of the maharani's correspondent. She and Mrs. Watson hadn't written many letters to each other. They'd spent almost the entirety of their affair in physical proximity, for one thing. For another, the maharani had wished the true nature of their relationship tightly concealed from her courtiers and servants and considered passionate love notes too risky to be kept.

Had she become less careful in the intervening years?

Miss Charlotte reached for the sugar tongs — and pulled her hand back, no doubt recalling that she had lately given up milk and sugar in her tea. "The person who acquires the painting may have no interest at all in some old letters," she pointed out.

"Except the one most interested in purchasing the piece is rumored to be Sir William Pershing. He served under the Viceroy of India and knows exactly who I am."

Miss Charlotte drank her black tea with a look of resignation. "Have you considered buying the painting yourself, Your Highness?"

The maharani made a dismissive sound. "The Van Dyck is expected to fetch in excess of twenty thousand pounds. We are not the Maharaja of Jaipur or the Nizam of Hyderabad, Miss Charlotte. We are a small kingdom of relative insignificance and few resources. Even if I were still the queen regent, I would have had trouble coming up with such a sum. And now I am no longer in charge of the treasury, it is completely beyond me to produce the funds necessary to purchase the painting outright."

"I see," said Miss Charlotte. "When is this year's ball expected to take place?"

"In little more than a fortnight."

Mrs. Watson sucked in a breath. So soon. She thought of yuletide as the twelve days after winter solstice, but this would be several days before.

"Surely you must have some other plans in place for dealing with this situation?" asked Miss Charlotte.

"I did. I didn't have enough money to buy the painting, but I still had enough to tempt a thief — or so I believed. I made a stop in France on my way to London. But those who I asked to make inquiries all returned the same report: that no thief who could be

108

relied on to do the job properly would take the job in the first place.

"And then, during the Channel crossing, I overheard some people discuss Sherlock Holmes. To be sure, they were more interested in gossiping about his client, a gentleman who was on the verge of being scapegoated for his wife's murder. At that point, I didn't have much to lose by consulting this sage. So I did. And now here we are."

Miss Charlotte nodded, as if satisfied with the maharani's account. "What else can you tell us, Your Highness, about either the château or the event?"

"Before I met Sherlock Holmes, I wrote down everything I knew, in case I decided to retain his services. I still have that document." The maharani rose — and abruptly sat down again. "Will the two of you really attempt this? It is orders of magnitude more difficult and dangerous than taking one jewel box out of my hotel safe."

Her gaze met Mrs. Watson's. Was there something other than doubt in the maharani's eyes? Was there a hint of worry, even anxiety?

A bittersweet sensation unfurled in Mrs. Watson's heart.

It was Miss Charlotte who answered, "We do not promise success. But we will do our utmost."

The maharani glanced down. The next moment she left the room and returned a minute later with an envelope, which she entrusted to Mrs. Watson. "Shall we discuss your compensation?"

"Let's discuss it after we have what you want," said Mrs. Watson, determined not to charge the maharani a single penny even then. "If you have no more information to impart, Your Highness, we must start on our work. There is very little time."

"Everything I know is in the envelope. Good luck, ladies."

Miss Charlotte rose. "I thank you for your sentiment, Your Highness. But it would help us more if we knew the reason you are being blackmailed — and the identity of your extortionist."

"I would like nothing more than to better your chances of success, Miss Holmes," said the maharani smoothly. "But I do not know the identity of the person who holds my letters — and the nature of their contents is immaterial to your task."

Miss Charlotte inclined her head. "If you say so, Your Highness."

It wasn't until they were on the pavement, waiting for her carriage to come around,

110

that Mrs. Watson gulped. "Good heavens, what have I done? And what do we do now?"

To steal an Old Master painting worth twenty thousand pounds at a crowded ball in a château she'd never visited — and in a foreign country, no less. She might as well have signed up to wipe all discolorations from the surface of the moon.

"We will get some help," said Miss Charlotte decisively. "You can speak to Lord Ingram. I will see whether we can engage Mr. Marbleton. There should be enough time left for me to go to the newspaper offices and put in a small advertisement for the morning editions."

"Engage . . . as in hiring his services?"

"He should not devote his time and expertise to our cause solely out of admiration for my sister — I would pay Lord Ingram too, but I would be wasting my time. And then we shall need to either explain to my sister why she must remain behind in London or tell her everything and bring her to France," continued Miss Charlotte.

Good gracious! Mrs. Watson had forgotten about Miss Olivia. And the poor girl had come only the day before with such happy anticipation of spending all of December with her sisters. "What — what do you propose we do?"

"I leave the decision to you, ma'am. I will abide by it, and I'm sure so will she."

Mrs. Watson's head throbbed. "But she will be so very unhappy to be left behind here."

"Life is imperfect," said Miss Charlotte, thoroughly unperturbed. "And Livia knows that as well as anyone."

Livia's second day in London did not proceed as expected. As soon as she went down for breakfast, she was informed by Mr. Mears that Charlotte and Mrs. Watson had gone out. Charlotte had left her a note, apologizing for their absence and telling Livia not to wait for them for luncheon. But she, like Mr. Mears, gave no reason for that absence except to say that it had to do with a client.

Livia felt rather bereft. She would have dearly loved to be part of what they were doing — or even just to bring up a tea tray at 18 Upper Baker Street. But since that didn't seem to be in the cards, she spent the day working on her Sherlock Holmes story.

Here, something even more unexpected happened. She thought she still had weeks of work left, but around two o'clock in the afternoon she realized that she was approaching the end of the story, that after another ten or fifteen pages in her notebook she could very well be scrawling *finis* to mark her first complete manuscript.

And then she couldn't write another word.

A nervous energy shot through her. She became so jittery she couldn't stay still. Even pacing in her room made her feel caged. She kept sitting down and standing up, and rushed over to the window every time she heard a carriage pass.

At last, late in the afternoon, Mrs. Watson returned by herself.

Livia met her coming up the stairs. "Did my sister not come back with you, ma'am? And are you quite all right after your indisposition last night?"

Mrs. Watson didn't look unwell, but she was obviously under-rested. And tense, the fine lines around her eyes etched deeper with distress. She gave Livia a game smile. "Yes, I'm all right, Miss Olivia. Miss Charlotte and I had different tasks to see to after meeting with the client. Ah, that might be her now."

And it was indeed Charlotte, coming through the front door. She gave her hat and gloves to Mr. Mears, and they all headed up to the afternoon parlor. "I have sent out signals for Mr. Marbleton," she said, once she took a seat. "Now we wait and see."

"Mr. Marbleton?" Livia exclaimed. And immediately blushed. Did Charlotte contact him for *her*?

"Yes, Mr. Marbleton. We will need him."

"For what? Surely Lord Ingram isn't in any kind of difficulty again."

"No, but I have a friend in trouble," said Mrs. Watson, her tone calm enough but her eyes plainly apprehensive. "We might have to go to France to help her."

Did this *we* include Livia? She looked from Charlotte to Mrs. Watson and back again, but neither seemed inclined to offer any clarification.

"This . . . this trip to France, is it imminent?" asked Livia, not feeling courageous enough to ask outright whether she would be part of it — or left behind.

France. How she longed to see France. To be anywhere, really, on a journey of freedom. But would she be in the way? It was one thing to bring up a tea tray to 18 Upper Baker Street, quite another to take part in an actual mission.

"It will be soon," answered Mrs. Watson. "No later than the day after tomorrow."

Again, no elucidation on what role she was

to play, if any.

Charlotte was daintily eating a potted beef sandwich. Mrs. Watson gazed into her tea, her forehead creased. Livia's deductive powers might not approach Charlotte's in scope or trenchancy, but the situation before her was hardly opaque.

Whatever they intended to accomplish in France would be difficult, very possibly dangerous. And they didn't know what to do with Livia. Charlotte must have left the decision to Mrs. Watson, given that they were under Mrs. Watson's roof and that their task concerned Mrs. Watson's friend. And Mrs. Watson was reluctant either to tell Livia to stay put or to involve her in a perilous undertaking.

"How long will this trip last?" she asked.

She could wait, if they would be gone for only a day or two.

"A good fortnight," said Charlotte. Livia's heart fell. She'd kept telling herself and anyone who would listen that she planned to stay away from home for as long as possible. But that wouldn't be wise. She shouldn't be gone for longer than two weeks, three at the very most — not if she wanted more such excursions in the future.

If she stayed behind, Charlotte and Mrs. Watson would be away for most of her visit.

On the other hand, she had very little appetite for danger and no useful skills. She didn't even have Mrs. Watson's reservoir of experience or Charlotte's nerves of steel.

"I would like to go with you," she said. "I don't know whether I'll be able to make any contributions, but I will do what I can. And I do know that I'll be much happier with you in France."

"It will be dangerous," said Charlotte.

Mrs. Watson nodded — slowly, as if she were unwilling to admit that to herself.

Livia wiped her suddenly damp palms on her skirt. "If it isn't too dangerous for you, it can't be too dangerous for me."

Charlotte took another bite of her sandwich. "It's true that we aren't speaking of life-threatening dangers. But we know very little about where we are going or what we will find when we get there. And given our relative inexperience as cat burglars, a stint in a French jail isn't out of the realm of possibility."

Livia sucked in a breath. Cat burglars?

Mrs. Watson gasped, too. "I've been fretting about the consequences to my friend if we don't succeed, but not yet the consequences to ourselves. Miss Olivia, in that case, perhaps you —"

"No!" cried Livia. "In that case, I shall be

116

that much worse off if I remained in England. I will worry until I make myself sick, especially if — especially if —"

Especially if Mr. Marbleton went with them.

Mrs. Watson looked beseechingly at Charlotte, who said only, "We will abide by your decisions, ma'am."

Livia went to Mrs. Watson, sank to her haunches, and took Mrs. Watson's hands. "Please, ma'am, I shall be extremely unhappy — not to mention tormented by the most terrible thoughts — if I were to stay behind. Please, Mrs. Watson, let me come with you."

Mrs. Watson shut her eyes tight for a moment, then she pulled Livia to her feet. "Very well, then. Let's all go together. But you must promise me, Miss Olivia, that your own safety will be your first and foremost concern."

"I promise. Thank you, ma'am!" Livia cried, smiling hugely. "Thank you! Thank you!"

Her euphoria evaporated somewhat when no one else smiled.

FIVE

The house near Portman Square had been outfitted some years ago by Lord Bancroft Ashburton, Lord Ingram's brother, when the latter thought Charlotte would accept his proposal and become his wife. Charlotte, however, hadn't learned of it until this past summer, after she'd lost her respectability. Livia, by turn, learned even later and still remained unsure that it wasn't a fable.

A house that *Charlotte* thought to be "slightly extravagant"? Charlotte, who had never met a garish color combination she didn't immediately wish to add to her own wardrobe?

Though Livia had prepared herself, the anteroom itself made her jaw drop, with its gilded mirrors and dozens of red-and-white chinoiserie plates set inside a large niche painted a brilliant shade of coral.

"It's too much! Too much!" she hissed, as soon as the maid who had opened the door

118

for them left to announce the Holmes sisters and Mrs. Watson. "How can you like this house, Charlotte? Are you sure that you are not *actually* color-blind?"

"I forgot to tell you?" said Charlotte mildly. "After you accused me of being color-blind the first few times, I performed some tests and determined that there is nothing the matter with my sight."

"But there is already so much red and coral on this side, and that is all green." Livia pointed an accusing finger at the opposite wall, behind one large gilded mirror.

"It's a nice green."

"It's a wrong green," said Livia, half shuddering.

And it was worse, so much worse, beyond the anteroom. By the time they reached the drawing room, which featured enough tassels, fringes, and flounces to outfit every bordello in London, Livia was slack-jawed with dismay. "Charlotte, this is a brothel *and* a circus."

"And I am both a woman of ill repute and a conjurer of tricks," said Charlotte. "My tastes are commensurate with my stature."

"You had the exact same tastes before you arrived at your current stature," said Lord Ingram, walking in.

"Ha!" cried Livia.

Mrs. Watson chuckled. Even Charlotte smiled slightly. They exchanged greetings and the maid brought in a large tea tray.

"Well, everyone is here," said Charlotte.

Livia glanced at her quizzically. "But I thought Mr. Marbleton would be joining us."

Or did he not get their message, after all? But the small notice from Charlotte was in the papers this morning, and he most certainly paid attention to the small notices.

"He *has* joined us," said Charlotte.

Livia looked around the room. Was there a piece of furniture large enough to hide him?

Lord Ingram looked amused. Charlotte was examining the plates of cake that the maid was placing on the table. It was Mrs. Watson whose gaze first settled on the maid.

Surely —

The maid laughed. With Stephen Marbleton's voice. But in reality he looked nothing like this woman.

"How did you know, Miss Charlotte?" he asked.

"Well, for one thing, I've never seen a female servant at this establishment before. The appearance of one now, after a number of visits, made me pay closer attention than I otherwise would. Two, I have seen you dressed as a woman before. Even though you've made greater changes to your face this time, there is still something familiar about you.

"And three, you have not been subtle about telling us who you are. Or perhaps I should say, you have not been subtle about signaling your true identity to one particular person in this party."

Livia lifted her fingers to her lips. She noticed for the first time that the pretend-maid was wearing a pendant of moonstone. The first time they met, they'd discussed, among other things, a book called *The Moonstone.* Later he had sent her a cabochon of moonstone as a present.

Mr. Marbleton smiled. He made for a winsome woman. "Shall I pour tea for everyone?"

"Please," said Lord Ingram.

Once everyone had their tea, Mrs. Watson cleared her throat. "Thank you all for coming — to help me. Because this is most certainly something *I* undertook, and I did so knowing that I could not manage it by myself. That I'd need a great deal of help. Mr. Marbleton, shall I explain something of the circumstances?"

"Lord Ingram has kindly informed me of the general contours of the situation. So if everyone else has been filled in . . ."

He looked at Livia. She gave him a small nod, feeling a surge of warmth in her chest.

"In that case," said Mrs. Watson, "here is the summary of our task: to liberate certain letters from the back of a portrait by Van Dyck, currently held at Château Vaudrieu outside of Paris, and which will find itself under new ownership in a fortnight, as part of the proceedings at the château's annual masquerade ball.

"Miss Charlotte Holmes visited the offices of two magazines today and was fortunate enough to be permitted into their archives without a prior appointment. Will you care to tell us what you have learned, Miss Charlotte?"

"I couldn't find out very much, except that the château changed hands about fifteen years ago. The current owner, a Monsieur Albrecht, is said to be a Swiss manufacturer. His mistress, Madame Desrosiers, lives at Château Vaudrieu and organizes the ball. And her brother arranges for these private art sales."

"Thank you, Miss Holmes." Mrs. Watson turned to Lord Ingram. "My lord, after we met yesterday, you made some inquiries, too. Did you learn anything?"

"I did. Given that we have scant time and

much to do, we need someone in France immediately. Under different circumstances I would have already crossed the Channel, but now I cannot move as easily. I will head to Paris after I escort my children to my eldest brother's estate, but until then, I must appoint someone to act on my behalf.

"Fortunately, I have an ally who happens to be passing through France. My cable caught him in Paris, and he has since learned that there will be a reception ahead of the ball for those wishing to submit private bids to view the artworks. He has also found out that when the château was purchased by M. Albrecht, the architect firm of Balzac & Girault redesigned portions of the interior. My ally will pay the firm a visit, in the hope of securing the architectural plans."

"Your ally sounds inordinately competent — and proficient," said Mrs. Watson. "We are not speaking of Lord Remington, are we?"

Lord Remington, Lord Ingram's second-eldest brother, had left for India not long ago.

"No, not my brother, but someone I trust."

"If he can find the architectural plans, it

would be of great help to us," said Charlotte.

"If they are to be found, he will find them," answered Lord Ingram. "In addition to my ally, I also cabled the French branch of my godfather's family."

The French branch of that family was one of the wealthiest and most powerful in the country.

"I asked for help with invitations to the masquerade ball. I have been assured invitations will be forthcoming. And a house will be waiting in Paris, when we get there."

"But that's marvelous," exclaimed Mrs. Watson, "especially the invitations."

"You seem to have everything well in hand. Are you sure you will need my services?" asked Mr. Marbleton with a grin.

"We have nothing in hand," said Charlotte. "We have no plan on how to go about this and cannot formulate one until we see and know more. Which is why, though I cannot tell you what we might need you to do, Mr. Marbleton, I prefer to have you with us. If nothing else, think of it as a sponsored trip to Paris."

"Why not?" Mr. Marbleton turned to Miss Livia. "If nothing else, may I squire you about Paris? Perhaps for a walk in the Jardin des Tuileries, if weather permits?"

Livia thought she would stammer, her heart was beating so fast. But her voice sounded even, as if gentlemen escorting her around foreign capitals was a regular occurrence. "I should like that."

"And the Louvre, too?"

"If you won't be too busy."

"You might both be too busy," said Charlotte. "But you will come with us, Mr. Marbleton?"

He smiled at Livia. "That would be my great pleasure and privilege."

You are a romantic, Holmes had told Lord Ingram shortly before the troubles at Stern Hollow.

He'd protested that he hadn't been a romantic in a long time.

She'd corrected him. *Being disappointed in love does not change a man's fundamental nature. You are more cautious, you wonder whether you can ever make a good choice, but you do not question the validity of romantic love in and of itself.*

She was right. For someone whose own love story had ended catastrophically, he was nowhere as cynical as he should be. He felt no scorn at all toward Mr. Marbleton's undisguised sentiments, only concern for the obstacles he and Miss Olivia faced. He wanted to shield them from everything that could damage or pollute their affections.

From life itself.

He could see in Mrs. Watson's indulgent and slightly anxious expression that she felt the same. Holmes, on the other hand, was almost aggressive in her neutrality.

He felt a pang in his chest. What did a man who still believed deeply in "the validity of romantic love in and of itself" do with a woman who believed deeply otherwise?

The company was dispersing. He must first take his children to his brother's place, but everyone else would take the tidal express service from Victoria Station that evening. Mr. Marbleton slipped out first, via a service door. Lord Ingram accompanied the ladies to their waiting carriage in front, but Holmes surprised him by seeing them off and then asking if he would take her home in a hackney.

"Yes, of course," he said, his heart thudding.

She was wrapped in a midnight blue mantle with prominent streaks of light green. Pedestrians on both sides of the street craned their necks to get a better look at it. Years ago, the sight of this very garment had made him ask why she chose to array herself in such a cacophony of colors.

His irritation had been building with regard to her wardrobe. She possessed a fine figure and eyes that could fetch a man from across a ballroom. Why did a woman with such obvious assets — and a frightfully perceptive mind to boot — feel the need to wear garish and frequently over-festooned clothes?

She'd looked at him for a minute and said, *Unbroken stretches of a single color or texture, especially in clothes and interiors, over-whelmed me as a child. I had to close my eyes to ward off headaches. I'm no longer af-fected to the same extent, but I still have an instinctive preference for more colors and textures over fewer.*

Until then he had thought of her clothes only in terms of the unnecessary attention they'd precipitated — he himself greatly disliked unnecessary attention. It had never occurred to him that those multitudes of hues and trimmings could serve any purpose besides making both men and women whip around for a closer study.

But he'd been arrogant and self-righteous in those days. Rather than feeling ashamed for having been so wrong in his assumptions, he had instead become annoyed by just how strange she was. And by the fact that he was and would continue to be friends with a girl so far from normality she'd need a sextant and an ocean voyage to find it.

"You still have this mantle," he said softly.

"Livia brought it from home. She hates it, so she knows it must be one of my favorites."

"It's striking."

"You hated it, too."

Not so much anymore.

A hackney arrived. He handed her up and gave Mrs. Watson's address.

"What do you think of the situation with the maharani?" she asked, once they were on their way.

This was the discussion he'd expected; still he felt a sharp kick of disappointment. Already he wondered whether their days of greater intimacy were behind them; her demeanor, all coolness and efficiency, certainly gave him no hope otherwise. He sighed inwardly, feeling like a child separated from an avalanche of sweets by the largest, thickest display window in the entire world.

"I wish we knew what the maharani is being blackmailed for — and who is her blackmailer," he said. "That would shed a great deal of light on the situation."

"I posed those exact questions to the

maharani and received no answers," she said. Then, after a pause, "Mrs. Watson actually named her?"

"Not initially. But I told Mrs. Watson that I must know the exact identity of this friend of hers." A man became a little more suspicious after his wife turned out to be Moriarty's agent.

"And did knowing her identity ease any of your concerns?"

"Somewhat. No one meets the queen without a clean dossier. I read hers last night. She was considered a fair and forward-thinking regent who made substantial improvements to her realm. It is solvent and stands in good stead with its neighbors and with the government of India."

The government of India being the British.

She nodded slowly. "Do you not find it strange that someone like her is being blackmailed?"

Her hat was veiled. The netting did not truly conceal her features, but directed attention to her full lips, the only exposed part of her face. He stared at her mouth a moment too long, before he lifted his eyes to meet her veiled gaze. "No stranger than someone like you becoming one of the biggest scandals of the decade."

The tiny jet beads on the netting caught and refracted the grey light of an overcast afternoon. "Any theory on what her misstep might have been?"

"My first assumption was that her letters were sent to an illicit lover — and contain embarrassing, possibly lurid passages. But that is too easy a line of thinking when the person being blackmailed is a beautiful woman. You?"

"I do believe that she is being blackmailed. I do not understand how those letters ended up at Château Vaudrieu. Or why, for that matter, she was *informed* about their location."

That was the reason he had wanted to know who was blackmailing her and with what. "I wonder whether the intended target is in fact the Van Dyck piece itself. If the people at Château Vaudrieu have been doing this for a while, they know how to secure their artworks. And if French criminals are unwilling to infiltrate the château, then that means the château has made sure its objets d'art are more trouble than they are worth as stolen goods. But if you find a woman desperate to keep her secrets, then you just might get your Van Dyck for a song."

She didn't say anything for a while.

To keep himself from staring at her again,

he turned and looked out the window. But he remained conscious both of her nearness and of the perennial distance between them.

"Are you concerned about the theft itself — the moral aspect of it?" she asked suddenly.

"You ascribe more scruples to me than I actually possess. On the other hand, if what the maharani declared is her actual intention, that she wants only the letters, then it would hardly be theft to return them to her. Which doesn't mean that should we manage the feat, I wouldn't read them to make sure that they are what she says they are."

They were silent again. He didn't know what to make of the silence. In some ways, things had been simpler when he'd been a married man who believed that he'd always be a married man. She'd been an impossibility, no less, no more. But now, with his divorce to be granted by the beginning of summer at the very latest, he had no idea what to do.

"What's the matter?" she asked.

He looked back at her.

"Something is bothering you."

What could he tell her? *My children's governess specifically mentioned you in her bid to become the next Lady Ingram. Is there anyone under the sun who doesn't know that*

I am in love with you? And God help me, but I'm beginning to wonder whether a marriage of convenience isn't a better idea than I first thought.

Could he and Holmes ever come to an agreement on what they wanted from each other? And if they couldn't, then ought he not do the best thing for his children and marry Miss Yarmouth to keep her from leaving?

He did not reply.

Silence had long been the usual state of things between them; he was prepared to let this one last until the hackney reached Mrs. Watson's house. To his surprise, Holmes spoke again.

"I might have some ideas as to what's in those letters the maharani wants back. But the knowledge could put you in an awkward position."

Livia was a good sailor. She hadn't known it — she'd never been on a steamship before and had expected to do poorly. But the pitching and rolling of the ship, on the infamous English Channel, no less, did not affect her at all and she was jubilant to have been spared.

"I know seasickness is an ordeal. Still, I've never seen anyone so happy not to be seasick," teased Mr. Marbleton, as they took a turn on the deck.

"I'm always looking for hints from the universe to tell me how the future will proceed. If I were ejecting the contents of my stomach right now, I'd take it as an ill omen: Not only shouldn't I be here, but no one should and everything will turn out badly," she answered, a broad smile on her face, speaking over the waves striking the prow of the ferry and the steady hum of the engine. "But now that I'm practically dancing across the English Channel? I can't help but interpret it as an auspicious sign.

"But of course, my happiness will be short-lived. Because I suspect the universe to be full of malice and pranks. Soon I will wonder how I am going to pay for this moment of reckless exuberance. And what grand disenchantment will come my way to reduce me to my usual sullen and down-trodden self."

Mr. Marbleton tilted his head. "Do you really think of happiness as such a fragile entity?"

"Mine is," she answered, still smiling. "I don't know that I've ever been properly happy. I simply careen between moments of intense buoyancy and moments of intense misery. Only my anxiety is constant: When I hope, I'm anxious that my hopes will come to nothing; when I fear, I'm anxious that my fears will all come true."

He didn't say anything.

Some of her reckless exuberance faded, as did her smile. "I'm sorry."

Perhaps she'd been too honest. So few people liked her as she was. That he seemed to make her want to *be* herself, fully and unapologetically, without stopping to wonder whether she was meeting some arbitrary standard of normalcy and likability.

"Why?" he said sincerely. "Have your fears ever hurt or even inconvenienced anyone?"

She exhaled in relief — she still hadn't managed to repel him. "Me, I suppose. How I hate always being so anxious. How is it that you are *not*?"

A fresh wave of anxiety struck her. "You aren't just putting on a brave front, are you?"

He shook his head. "My parents have always told my sister and me that we are living on borrowed time. They said that not to make us live in fear but so that we would rejoice in each day that we have managed to stay ahead of Moriarty. Did you not feel a great joy, running away from home — without your parents being any the wiser?"

"*Such* joy."

"That's how I feel morning and night — and often in the middle of the day, too — that I am still at large, that everyone I love is still safe, and that my life is still my own."

The clouds stretched from horizon to horizon, yet she saw nothing but starlight in his eyes. She had never known such an unpolluted soul, such purity of spirit. "I envy you," she said.

"Because I'm happy?" He grinned. "My sister says I'm too young to know any better."

Ah, here was something she'd been wondering about. Charlotte had told her that he was at least five years younger than her, but she'd been hoping that perhaps Charlotte was wrong, for once. "How old are you, if you don't mind my asking?"

"I will be twenty-one soon."

Good heavens, he was even younger than she'd feared. There must be a full seven-year difference in their ages, as she was not far from her twenty-eighth birthday. "I — feel like a fossil standing next to you."

"I happen to adore fossils. I have visited every museum of natural history in every major city we have passed through to see their paleontological collection. I even dragged my family to Lyme Regis in the hope of discovering some fossils myself."

She laughed. It was so easy to laugh with him.

He reached across and took her hand. Her heart pounded. The boat tilted up all of a sudden, sending them both skidding across the deck. They ended up against a railing, her falling into him.

"Do you mind my age?" he asks.

"Somewhat. But I worry more that you will mind my age — or that other people will find our age difference ridiculous."

"Well, our age difference will always be the same, but at least I'll never be as young as I am now."

They still clasped each other's hands, still stood chest to chest.

"Maybe . . . I don't mind your age at all. Maybe I like that you are young and kind and not at all cynical."

She lifted a gloved hand and touched it to his face. She could not feel his skin, of course, but just the fact that she was doing something she had never dared in her life — somehow that made it less important that she was fast approaching the cliff of thirty, beyond which unmarried ladies plunged into utter uselessness and undesirability.

She pulled her hand back, shocked by her forwardness, after all. "I should — I should go see how Charlotte is getting on."

The ferry reached Dieppe before dawn. By the time their train pulled into Gare du Nord in Paris, it was barely past eight in the morning. A cold drizzle greeted them, along with staff from the house that had been put under Lord Ingram's disposal.

Paris was a better planned, more impressively laid-out city than London, which simply grew and spread however it liked. The thoroughfares were straight and wide, the grand houses that lined them, with pale stone stucco facades and slate-colored roofs, uniformly imposing. And the city as a whole seemed cleaner, less grimy than its English counterpart.

Livia expected to pull up at a town house rather similar to Lord Ingram's dwelling in London. Instead, they were brought to a four-story, green-roofed *hôtel particulier,* a private mansion, set some distance back from the street and surrounded by high walls.

When Livia was younger, she'd been confused that the rich and powerful people of France all seemed to live in this or that hotel. Her governess had chuckled at her question and explained that an *hôtel* was simply a large town residence, not necessarily an inn, the same way that a château was but a large country residence, and usually not a castle.

This one had an unusual name, Hôtel Papillon: Butterfly Residence. At the moment, the family that lived in the house was away and it was served by a skeleton staff. A manservant named Forêt, who spoke English with a pronounced French accent, welcomed Livia & co. and showed them to a dining table laden with coffee, hot chocolate, croissants, and *pain au chocolat.*

"I have been given to understand," he said — *I 'ave been giveng to undairzdang* — "that the *Anglais* prefer eggs for breakfast. I hope these *oeufs au cocotte* will serve?"

He lifted a large domed lid to reveal a platter of ramekins, which turned out to contain baked eggs, made with cheese and ham. The *Anglais* gave their hearty approval and fell upon their meal, with the exception of Charlotte, who ate slowly, gazing at the spread with the lasting regret of a monk who'd taken his vows immediately before inheriting a harem.

At the end of the meal, Forêt led them to a large library with a comfortable reading area and presented them with a dossier. "Mesdames, Monsieur, milord's friend brought this for you."

They thanked him and waited until he'd left to open the dossier.

"My goodness," Mrs. Watson immediately exclaimed, "but Lord Ingram's ally works fast. These must be the architectural plans for Château Vaudrieu."

While she, Charlotte, and Mr. Marbleton bent over the architectural plans, Livia picked up a magazine from the dossier, which happened to be an omnibus that reprinted articles from other publications. She flipped through a feature from the *Journal of the Royal Geographic Society* on Chinese Turkestan, another on the current and future development of railway tunnels in the Italian Alps, before landing on a piece concerning the Château Vaudrieu masquerade ball.

The article, which originally appeared in an American magazine, presupposed its readers to be unfamiliar with everything about the ball. That assumption of ignorance grated on Livia, but because of it, the author omitted no details or explanations.

The château was described as sitting on extensive grounds, with its own apple orchard and a herd of dairy cows. One approached via a splendid tree-lined boulevard, lit for the occasion with thousands of paper lanterns. The would-be revelers then traversed a formal garden with extensive parterres, abundant sculptures, and dramatic fountains, before — and here the writer nearly swooned with excitement — crossing a handsome stone bridge that led to the actual manor.

For the edifice itself was situated on an island one third of the way into a lake, which acted as a natural moat, and the bridge was the only access. At either end of the bridge stood gates that could be locked. As if those weren't enough, a third gate barred the way on the island itself, in the center of high wrought iron railings that surrounded a courtyard that was also a miniature formal garden.

For those still entertaining the idea of an unauthorized entry, perish the thought. The château had been constructed on the foundation of a former fortress, the base of which rose directly from the water and retained rows of downward-pointing spikes as sharp as shark's teeth.

The writer went on to proclaim, smugly in Livia's opinion, that he had been invited to the dinner, a more intimate gathering before *tout le monde* arrived for the ball. She carefully read the description of the entry, the grand drawing room, and the dining room but skimmed over the dissertation on the food, the wine, and the guests who were favored enough to partake of this meal.

"Something is missing," said Charlotte.

Livia looked up, as did everyone else.

"I don't see anything amiss, but I do wonder what this is." Mrs. Watson pointed at something on the plans, which Livia, from where she sat, couldn't see. "It's labeled *C. E.*"

"I would guess that is the electrical plant, *le centrale électrique,*" said Mr. Marbleton. "What were you saying about the missing item, Miss Charlotte?"

"I understand the château is built atop the remains of a medieval fort," said Charlotte.

"I'm reading about that now," interjected Livia. "A fort with downward-pointing spikes and whatnot at its base."

"Ah, I see," said Mr. Marbleton. "The fort would have existed in dangerous times. It would have been built to withstand a siege. There should have been a tunnel that would have allowed the family to leave undetected."

"Perhaps that knowledge was lost over the centuries," said Mrs. Watson.

"Perhaps," said Charlotte.

She went back to studying the architectural plans, and Livia resumed reading, only to pipe up excitedly a minute later, "There's a private art museum at Château Vaudrieu — or at least that's what this article is choosing to call it."

Everyone looked at her.

"Is that so?" said Mrs. Watson, sounding a little breathless.

"Let me read this to you." Livia cleared her throat. " 'Upon rising from dinner, Madame Desrosiers, our elegant and effervescent hostess, invites us to tour the private museum. The guests chatter about the legendary fireworks display to come as we mount the stunning double-returned staircase and walk down a wide passage, lit in such a way as to draw the eyes up to the painted ceiling. A collective gasp of delight echoes against the murals. Besides the Sistine Chapel, I have rarely seen another ceiling as grandly and gloriously illustrated. But here the themes are mythological rather than biblical, and the tableaux consist of the births of Athena and Aphrodite, Perseus killing Polydectes with Medusa's head, Daphne turning into a laurel tree to escape Apollo's insistent pursuit, and other dramatic renderings of classical themes.'

" 'The space dedicated to the private museum doesn't have such dramatic murals, but muted walls to better display the artistic treasures thereupon. We the gathered exclaim with exulted admiration at the richness before our eyes — canvases by the greatest masters of the Renaissance sit side by side with works of Flemish maestros and more recent oeuvres from this current century."

Livia turned the page. " 'I was surprised to see a number of English portraits and landscapes. They are indeed very magnificent specimen and a worthy addition to any collection, but simply not what I have expected in this collection. A gentleman whom I later learned to be our hostess's brother informed me that though the English pieces were unexpected, they were possibly the most valuable in the collection, as the English government did not hesitate to part with tens of thousands of guineas to acquire the finest works of its native sons for the National Gallery.' "

"But that is marvelous information," said Mrs. Watson.

"Indeed. Very helpful," added Charlotte.

Livia's cheeks warmed with pleasure. Of course everyone present would have read the article eventually and learned all it had to impart, whether she had brought it to their attention or not. But still, she felt as if she'd actually contributed something, however minor that contribution.

Forêt returned. *"Mesdames, Monsieur,"* said the manservant. "Milord said that you wish to see the *marché de Nöel* at Mouret today. Shall I order your carriage? There is a train that leaves for Mouret in an hour. The *gare* isn't far, but the roads can be terribly congested these days. And you wouldn't wish to leave any later or the *marché* will have dispersed by the time you reach."

Why would they want to rush off to some Christmas market at a place they'd never heard of?

"You may order the carriage now, M. Forêt," said Charlotte. "We will all of us be ready in a quarter of an hour."

When the manservant had exited, Charlotte showed everyone a map of Paris and its surroundings.

Mouret was the village nearest Château Vaudrieu.

Livia's heart pounded. Their adventure was about to begin.

SIX

Mouret didn't have a true Christmas market, only the usual village market with the addition of some seasonal items. Still, its small square was filled to the brim, with cattle and a herd of turkeys milling about at one end and stalls crowding the rest of the space, selling everything from tablecloths to Christmas crèches to hams the size of small boars.

Mrs. Watson purchased bottles of mulled wine, Mr. Marbleton a wheel of local Brie cheese. Charlotte, after much contemplation of loaves of *pain d'épice,* acquired skeins of homespun yarn. Livia, while nobody was looking, bought lace-edged handkerchiefs — she could monogram them and give them as Christmas presents.

They spoke in German to one another. Livia and Charlotte's governess had been from Alsace, and they could get by in both German and French. Mr. Marbleton, ac-

145

cording to himself, spoke only enough German to fool the French. Mrs. Watson had the least acquaintance with the language and didn't speak much except to the locals, in French that had a heavy German accent.

When Charlotte deemed that they'd made as many purchases as any quartet of genuine tourists, they entrusted their new possessions to Forêt and headed into an establishment that seemed to be both a pub and a coffeehouse.

While they lunched on pot-au-feu, Charlotte spreading only a fraction of her customary amount of butter on a slice of rustic bread, Mr. Marbleton, in very decent French, asked for directions to the château from a local farmer. He also asked whether the château admitted visitors, as most stately manors in Britain, which they had just visited, surely did.

The farmer shook his head. *"Pas celui-ci."* *Not this one.*

They finished their meal and strolled in the direction of the château. The sky had cleared, the sun shone, and though it remained chilly, Livia's heart lifted at the sight of the pale blue sky.

The buildings of the village, largely clustered around the square, quickly thinned. Cobblestoned streets gave away to dirt lanes cutting between fallow fields and stubbly pastures where goats and donkeys foraged.

The ground dipped and rose, both gently. To Livia's surprise, from atop the next rise, she saw their quarry.

When the article had mentioned *extensive grounds,* she had envisioned something on the scale of Stern Hollow. But one glance was enough to take in the entirety of the estate.

Granted, the avenue that ran straight from the gate to the bridge was impressive. The formal gardens, even from a distance, was geometric grandeur. And the château itself, slate-roofed, clear-windowed, almost golden in the slanting sun of the afternoon, was indubitably beautiful. But there was hardly any extra acreage, parkland or farmland. The whole thing made Livia think of a massive wedding cake perched on a too-small table, leaving barely enough room for a cake knife.

A ten-foot-high wrought iron fence surrounded the entire estate. They walked alongside it, stopping from time to time to admire the view inside. Mr. Marbleton carried a rucksack. Livia had assumed it contained a water canteen and some extra food. But the first time they stopped, he took out from the rucksack a book that wasn't big but rather thick — and held it so that it pointed toward the château.

"Is that a detective camera?" asked Charlotte. "Custom-made?"

"Frances and I made it with parts from other cameras," he answered happily. "And we did some additional bits of tinkering so we could use sensitized paper rather than plates."

Livia remembered that he and his sister had passed themselves off as a photographer and his assistant during the summer.

Mr. Marbleton took a number of other images as they circum-navigated the estate. There was indeed an orchard, if two dozen apple trees could be called an orchard. At the back of the estate, there was in truth a herd of dairy cows, too, comprised of all of three heads. Occasionally dogs barked; Charlotte listened carefully, as if trying to deduce their numbers.

"I don't think we'll be able to learn much more than we have, promenading on the periphery," said Charlotte once they'd done an entire circuit. "It's getting a bit late. We should head back."

They had almost reached the village when Mr. Marbleton said, "You ladies have a safe trip back to Paris. I'll stay here tonight."

It made sense, his plan; they should know

what the place would be like at night. But still Livia's heartbeat stalled. "Will it be safe?"

"For an observer, I don't see why not."

"What if there are guard dogs?" Charlotte wouldn't have paid attention to the barking otherwise.

"What if there are? I don't see how that should endanger me sitting in the café, listening to gossip."

She looked at him incredulously. "Is that really all you are going to do?"

He winced. And then groaned. "I would have preferred to lie to you, Miss Olivia, but alas, all the inculcation from my parents is preventing me from withholding the truth. No, that is not all I am going to do, if you must know. I also mean to take myself back to the château, climb the fence, and get as close to the manor itself as possible."

Livia bit her lower lip. "Then I'll also stay here tonight. I won't tag along when you venture out, since I'll most likely get stuck on the fence and spoil your entire plan. But I'd rather be worrying here than worrying in Paris."

"Then I suppose I should remain here as chaperone," said Mrs. Watson.

Charlotte glanced at the three who had declared their intentions. "I will go back to

149

Paris. I haven't read everything that has been furnished to us in that dossier."

Ah, Lord Ingram was due this evening. And Charlotte wouldn't wish to miss his arrival.

Charlotte read everything in the dossier twice, except the article on the masquerade ball. That one she read three times. By the time she finished, she could recite, word for word, the final paragraph extolling the fireworks display that marked the end of the night. Then she bathed, dressed for dinner, and studied the architectural plans until the dinner bell rang.

In the dining room, she was the only person at table. Forêt, after ladling out a bowl of thick potage, stood back against the wall and seemed to disappear into it. He was unobtrusive, this man, effortless at making himself unnoticed — an interesting talent, given that he happened to be very good-looking.

"It's just the two of us," she said in English. "Why don't you take a seat, sir?"

"I beg your pardon, Miss?"

She looked at him. "My father is a man of little significance. But his cousin, Mrs. Newell, is very well connected. She is related, by marriage and somewhat strenuously, to the Ashburtons of Derbyshire, the current Duke of Wycliffe among them."

At the mention of the Ashburtons, something flickered in Forêt's dark green eyes.

"Some years ago," continued Charlotte, "when she still moved in Society, Mrs. Newell brought my sister and me to Eastleigh Park, the Duke of Wycliffe's country seat, for a house party. When I was there I saw a photograph that caught my attention: The people in the picture were draped in garlands of tropical flowers, on an island with a dramatic landscape.

"I asked and was told that the lady in the picture was born an Ashburton, a cousin of the late duke. And those in the photograph with her were her husband and her two sons from a previous marriage. I may not remember every face in every photograph I have ever seen, but yours was a memorable face in a memorable photograph, sir."

"Ah," said Forêt, this time in perfect English, "Ash did warn me that my disguises would be too paltry for your penetrative gaze."

"The lady's late husband was an Atwood of Sussex. That would make you Mr. Atwood."

"Lieutenant Atwood."

"Pleased to make your acquaintance,

151

Lieutenant." She gestured at the chair at the opposite end of the table. "Won't you join me for dinner?"

Lieutenant Atwood did not hesitate this time. He set a place, served himself a bowl of soup, and sat down.

"Lord Ingram mentioned that you were passing through France. Were you on your way back to India?"

"That is correct."

"Did you come to England with Lord Remington?"

This time Lieutenant Atwood's answer was slightly slower in coming. "Yes."

Lord Remington, youngest of Lord Ingram's three elder brothers, was attached to the viceroy's office in Calcutta in an officially vague capacity. Charlotte would call him a spymaster, except she wasn't sure that was all he did.

"I investigated a case for Lord Ingram at Stern Hollow. At the time, he mentioned that he'd entrusted his children to Lord Remington. But it became apparent later that the children had not been, in fact, with Lord Remington himself. Were they by some chance with you?"

Lieutenant Atwood inclined his head — this line of inquiry apparently did not bother him. "The children and their governess were at my place in Sussex. I was happy to host them, as I myself was needed at the estate, to make decisions and see to its upkeep."

It was rare for a firstborn heir to join the military, which was more typically the lot of younger sons.

"It sounds as if you hadn't been home for some time."

"Years."

"May I venture to guess that you have been saving your home leaves for more travel, such as to Chinese Turkestan?"

Her dinner companion was reaching for a slice of baguette. His hand hovered for a moment above the basket. His eyes cast briefly downward, before he met Charlotte's gaze. "Chinese Turkestan is a politically sensitive area," he said evenly. "The Chinese would be quite miffed if the English were mucking about. The Russians wouldn't be pleased either."

"Which is why the English would be mucking about, I take it."

"Just because the magazine I put in the dossier has an article on Chinese Turkestan doesn't mean I have visited or plan to visit the area."

Even though those pages had been read repeatedly and the rest of the magazine hardly riffled through?

"Of course you're right about your own plans," said Charlotte, deciding not to further press the point. "But I'm glad you came back to England with Lord Remington. Nothing matters more to Ash than the safety of his children. I'm sure he was supremely grateful that they found timely refuge in your home."

Lieutenant Atwood inclined his head again. "It was very little trouble on my part."

Charlotte judged that had been enough small talk. She took a bite of her unbuttered bread. "Our current venture, however, promises to be much more troublesome. Have you already seen the château?"

"Yes."

"And obviously you have also seen the architectural plans. What do you think?"

"That would depend on whether we are taking the painting by force or by stealth."

She raised a brow. "You are open to taking it by force, Lieutenant?"

He shrugged. "We are going to commit a crime. Armed robbery is but another criminal option."

"What, then, are your thoughts on taking the Van Dyck by force?"

"On the main it seems inadvisable. The private gallery is at the rear of the château,

154

directly above the lake. Let's say we slash the painting from its frame and carry the canvas through the rest of the building. The multitudes on the night of the ball will make that a fraught endeavor, even if the gates on the bridges wouldn't already be locked in anticipation against such blatant thievery.

"The only other option would be to throw it out of one of the windows and hope that someone stationed below in a boat can catch it. There were no boats on the lake when I went. I'm not sure how we get one there. And I'm not sure that the person in the boat will have time to row the boat to shore and climb over the fences before the dogs get there."

Charlotte had noticed the kennels in the afternoon. She'd chosen not to mention the guard dogs to either Livia or Mrs. Watson, but had spoken with Mr. Marbleton before she left. He assured her that he'd seen the kennels and planned to avoid all canine entanglements on his second outing to the château.

"What if we proceed by stealth?"

"Stealth requires far more preparation, preferably from inside the château. Which will be difficult to accomplish, given that at the moment, we have no one inside. It also requires that in the midst of a large gathering, we remove a sizable painting not only from the wall but from the premises, with no one being the wiser." He took a sip of his soup. "I would not even consider stealth, except the alternative seems certain to end in a very public disaster. With stealth, we might yet have the luxury of failing unnoticed."

"You are not very optimistic about our chances."

"Are you?"

"No."

"In that case, Miss Charlotte" — he smiled slightly — "bon appétit."

Oddly enough, in spending time with the quiet, competent, and handsome Lieutenant Atwood, Charlotte began to understand the impasse between herself and Lord Ingram.

For years their interactions had been characterized by a deep, sharp-edged tension, the friction between the pull of physical desire and the restraining force of everything else. The rules that governed a respectable woman's conduct, the rules that decreed what a man could or could not do with a respectable woman, and the rules that he placed on himself, a begrudging yet

156

implacable respect for his foundering marriage.

But since summer, one by one those restraints had fallen by the wayside. She was no longer a respectable woman, and his marriage had met its demise, needing only the High Court to officially pronounce it well and truly dissolved.

And only now, trudging along in uncharted territory, could she appreciate the significance of those restraints.

They had not been restraints, in reality, but a safety net, something she counted on to make sure that they could proceed this far but no further. That he would observe all those restraints was what made it possible for her to repeatedly proposition him, knowing that he would refuse her advances.

Even when she'd cajoled him into bed, she'd known it would be only temporary, that he would not allow it to continue beyond the conclusion of the case at Stern Hollow.

But along with the disappearance of societal restraints, they had also changed. The affair had changed them, and instead of the old chaste yearning, there was now a hunger for more of the forbidden fruit.

Which had tasted sweet indeed.

But a forbidden fruit that one could bite

157

into at will was just another apple.

And Charlotte Holmes and Lord Ingram, without everything holding them back, might come together in a storm of sparks while the physical pleasures were new. But, as time went on, they would reveal themselves to be what they had always been: two highly mismatched individuals.

The atmosphere between herself and Lieutenant Atwood was easy because they had no history, tortured or otherwise, to color their interactions. She could make such a man her lover — or never see him again — without worrying about losing a friend of long-standing.

With Lord Ingram, the potential for catastrophic loss hung in the balance.

She sighed and returned her attention to her dinner companion. "There is something I need to discuss with you, Lieutenant. It concerns the actual contents of the maharani's letters."

SEVEN

Lord Ingram was not terribly surprised to see Mr. Marbleton at the inn, though he had not expected Mrs. Watson and Miss Olivia Holmes at the same table. The ladies, on the other hand, were a little distressed by the sight of him.

"But Charlotte returned to Paris — and now you are here," cried Miss Olivia, in fluent, if regional, German.

He smiled slightly. "I am fairly confident that when Miss Charlotte left, she foresaw that I would be here tonight."

"She did say that she wanted to finish studying the contents of the dossier provided by your ally," said Miss Olivia, still looking rather crestfallen. "I thought it was an excuse to meet your train or some such."

He couldn't imagine Holmes doing such a thing. Not that she wouldn't ever meet his train if she needed to, but that her emotions should run away with her to such an extent

159

that she would rush back to town just so that she could see him half a day sooner.

He was very much that sort of person. She, not in the very least.

"Forêt, is he here, or did he accompany her back to Paris?"

"Back to Paris," answered Mr. Marbleton.

That might also explain why she took herself there, so she could have a private conversation with Leighton Atwood, away from the others in their company. The good lieutenant was traveling on official business — granted, it was only the return trip. That he was participating now in a private inquiry probably wouldn't raise too many brows, but he had not wished his identity to be made known, and Lord Ingram had acceded to that.

"Good," he said. "With Forêt on hand, her tea and supper will be seen to."

He ordered his supper. Then the company moved to Mrs. Watson's room, so as not to be overheard in their discussions.

"I was just talking to the innkeeper," said Mr. Marbleton. "It would appear that the occupants of the château have not been frequently seen in the village. And they rarely employ anyone local, not even for the ball. Instead Madame Desrosiers brings in additional servants from Paris. We'll need to find out where in Paris they get those servants. Properly trained footmen aren't everywhere to be had."

"There are agencies specializing in providing temporary staff," answered Lord Ingram. "My godfather's French relatives should be able to furnish us with a list of the reputable ones."

Reassured on that front, his companions proceeded to describe their rudimentary tour of the château, outside its fences.

"Seems a rather idyllic setting," said Miss Olivia, "but the grounds are far too small for the manor. It's sitting on a handkerchief."

France had experienced great upheavals in the past century and a half. The château would have lost most of its demesne, the attendant territory that would have rendered it self-sufficient, during the more turbulent times. These days it was but a costly country house that generated little income and required wealth to flow in from elsewhere for its maintenance.

The reason it was currently owned by a Swiss manufacturer.

"It's also easier to patrol that way, with smaller grounds," said Mr. Marbleton sagely.

The talk turned to the night's plans. The

gentlemen would start from the inn at one o'clock in the morning and be back before dawn. Mr. Marbleton left to get a few hours of sleep.

Miss Holmes was the next to leave. "Please look after yourself, my lord. And please keep an eye on Mr. Marbleton."

"I will," he assured her.

And now it was just him and Mrs. Watson, who had been quiet and not at all her usual ebullient self.

"Are you all right, ma'am?"

"I don't know, Ash. I don't know." She poured amber liquid into a glass — Calvados, by its aroma — and downed two fingers in one draught. "Until this afternoon I was full of fear for the maharani. But when Mr. Marbleton said he planned to visit the château at night, to go over the fence and get as close to the manor as possible, I — I suddenly became afraid for *us*. Is it really necessary to reconnoiter in the middle of the night?"

"I'm afraid so."

Her anxiety was a feeling of constriction around his own heart. Other than for his children, it was for Mrs. Watson that he'd always felt the purest affection, this woman who had watched him grow up and been unwavering in her warm devotion.

She clutched at the empty glass. "But you said invitations would be forthcoming. We'll be able to walk in the front door."

"And steal from a place we've never seen?" He shook his head. "If we were able to walk through the front door again and again, that would be a different matter. But since we will only be able to do so on the night of the ball — and at the earlier reception, if all goes well — we must know as much about the place and its surroundings as possible. Since there will be few opportunities for approaching during daytime, we have to do what we can at night."

"I can't help but think of the people in the château — I don't know how they are related to those who blackmail Her Highness, but they must be somehow."

This was his worry, too. And no doubt Holmes's.

"I'm well aware of the potential dangers, ma'am, as is everyone else here."

Maybe not so much Miss Olivia, who wasn't, as of yet, accustomed to thinking of the world in such terms, but certainly Holmes. And most certainly Mr. Marbleton.

"And I am excruciatingly aware of the fact that you are all here because of me."

He moved closer, took the empty glass out

of her grip, and held her hands in his own. "Ma'am, this is exactly where I wish to be. When I needed help, you did everything in your power to provide it. Let me return the favor."

A sheen of tears came into Mrs. Watson's eyes. "But when we helped you, Ash, it was because you yourself were in peril. Whereas everyone is only here because of my guilt."

"You would be here by yourself, working on the maharani's behalf, if you had to. And you would do that for any of us. We are here not because of any guilt you may be feeling, but because you are the most gallant person any of us has ever had the good fortune to meet."

Her lips quivered.

He smiled at her and kissed her on the forehead. "So let us be gallant for you. For once."

If only gallantry required less suffering.

It started to rain around midnight. Lord Ingram's long, hooded mackintosh kept most of him dry, but still, it was a miserable business being outside on a wet December night.

Before they'd set out, he and Mr. Marbleton had studied a map of the estate that Mr. Marbleton had brought from Paris, part

164

of the architectural plans. The front gate was at the southern end of the property. The lake on which the manor sat was much closer to the fences on the north side than the front gate. *And there is also a chapel,* Mr. Marbleton had said, tapping its location on the map, not far from the northern fences, *which should hide us from view if we climb in behind it.*

They had come to the spot Mr. Marbleton had selected. Copses of woods stood between the château and the village, but outside the fences the trees had been pared back a considerable distance, leaving only bare ground. They waited for a few minutes under the trees, the rain coming down harder and harder. Distantly dogs barked.

Mr. Marbleton glanced at him. He nodded. With feline lightness, Mr. Marbleton shot over the fence. Lord Ingram shook his head — was he himself ever so acrobatic, even at that age? But the fence did not prove an obstacle, even if he made it past without quite the same panache.

A strong gust blew. He wiped the rain from his face. The air smelled faintly of cow manure. It made him think of Stern Hollow, of its herd of twenty that grazed behind the house.

Apropos of nothing at all, he wondered

what Holmes thought of the cream and butter produced on his estate.

They ran, crouched low, toward the chapel two hundred fifty feet away. The chapel, which faced east, stood athwart their direct path to the manor. They crept along its long side, until they could peek out a corner toward the château itself, dark except for lamps that burned in the small courtyard on the island.

Which only made everything look more shadowy.

It was another half furlong to the northern edge of the lake. But there would be no more covers of any kind: nothing but water and smooth, flat ground around the manor. The parterres of the formal gardens were a furlong south of the lake, the orchard too distant to even be seen.

"We have to get to the bridge to have a proper look at the château — and to have any kind of hope of concealment," said Mr. Marbleton, stating the conclusion Lord Ingram had also come to.

They went back to the fence. It offered no concealment, but it was farther away from the illumination — and a quicker way out if the dogs came near. He considered making their way outside of the fence. But they would leave a trail on the wet ground,

166

footprints that might or might not be washed away by the rain. Whereas inside, they had the advantage of an excellent lawn. In summer it would have been as luxuriant as any velvet carpet: He stepped on no mud, only an occasional puddle where the ground was slightly uneven.

They reached the formal garden before the dogs came along the eastern fences, several hundred feet away. Even in the din of the rain, the canine growls carried, low, menacing vibrations. He hoped those were only growls of displeasure, as even the best trained dogs wouldn't enjoy being out in this weather — and the rain should be enough to obscure their scents.

The dogs patrolled on. He exhaled. Mr. Marbleton was already hurrying in the direction of the château again. Lord Ingram followed suit, wondering if he was getting a little too old for this. He crouched behind the plinth of a statue, rushed to a small fountain, and then again forward to a conical yew.

Lightning flashed in the distance. In the distance, but too near. He swore under his breath. He didn't fear the lightning itself, but the illumination it threatened, should they be caught in the open.

The sky flashed again. Mr. Marbleton,

who had been at least twenty paces ahead, waited in the shadow of another ruthlessly trimmed yew for him to catch up. They were almost at the northern edge of the garden, nothing but boulevard and lawn between them and the edge of the lake.

"We can't do this if there is a risk of the entire sky lighting up any moment!" said Mr. Marbleton.

Lord Ingram exhaled again. "We crawl."

He supposed he should be thankful for the lawn — it was not the worst surface to be crawling on. But within a minute his lower half was soaked — a mackintosh was scarcely any use when a man was on his stomach, inching forward on elbows and knees.

The night turned brilliant. The château stood in sharp relief against roiling storm clouds. For a second he thought he saw the silhouette of a woman outlined against a window, but then darkness descended again and the château was but shadows and bulk, made more sinister by the guttering light of a few lamps.

He broke into a sweat. Had the woman seen them? They should be only a pair of dark streaks on the lawn, easily mistaken for puddles or other such unevenness. But what if she'd seen them for what they were?

With dots still dancing before his eyes, he crawled forward again. He must reach the bridge as soon as possible.

They were perhaps fifty feet away when what seemed like a hundred dogs barked all at once. The uproar came from behind and to their left, closing in fast.

"Run!" he cried.

Mr. Marbleton did not hesitate, leaping up from the grass. They dashed to the bridge. Then, as quietly as possible, they waded into the frigid water, which rose to chest level within three steps — the banks had clearly been excavated to achieve a steep drop — and swam under the bridge.

The temperature was in the mid-thirties. The water was so cold it burned, as if he were in some lower circles of hell. But fear was even colder, a spike of ice piercing through his lungs.

The barking and growling continued, coming closer and closer to the bridge. Footsteps, running fast in their wake. His breaths bellowed in his own ears.

There were no reeds nearby. How long could he hold his breath underwater?

And then the dogs ran *past* the bridge. Not over it, but around the lake to the east. He exhaled, his heart pounding. What had just happened? Where were the dogs going?

He lifted his arm, dripping and heavy, and settled a hand on Mr. Marbleton's shoulder. The younger man was shivering, but placed a deathly cold hand over his to show that he was all right. Together they swam toward the eastern edge of the wide bridge, almost outside of the shelter of its arc.

Another flash lit the sky. Dogs and men raced toward the chapel. No, toward the fence. The sky turned dark again. A long earsplitting crack of thunder overshadowed all other sounds.

And then there was only the din of rain striking the lake and the stone bridge overhead.

When another bolt of lightning radiated its harsh white light, there were no dogs and no men. As if they'd disappeared off the face of the earth.

As if the entire mad pursuit had never taken place.

EIGHT

Lord Ingram gritted his teeth so that they wouldn't chatter. The cold burned his nerve endings, an indescribable pain. But that he was feeling the bite of the frigid lake was no small consolation — if he stopped feeling cold, then he would be in real trouble.

Thunder rolled. But now lightning came only as faint flickers inside storm clouds. He couldn't see beyond his immediate vicinity, and rain slamming down on stone and water made it difficult to hear. Beside him Mr. Marbleton breathed rapidly, as if by doing that he could make himself warmer. But even his breaths shook with cold.

They needed to get out of the water as soon as possible. But the guards and their dogs couldn't really have disappeared. Where were they now?

He listened for some more time, staring blindly into the darkness, and heard nothing besides the rain. He was just about to clamp a hand on Mr. Marbleton's shoulder and signal him to move when dogs barked from barely fifteen feet away.

"Taisez-vous!" growled a man, ordering the dogs to shut up.

Lord Ingram pushed Mr. Marbleton down and submerged himself too, the cold on his scalp a shock even after all the time he'd spent treading near-freezing water.

He stayed under water for as long as he could, lifting his head into the air only when pain skewered his lungs and stars burst on his closed lids. Mr. Marbleton broke water at almost the same time, panting.

Lord Ingram gave him a push toward the bank. Under his hand, Mr. Marbleton turned around. He couldn't see the younger man's face but he understood his unspoken question. Were they not neck-deep in black-cold water, he, too, would have waited longer. But he had to weigh the risk of discovery against that of hypothermia, and the latter loomed larger with every passing second.

And now he gambled that the men and dogs that passed by would be the only party they needed to worry about, that the others had dispersed to other corners of the estate.

Mr. Marbleton, so quick and agile earlier,

had become slow and clumsy. Lord Ingram had to push him onto the bank before climbing up himself. Rain still poured, and would wash away any mud they might have dredged up from the bottom of the lake. He put his flask of whisky to Mr. Marbleton's lips and made him take several large gulps. Then he pulled the latter upright. "To the garden, then out the side at the nearest fence."

They ran. Or attempted to. But Mr. Marbleton wasn't the only one whose body had become unwieldy. Lord Ingram felt as if he trudged on limbs of clay — overwatered clay that threatened to collapse in a puddle. Beside him, Mr. Marbleton's teeth chattered continuously.

"My God," he mumbled. "Why am I so sleepy?"

Lord Ingram swore and placed Mr. Marbleton's arm over his own shoulders. "Move. Keep moving."

In the middle of the garden Mr. Marbleton tripped. They both went down hard. He didn't want to get up again. It was almost . . . comfortable to lie with his cheek on the garden path, as rain needled his exposed skin.

He forced himself up, dragged Mr. Marbleton to his feet, and headed for the

173

fence at a stumbling jog. Which soon degenerated into a drunken walk. Mr. Marbleton tripped again. Lord Ingram barely managed to catch him.

They were both on their knees in a puddle. *Get up,* Lord Ingram mouthed. But he didn't want to. He wanted to put his head down and curl into a ball. Anything but getting up.

Dogs barked. A jolt of panic filled him with a sudden, mad energy. He scrambled to hide behind the low shrubbery that formed the edge of a parterre, Mr. Marbleton following close behind on his own power.

The dogs barked again. Much closer. His heart pounding, he felt for his pistol. His heart pounded even harder when he remembered that his ammunition had been soaked.

Could he hear the dogs sniffing — or was he imagining things?

Excruciating seconds passed. More seconds passed. A whole minute passed and no growling beasts charged at him.

Which could only mean one thing. In their blind groping in the dark, they'd managed to come close to the fence. The dogs had passed on their regular patrol. But thanks to the rain and the fact that they were downwind from the dogs, they had not been detected.

Hope flared, a sensation like fire on a winter night. If they could get out of this infernal place, they might reach safety yet. He yanked Mr. Marbleton forward. In reality they were most likely doddering along, but it felt like a sprint.

He almost slammed his shoulder into wrought iron pickets before he realized they'd reached the fence. The burst of nervous energy from earlier still held. He helped shove Mr. Marbleton over the fence and got over himself on his third attempt.

By which time Mr. Marbleton had sat down and was already dozing. His heart sank. "Move, young man. You fall asleep here and you'll never see Olivia Holmes again."

Mr. Marbleton mumbled something unintelligible.

He pulled Mr. Marbleton upright yet again. "We have to go. Think of some place warm. Think of being there again."

It was a whole league to Mouret, an hour on foot under normal circumstances. But they — who didn't have spare clothes — must walk in the same sodden garments. He didn't know whether they could make the trip in an hour and a half. Or even two hours.

Within twenty minutes he was as exhausted as he'd ever been. It still rained, and the wind had picked up. Cold cut into his skin like surgical scalpels. His mind was becoming duller, and Mr. Marbleton, whom he half supported, grew heavier with each step.

"Don't fall asleep," he repeated mechanically. "Say something. Think of the sun in summer."

No reply. Mr. Marbleton hadn't said anything in at least five minutes. He suspected that the young man was asleep on his feet. He should halt and shake him until he was sure the latter was awake, but he was afraid that if he stopped moving forward, even if it was only for a second, they would both collapse in a heap.

Mr. Marbleton croaked something.

He gave Mr. Marbleton more whisky.

"Andal— Andalusia," said Mr. Marbleton hoarsely. "Warm. Hot."

Even in his reduced state Lord Ingram recognized that Mr. Marbleton was making a herculean effort. He walked a little faster. His heart, which was beating most sluggishly, sped up some. "Tell me more about Andalusia."

"I like it." Mr. Marbleton dropped his head on Lord Ingram's shoulder. "I love it."

"You lived there?"

"Years ago." The answer came after a long pause. "Do you think — do you think that Miss Olivia will like it?"

Lord Ingram realized dimly that he knew a great deal about Miss Olivia via his long correspondence with her younger sister. "Yes, I think so. Miss Olivia enjoys warmth and brightness. She will find Andalusia much to her taste."

Another long pause. "That's wonderful. Will you help us forge another letter from my mother one of those days, my lord?"

Ah, so he was already thinking ahead to the future. Despite his numb cheeks, Lord Ingram smiled. "It would be my pleasure."

Mr. Marbleton spoke some more of Andalusia. Their conversation slowed as they plodded on. After some time, even Lord Ingram stopped speaking. It took all his energy to put one foot in front of the other.

He imagined Holmes in her comfortable, four-poster bed at Hôtel Papillon in Paris. He imagined climbing into that bed, holding her tight, her warmth spreading along his skin and into his sinews.

The vision kept him going, dragging Mr. Marbleton along.

When the inn came into view, he was too worn out to feel any proper jubilation. To the contrary, he remembered, with a rattle of dismay, that because the inn's proprietor bolted the front door at night, he and Mr. Marbleton had climbed out of the window on knotted sheets.

The thought of the sheet rope inundated him with despair. In his current state, he wouldn't be able to get himself up, let alone Mr. Marbleton.

But when he got close to the inn, the front door creaked open. Mrs. Watson and Miss Olivia stood before it, their anxious faces the most beautiful sight he'd ever beheld.

The ladies rushed out and took over supporting Mr. Marbleton. One under each of his arms, they helped him up the stairs. Lord Ingram somehow remembered to bolt the door after himself, before he half-climbed, half-crawled up the steps.

As soon as they were in Mrs. Watson's room, with the door closed, Mrs. Watson said, "Miss Olivia, I need you to help me take off Mr. Marbleton's clothes. Every item."

She glanced at Lord Ingram.

"I can disrobe myself," he said, when all he wanted was to drop to the floor in a heap and sleep until the end of the world.

Helpfully she provided a dressing robe. He groped his way to behind a screen and stripped. His wet clothes seemed glued to his body, and his hands were about as useful as those of an eighty-year-old arthritic. But he pulled and shoved every last thread of fabric from his body and put on the robe.

He had never been naked in a room with two women present, and certainly not two women whose sole focus was undressing a different man — he almost laughed as he came out from behind the screen.

Mrs. Watson and Miss Holmes already had Mr. Marbleton, also in a robe, in a chair near the potbellied stove. They'd put hot water bottles — pressing into service their canteens and even a few wine bottles wrapped in pillow cases — around him. Mrs. Watson set Miss Holmes to rubbing his feet. She herself pulled Lord Ingram into another chair, thrust a hot water bottle into his hands, and rubbed his feet.

"I would think myself in Heaven, Miss Olivia, if I could feel anything in my feet," mumbled Mr. Marbleton.

Lord Ingram let out a breath he didn't know he'd been holding. The young man was going to be all right.

They were both going to be all right.

In the morning, Charlotte and Lieutenant Atwood visited the offices of *Le Temps,* the

Parisian newspaper of record, where Lieutenant Atwood had made an appointment for them to consult the archives. They worked quickly, checking indexes, pulling volumes, one person copying down relevant information while the other moved on to the next article.

After lunch, taken at a café, they went to their next appointment, a consultation with Monsieur Sauveterre, a mostly retired art dealer who remained highly respected for his encyclopedic knowledge. They hoped to find out what an expert thought of the art sales at Château Vaudrieu, though they planned to approach the subject obliquely.

They arrived in disguise, Lieutenant Atwood as Mr. Nariman, a scion of a prominent and wealthy Bombay Parsi family, and Charlotte as his rotund, bespectacled English friend Mr. Hurst.

Normally Monsieur Sauveterre might not be inclined to grant an audience to two strangers, but Lieutenant Atwood, along with his request, had sent along two bottles of vintage claret from Hôtel Papillon's cellar. For that, they were received warmly.

After some pleasantries, Charlotte, as Mr. Hurst, got to the gist of the matter.

"You see, Monsieur, my friend here has put me in something of a dilemma. We have been traveling together, trying to see as much of the world as possible. I am not as well funded as he is and would have been obliged to stop soon, but for the fact that I recently inherited some paintings.

"I have no eye myself and little expertise in the arena. Those I've asked to appraise my new possessions have said anything from a thousand pounds for the lot — a dozen paintings in all —- to four hundred pounds for this piece alone."

She brought out a large envelope and extracted from it a watercolor measuring eighteen inches by twenty-four inches. Monsieur Sauveterre perched a pair of glasses on his nose and leaned in for a closer look.

"Ah, a work by Monsieur Turner. Very English."

"My late aunt had very English tastes," said Charlotte. "Mr. Nariman has grown impatient, waiting for me to affix a value to this Turner, and offered to buy it for sixteen hundred pounds."

"Sixteen hundred pounds?" Monsieur Sauveterre's brow raised. "That would be forty thousand francs."

"Indeed, a small fortune — which is why I declined his offer."

"And yet, from what I understand, a

similar work exchanged hands for fifty thousand francs right here in Paris a few years ago," pointed out Lieutenant Atwood, as Mr. Nariman.

This they did not glean from the archives of *Le Temps,* but from Lieutenant Atwood's mother, who, according to him, had purchased two Turner pieces some time ago and was pleased to inform him, about a year ago, that she'd heard, via private channels, that a similar Turner watercolor in Paris had gone for twice what she had paid, no doubt presaging a rise in value for her own acquisitions.

"I have heard of that myself," Monsieur Sauveterre admitted. "Although personally I would not take prices achieved at Château Vaudrieu as a benchmark."

Aha, so that particular transaction *had* taken place at Château Vaudrieu.

"Château Vaudrieu?" repeated Charlotte. "Is that the name of a Parisian gallery?"

"No, it is an actual château not far outside the city. In recent years, it's become well-known for an annual December ball. But the ball is also the occasion of an art sale — and at times the prices fetched there have been spectacular."

"Hmm," said Charlotte. "Is everything there sold at prices you would consider inflated, Monsieur?"

"No indeed!" cried Mr. Sauveterre. "Sometimes pieces go for reasonable prices. Sometimes there are excellent bargains to be had — or so I've heard."

He rather hastened to give the appearance of evenhandedness, to make sure that on the whole, he could not be accused of having pronounced Château Vaudrieu's prices too high.

"In other words, exactly as it would be at any other marketplace for art." Lieutenant Atwood turned to Charlotte. "Art isn't corn, my friend. There is no fixed price. For me to pay you anything less than the highest price your Turner could fetch would be highway robbery."

"Ah, but Monsieur," said Monsieur Sauveterre, now more unhurried in his speech, "you did come seeking my opinion. Château Vaudrieu notwithstanding, my professional honor would not allow me to let anyone pay forty thousand francs for a forty-five-centimeter-by-sixty-centimeter watercolor.

"On the other hand, the trend in favor of Mr. Turner's work has been clear. In the thirty-odd years since his passing, his reputation has grown and the value placed on his oeuvre has appreciated considerably. I see no reason why that should come to an abrupt halt: England is wealthy, and there remains a large supply of men and women willing to pay premium prices for one of the country's foremost artists.

"Everything considered, I would decree twenty-one thousand five hundred francs as a fair price for this transaction between friends."

"So . . . eight hundred and sixty pounds? Done," said Charlotte. "I will not take one penny more than what Monsieur has declared fair."

Lieutenant Atwood scoffed. "I still think it's highway robbery, but it was my idea to let the matter be settled by a professional, so I must abide by Monsieur's price."

"Deal!" said Charlotte.

"Deal," said Lieutenant Atwood

They shook hands and thanked Monsieur Sauveterre for his help. The art dealer, in return, thanked them again for their earlier gift of wine. "My supplier ran out of his last bottle of this particular vintage five years ago. I shall lord it over him next time we meet."

As they rose to take their leave, Charlotte asked, as if it were an afterthought, "Monsieur, although our little problem is solved, I can't help but be curious about the prices at Château Vaudrieu. In general, do they skew high or low?"

"That is hard to say," answered Monsieur Sauveterre, sounding cautious. "I have never been to Château Vaudrieu myself, and everything I hear is second-, sometimes thirdhand. I do not have the complete picture."

"Nobody has the complete picture on anything," Charlotte persisted. "We glean what information we can, and we make our judgment based on that. Given what you know, which is probably more than most, what do you think?"

Monsieur Sauveterre laughed dryly. "I think that the presence of unlimited champagne and beautiful women can muddle the thinking of otherwise clearheaded men. And that's all I can say on the matter."

So he did believe that prices there were inflated, but would not state so outright.

Charlotte turned to Lieutenant Atwood. "I say, old chap, we should get ourselves invited to the ball and see with our own eyes what kind of champagne and women make otherwise clearheaded fellows pay double for art."

"Well, why not?" said Lieutenant Atwood. "We'll be in town until after Christmas. When is the ball?"

They looked toward Monsieur Sauveterre,

who said, with almost visible reluctance, "Oh, ten or twelve days from now, I believe."

"I can find out the exact date," said Charlotte. She patted Lieutenant Atwood on the back. "And you, Nariman, can get us into any gathering."

Mr. Nariman inclined his head. "But of course, my friend."

Monsieur Sauveterre saw them out, smiling. But it was the kind of smile that would turn into a frown as soon as the door closed behind them.

Mrs. Watson, whose warmth belied her ferocity, did not let either Lord Ingram or Mr. Marbleton close their eyes until they'd reached Hôtel Papillon in Paris.

Lord Ingram was installed in an opulently appointed bedroom. Mrs. Watson repeatedly questioned him to make sure that he was lucid. After checking his hands and feet one last time, she gave him a cup of hot chocolate that was at least half whisky, packed him with three hot water bottles — proper vulcanized rubber ones — and at last allowed him to sleep.

He woke up to the sight of Holmes sitting in a chair, her head bent. He didn't get too many opportunities to study her closely. Even when they found themselves in physical proximity, there was still the matter of her unnerving, sometimes all-seeing gaze.

With something of a shock he realized that after the near misadventure the night before, what he wanted was for her to raise her face and settle that exact unnerving, sometimes all-seeing gaze upon him.

He opened his mouth to speak and closed it again. He'd almost asked her what she was reading, but she wasn't reading. She was knitting. He sat up to make sure he wasn't dreaming.

"What are you knitting?"

The question he really wanted to ask was *You knit?* But that would probably net him only a blank stare, the thought of which made him smile on the inside.

She looked up, wearing her usual expression of utter serenity. "A cozy for a hot water bottle."

A what?

He laughed. All at once he could see her as a plump, white-haired old woman with a half-finished muffler on her lap, her grandmotherly demeanor fooling all those who didn't know her. Maybe he'd suffered too much last night and gone a little cracked, but he felt an extraordinary glee at the image in his head.

"I see you are well," she said. "No lingering ill effects from your prolonged soaking at Château Vaudrieu."

"I'm a little groggy but otherwise fine."

She nodded, seeming not at all worried. But that she was here, waiting for him to wake up, was evidence enough of her concern. "Mrs. Watson has instructed me to be highly solicitous. Are you hungry?"

He was and said so. She left and returned with a large footed tray and set it down over his lap. Leaning her hip against the side of the bed, she poured him a cup of coffee.

"Mrs. Watson has decided that plain toast and French baked eggs make for acceptable convalescent fare," she said. "You take your coffee black, as I recall."

They'd never had coffee together. And he was sure he'd mentioned coffee only once in their entire acquaintance, many years ago, when she was lamenting the fact that he'd visited France without bothering to set foot inside a patisserie. In that same conversation she'd wanted to know what he'd had for breakfast during his French holiday and had been scandalized when he'd said black coffee and maybe, when he was in the mood, a slice of toast — but only when he was in the mood.

Come to think of it, he'd been pleased to find out that Lady Ingram had as little interest in breakfast as he did. Had thought it a further sign that they were true soul mates. Which only went to show that the choice of soul mates should not be left to barely post-adolescent young men.

Holmes, of course, would dispute the validity of the concept of soul mates in the first place.

"Yes, black coffee," he said.

She left the bed, pulled up a chair nearby, and resumed her knitting. He grinned with that same glee and put on a grown-up expression only when she looked up. But she'd seen his delight, and for a moment, he thought he again saw that smile in her eyes.

His heart floated.

"What happened at the château?" she asked. "Mrs. Watson said all she could get out of you was 'dogs' and 'lake.' "

He cleared his throat and turned his focus back to their task.

" 'Dogs' and 'lake' comprise, more or less, the sum total of what happened." When Mrs. Watson had asked her question, he'd been so sleepy, his mind so dull, that even those two words had taken superhuman effort. "Is Mr. Marbleton all right?"

"He is still sleeping. But he was briefly awake two hours ago and he was fine then."

"The ladies?"

"Mrs. Watson has retired for the night. Livia is still with Mr. Marbleton."

"She should rest, too."

"I have told her that, but I don't believe she will until she is convinced he is out of danger," said Holmes. "Now let me hear some details about dogs and lake."

He gave her an account of the night. She listened attentively, though her knitting needles never stopped clicking.

He loved that gentle, rhythmic sound.

Although . . . perhaps that was simply because it was easier to admit that he loved the sound rather than that he loved the woman.

"So they were all headed to a particular section of the fence, not far from the chapel. And then they all disappeared in the space of a minute or so."

"That's correct."

"I see."

"You mean that you heard me — or that you know what happened?" With Holmes, he wouldn't be surprised if it was the latter.

She didn't answer but took photographs out of an envelope. "Have you seen the château by day?"

He shook his head.

"These are pictures Mr. Marbleton took

190

with his detective camera — I brought the exposed roll of photographic paper back to Paris and Lieutenant Atwood developed them." She handed him one of the images. "This is the chapel. From outside the fence, I couldn't see the bridge for the chapel. I assume then you couldn't see the other side of the chapel either, from under the bridge?"

"No, we couldn't."

"Could you see the door of the chapel?"

"I think not. We could see the back and the southern side of the chapel. It faced away from us."

She nodded.

"You think dogs and men all disappeared inside the chapel and later reemerged?"

"Or that they were on the far side of the chapel from you."

"They were chasing something. Neither dogs nor people run like that unless they have a goal in mind. But I never saw what they were chasing."

"How can you be sure they weren't *being* chased?"

He stumbled over the question, the toast halfway to his mouth forgotten. Only after a few seconds was he able to say, with some certainty, "They weren't being chased — they never looked back."

"Speaking from experience?"

"You can deduce that even with logic," he said. "The pursuers can see the quarry. The quarry must look back to gauge whether his pursuers are gaining on him, whether more are joining from different directions, whether they have firearms and are willing to use them. The men and the dogs I saw were pursuers."

She nodded. "I trust you to know the difference."

He exhaled and finished his toast. She came out of her seat and leaned over the bed. He again forgot about his food, but she only pilfered a slice of bread, spread it with a bit of butter, and took a bite.

At least once in his life, he would like for her to look at him as she would a morsel of fine French pastry. Or a slice of Victoria sandwich. Or even a humble piece of buttered bread.

Something came over her when she relished her food. At afternoon tea parties, when she was still an eligible young lady, she frequently ignored the gentlemen in favor of a plate of miniature iced cakes. And the gentlemen, subtly or unsubtly, from every corner of the room, would peer at her, sometimes over the shoulders of young ladies they were ostensibly talking to, because of the unabashed desire on her face

— and the potent pleasure she emanated in consuming those objects of desire.

"I've never seen you take so little butter," he said.

"I shouldn't have any butter at all. But it is high misery indeed, to be battling Maximum Tolerable Chins in France, of all places. A little butter eases the suffering."

"You look fine to me."

Everything about her was slightly fuller — her bodice, most notably. It was a test of his own self-control not to let his eyes stray to her bosom, to those few buttons that seemed to be in imminent danger of popping open.

"Alas," she said lightly but firmly, "in this case, I am the only one who can judge whether and how the battle should be fought. But by all means rain down further compliments, while I order my troops and weigh my strategies."

She was only a fraction as vain as she was perceptive. But given her tremendous perspicacity, her concern for her appearance was no insignificant matter. He sighed in resignation. *"Oui, mon général."*

She glanced at him. Her eyes were her best features, wide set, thickly lashed, and deceptively transparent, hinting at a guileless sweetness antithetical to her true nature.

Silence. Only the barely audible flickers of

the gas lamps reached his ears — and the sounds of her soft breaths.

He found himself staring at her lips. Her lips were decadent. All of her was decadent. She leaned closer, her pupils turning dark. And he was only hunger, only need.

"Yes," she murmured. "I do believe you are quite all right. I have some matters to see to. Shall I send Forêt up?"

Mrs. Watson, sitting on an opulent, canopied bed, could not stop herself from shaking, not even in front of Miss Charlotte. Every time she thought of poor Mr. Marbleton, of how ice-cold and confused he had been, fresh tremors would seize her.

Miss Charlotte had informed her that Lord Ingram did not appear to be suffering any lingering effects from his unplanned night swim. And that Mr. Marbleton, too, had awakened and dined, and was now luxuriating in a bath with a French novel that Miss Olivia had selected from Hôtel Papillon's library.

Still . . .

"My God," Mrs. Watson murmured to herself. "But what if we'd been less fortunate? What if something *had* happened?"

She'd been repeating those questions — and using the Lord's name in vain — for

194

goodness knew how long. Miss Charlotte had asked whether she wished to see the gentlemen for herself. But how could she face them again, after having put them in such danger?

And she was so cold, almost as if she, too, had fallen into that frigid lake. She pulled the covers more tightly about herself, but she knew it wouldn't help, not as long as a glacier of fear and guilt advanced inexorably inside her.

After a while Miss Charlotte left. Mrs. Watson, at first relieved to no longer have an audience for her wretchedness, soon felt bereft, her misery doubling, tripling.

But two minutes later her young friend returned with a knitting basket and retook her seat near the foot of the bed. She didn't say anything, only knitted.

At an extraordinarily even tempo. One could keep time by counting the unhurried clicking of her needles.

Gradually, the gentle rhythm mesmerized Mrs. Watson. And gradually, she, who had not slept in more than thirty-six hours, closed her eyes and lost herself in welcome oblivion.

Livia was astonished at herself, in that she hadn't devolved into a blubbering mess that

195

needed to be scraped from the floor. After Mr. Marbleton's bath, they had spent some time reading aloud to each other from the French novel she'd chosen for his amusement. And then she'd been content for him to shoo her out so she could get some rest.

She didn't feel sleepy yet, only dull and uncoordinated. She walked slowly, occasionally bracing a hand on the wall.

Someone took hold of her arm. "Did you eat?"

Charlotte.

Livia nodded, though she could no longer remember what she had eaten.

"And how is Mr. Marbleton?"

"When I left him, he was planning to read a little more," answered Livia, smiling to herself. "Lord Ingram?"

"He's fine. Monsieur Forêt is looking after him."

Livia had a vague memory of someone urging a plate on her, reminding her that she must keep up her strength. That would have been Monsieur Forêt. The implication of Charlotte's words sank in a moment later. "You weren't with Lord Ingram just now?"

"I was with Mrs. Watson."

Livia's heart pinched. "How is she?"

"Racked by guilt that the gentlemen went

196

into danger for her cause — and that the outcome could have been much worse."

Livia rather thought that she, too, would have been tortured by her conscience. After all, Mr. Marbleton wouldn't be here if it hadn't been for her. Instead she was simply glad that he had recovered. Every cell in her body sang with relief, leaving no room for self-recrimination.

Or maybe she was simply too tired to feel anything else.

"Mrs. Watson ought to be proud of herself," she said. "You should have seen her ministering to the gentlemen. They are far better off than they would be otherwise."

"One can always count on Mrs. Watson in an emergency," said Charlotte. "But at the moment, she is far from appreciative of herself."

Livia shook her head and allowed herself to be guided by Charlotte, as she was too muddled to remember which room she had been assigned. But when they stopped before a door, a thought dropped into her head and knocked her sideways.

"Charlotte, you don't suppose — you don't suppose Mrs. Watson will call the whole thing off tomorrow, do you?"

If she did . . . Livia didn't know how she'd feel about that.

Charlotte opened the door for her. "At the moment," she said, "I believe that is what Mrs. Watson intends to do."

NINE

Mrs. Watson opened her heavy eyes. Her neck was stiff. Her right hand, caught under her body during the night, had turned numb. And somewhere in the back of her mind throbbed a dull yet persistent dread.

She blinked a few times. Light seeped into the unfamiliar room from behind curtains. Her travel alarm clock, on the nightstand, read a quarter after eight.

So late.

Memories rushed back. She bolted upright and flung aside the covers — she must see how the gentlemen were doing this morning. Then she dropped her head into her hands. Her entire body sagged. No, she couldn't face them, not after having put them through so much danger and suffering.

A soft knock came at the door.

"Yes?"

"A letter for you, Madame Watson," came

Forêt's soft voice. "I'll put it in under the door."

A letter for her? Here? Even Penelope didn't know she was in town.

She scrambled off her bed, pulled on a dressing gown, and went to the door. When she picked up the envelope, she recognized the handwriting immediately. Mr. Mears's.

Dear Mrs. Watson,
I hope this letter finds you, Miss Olivia, and Miss Charlotte well.

Her Highness the Maharani of Ajmer called just now. I told her that you were out of the country, as you authorized me to do. She asked if you had gone to France and I said I could not comment on the specifics of your itinerary.

After some hesitation, she declared that she was headed to Paris herself and asked that you please call on her at Hôtel de la Paix in Place Vendôme, at your earliest convenience.

My best wishes for your health and well-being.

Yours truly,
Mears

P.S. Miss Holmes is getting along well enough, in case her sisters worry.

Mrs. Watson clutched the letter and closed her eyes.

This was perfect. She would dress and head out immediately. And when she saw the maharani, she would apologize for biting off more than she could chew and that would be the end of it.

Miss Charlotte, already dressed for going out, rose from a chair in the foyer. "Good morning, ma'am. May I join you to call on the maharani?"

Mrs. Watson stopped in her tracks. How —

"I understand there has been a letter from home," said Miss Charlotte. "Had there been a true emergency, Mr. Mears would have cabled. I assume, since he used the post, that the maharani called at our house and told him she would be coming to Paris?"

This was — excellent. On her own, Mrs. Watson's resolution might waver. But with Miss Charlotte along, Miss Charlotte, who had been against being involved in the maharani's problems from the beginning, Mrs. Watson would be sure to hold the line.

"You are correct. And yes, please join me," she said. "Have you seen the gentlemen this morning? How are they?"

"I have not seen Lord Ingram, who has

201

gone for a walk. But I did see Mr. Marble-ton in the library just now, whispering to Monsieur Forêt, arranging for a bouquet of flowers to be delivered to my sister."

Such a romantic. And how could she ever have faced Miss Olivia again, if anything had happened to him? "It's good to know that they are up and about."

"They are doing well. And they are grate-ful that you knew exactly what to do in a case of incipient hypothermia."

Mrs. Watson immediately experienced another lashing of her conscience. "But they should never have been put in that situation in the first place."

"From what I understand, ma'am, *you* never suggested that they visit the estate at night and climb over the fences. The gentle-men did what they saw fit. They are grown-ups — or, in Mr. Marbleton's case, almost of age. And they are fully capable of choos-ing their course of action."

Mrs. Watson did not say anything, and Miss Charlotte did not persist.

Their walk to the hotel passed largely in silence.

The maharani opened the door herself.

At Mrs. Watson's surprised look, she said, "I left my servants behind."

She looked different. Not soft or open by any means, but not as rigid or closed as she had been in London. In fact, as her gaze landed on Mrs. Watson, her eyes were almost . . . welcoming.

When she saw that her caller had not come alone, however, her jaw tightened, slightly but noticeably. Mrs. Watson glanced quickly at Miss Charlotte. The latter, who missed nothing, did not appear at all bothered that their hostess didn't want her there.

Mrs. Watson debated what she ought to say. In the end, after everyone sat down, she opted for, "I understand you called after I left London, Your Highness. Was there some instruction you wished to relay?"

If she immediately announced she no longer planned to rob Château Vaudrieu, then she wouldn't hear what the maharani wanted to say. And Mrs. Watson had to admit, to herself at least, that she was terribly curious.

The maharani cast a look at Miss Charlotte, a not-so-subtle reminder that she wished the young woman would absent herself. Miss Charlotte reacted not at all. Mrs. Watson squirmed a little on the inside, even as her pulse accelerated.

"I only sought to thank you," said the maharani after a while. "My astonishment at finding out your involvement with Sherlock Holmes — alongside the temporary embezzlement of my jewelry — was such that it overrode all my other reactions. It wasn't until well after you'd left that it occurred to me what a gargantuan task you'd taken on.

"If it were remotely easy, I'd have found some way to do it myself. But it isn't easy at all." The maharani gazed at Mrs. Watson, her eyes dark, starlit wells. "I'm deeply moved by your gallantry."

Mrs. Watson's heart thudded, even as she was towed under by a tide of dismay. Dear God, how did she tell a woman who'd crossed the English Channel to express her gratitude that her gallantry had just reached its limits?

Her expression — and her uncomfortable silence — must have conveyed enough of her dilemma that the maharani looked away for a moment. "I see. You came to tell me that you have reconsidered your choice."

Mrs. Watson cursed herself. How could she hurt and disappoint the maharani again? Her heart and her throat burned, but she had no choice. "Please understand, Your Highness. If it were only myself involved, I wouldn't need to practice as much prudence. But I'm entirely out of my depth and entirely reliant on friends. Some of those friends have children, others ladies whom they love dearly. And now that I see the dangers before us —"

She shook her head. "I can risk myself, but I am finding it increasingly difficult to risk my friends."

The maharani said nothing, her eyes once again shuttered.

Mrs. Watson wished she could dig a hole and bury herself. "But I also loathe the threat of exposure hanging over your head like the sword of Damocles. Perhaps — perhaps if you could reveal the nature of the letters you wish to retrieve . . ."

"No, I have no desire to reveal that."

"Then, may I — may I make an assumption?"

"I cannot stop you."

Mrs. Watson winced at the coolness in that answer. "It's quite a vulgar assumption, of course. But the world is not a fair place, and women must pay a heavy price for certain infractions that do not seem to affect men at all."

The maharani showed no reaction.

Mrs. Watson girded herself and carried on. "If something of this nature took place, I beg you to please consider that however embarrassing exposure might be, we are perhaps past the age of maximum damage. As long as your son's legitimacy cannot be questioned . . ."

"As long as he can sit on his throne, it does not matter if I can never show my face in public again?"

"That might be too crude a manner of putting it. But . . ." Mrs. Watson inhaled. "But does your never being able to show your face again outweigh actual lives, Your Highness? That is the calculation I must make here."

"Then you must make the calculation that seems best to you."

"Which is why I am hoping, very much, that you will let me know what kind of threat you are dealing with."

"No, you will not know that," said the maharani, every inch the queen. "Make your calculations, Mrs. Watson."

"If I may," murmured Miss Charlotte, "I have a theory of my own with regard to the maharani's current difficulties."

Mrs. Watson had almost forgotten that she was still there, in the same room. The maharani, too, judging by her surprised and visibly irate expression.

"I propose," continued Miss Charlotte, "that this is not a matter involving, at its core, any kind of affair or liaison."

It wasn't?

"That Mrs. Watson should assume so is quite natural. Her place in life has been determined, for better or for worse, by such infractions. Her path in life — one might even say her success in life — has been paved with such infractions.

"But you, Your Highness, have led a very different existence. Your concern, as regent, was power and alliances. Which makes me think that your mistake, for which you are being blackmailed, also concerns statecraft.

"And yet it seems unlikely that your mistake arises from friendships and enmities between your house and other princely houses in the region. For one, letters to that effect have no reason to end up in a French château, among artworks that most likely came from elsewhere in Europe. For another, and this is the more important reason, if your current dilemma concerned schemes against your neighbor, you wouldn't be so adamant to keep it a secret from *us*.

"Which leads me to wonder whether you have been conspiring to rid India of its British empress."

Mrs. Watson leaped up from her chair, ready to defend the maharani against such an unthinkable charge.

"Though in my personal opinion," Miss

207

Charlotte continued calmly, "you are too seasoned a politician to make such a mistake. Your son, on the other hand . . ."

Surely — *surely* —

Yet seconds passed. Minutes. And no denial sallied forth from the maharani.

"You are a dangerous woman, Miss Charlotte Holmes," she said at last. "Even after our last meeting, knowing the theft you arranged from right underneath my nose, I still underestimated you."

Miss Charlotte inclined her head. Mrs. Watson tried to speak and could not. Did this mean that Miss Charlotte was right? That the current maharaja had rebellion on his mind?

"Please sit down, Mrs. Watson," said the maharani quietly. "I believe I shall ring for some coffee."

Mrs. Watson did as she was told, still stunned. Coffee came quickly, via a dumbwaiter that dinged pleasantly as it shunted into place. Miss Charlotte rose, went to the small compartment, and brought back the tray.

The maharani poured and handed a cup to Miss Charlotte. "A cream puff with your coffee?"

"Alas," said Miss Charlotte, "I already had breakfast. But thank you very much, Your

Highness."

"For you, Mrs. Watson?"

What Mrs. Watson needed was a stiff drink. She shook her head.

The maharani took a sip of her own coffee. "My son began to reign on his own three years ago. After the transition, I left for a pilgrimage tour. I had long wished to see our holy sites, but the more important reason was that I feared I might be tempted to interfere too much, if I were to remain at court.

"The maharaja had long been impatient to rule on his own. The court and I hesitated because of that very impatience. He had many ideas but we felt that his temperament was not even-keeled enough for the wise application of power.

"This, of course, led to many disagreements. I wouldn't go so far as to say that we were estranged, but we were no longer close. If I stayed, I would find faults with his decisions and he, having at last wrested power from me, would refuse to listen."

There was no trace of emotion in the maharani's tone but Mrs. Watson's heart ached. How frustrating it must have been, and how exhausting, to know that she must either give up being a mother, or fail her responsibilities to her realm.

"So I went away, to give him time to grow into kingship," the maharani went on, in that same unaffected demeanor. "I also hoped that his wife, a sensible woman, would prove to be a steadying influence. I returned home after a year to find that he had changed. That he had become both moodier and yet, somehow, more timid.

"His wife told me in secret what happened, because she was frightened not to have the advice of any elders on something so potentially catastrophic. And that was when I learned that shortly after I left, he took up corresponding with someone who claimed to be writing on behalf of the Margrave of B----------. That first letter was followed by precisely ten dashes, never one less, never one more, so he surmised that the name of the title was eleven letters long.

"He'd been tutored in European history and immediately thought of Brandenburg. The title was abolished when the Holy Roman Empire ceased to exist, but because the mark itself had long been ruled by the House of Hohenzollern, the head of that royal household is still styled 'Margrave of Brandenburg,' among other things."

The head of the House of Hohenzollern was the King of Prussia. And since the unification, also the emperor of Imperial

Germany.

Mrs. Watson's lips flapped a few times. "Your son thought he was writing to an intermediary of *Kaiser Wilhelm*?"

"Exactly. This so-called intermediary conveyed his master's interest in freeing India from the yoke of British rule. The said master would offer not merely moral support, but arms and military expertise so that those goals not realized in the great rebellion of 1857 might once again see light of day."

The maharani sighed. "Even if I believed the letter writer to be representing the kaiser, I would have wondered why he was contacting the very new maharaja of a minor kingdom. At the very least, I would have inquired whether others in our position have received similar offers. My son, of course, did not think of it. He dreamed of being as great as Akbar. Or Ashoka. Why shouldn't an imperial adversary of Britain contact him and him alone with such delicate and dangerous proposals?"

Mrs. Watson grew only more incredulous. "And he conveyed those sentiments *in writing*?"

"He did. The correspondence ceased as soon as that happened. My son realized at last that he had been bamboozled. It seemed to him that the confession had been drawn from him for the purpose of blackmail, so he wrote his extortionist one final time and explained that he didn't have any money to spare. He had invested in significant public works, and every other rupee in the treasury was already budgeted for other things."

"Then what?"

"Then nothing. For nearly two years nothing, and then a letter informing us about the Van Dyck at Château Vaudrieu."

The room fell silent. Mrs. Watson looked down at her lap. She wanted very much to embrace the maharani and tell her that everything would be all right. But she could only hold her hands tightly together.

"I hope this is not an intrusive question, Your Highness," said Miss Charlotte, after a while, "but why is the maharaja himself not in Europe, looking after this matter?"

"He is not well," said the maharani. Her throat moved, at last betraying a sign of emotion. "His ailment might have nothing to do with fearing every hour of every day that the might of the British Raj would be brought to bear on himself and his kingdom. But I for one shall never forgive the blackmailer for ruining his health and stealing all his joy at coming into manhood."

No one said anything for a long time.

The maharani took another sip of her coffee. "I will understand, of course, that you won't wish to help someone whose desires run contrary to British interests."

The last thing Mrs. Watson cared about now was British interests. There was very little chance of the young maharaja mounting any serious challenge to British rule in India, and every chance that he himself would be ground to dust under that vast machinery.

But Mrs. Watson wasn't alone in this venture. The Misses Holmes and Mr. Marbleton probably wouldn't mind, but what about Lord Ingram? He was, after all, an agent of the Crown and had risked his life for that very same.

Miss Charlotte turned toward her. "I have spoken to the gentleman you are thinking of about this matter, and he has judged that there would be very little harm done to the Crown to allow the maharaja's sentiments to remain private."

By now, Mrs. Watson should have become accustomed to being astonished by this young woman. Yet she was still very nearly speechless. "Ah, *when?*"

"Before we left London. And I've spoken to his ally, too. That gentleman also has no objections."

Mrs. Watson bit the inside of her lip. A lifetime ago, she had met the young maharaja. He'd been a beautiful, friendly toddler who'd loved it when she put on performances for him in her real theatrical costumes. She could not bear to think of him in such ill health that his mother worried for his life. She wanted even less for him to spend all his remaining days under the crushing weight of his greatest mistake.

She squared her shoulders. "In that case, if it's quite all right with you, Your Highness, we will carry on with our work."

The maharani looked from Mrs. Watson to Miss Charlotte and back again. Her gaze was contemplative, almost melancholy. "That will be quite all right with me. Thank you. Thank you both."

Mrs. Watson felt an upsurge of both warmth and terror. For the first time, they were all in this together.

Miss Charlotte, however, seemed to feel none of the emotions buffeting Mrs. Watson. She gave her coffee a leisurely stir, set it aside, and said, "Your Highness, you would best thank us by telling us what you have thus far held back."

TEN

It was not raining, but a wet sheen lay on the boulevards. The air was damp and cold. Despite the ermine-lined hood of her cloak, Mrs. Watson shivered.

"Miss Charlotte," she said, "did you happen to notice that even though the maharani disapproves strongly of her son's naivety and impetuousness, she never condemned, explicitly or implicitly, his desire to expel the British from India?"

"I did take note of that."

Mrs. Watson wrapped her cloak tighter about herself, but the cold air still penetrated. "Do you think then, that in her heart, the maharani also wishes to expel the British from India?"

"Yes," said Miss Charlotte without a moment's hesitation.

"But she never said anything to me!"

Mrs. Watson's words rushed out like pellets propelled by exploding black powder.

Miss Charlotte's answer, on the other hand, was slow in coming. "Do you, ma'am, disapprove of the existence of the British Raj?"

"I — I don't think I've ever thought about it one way or the other."

"To you, that Britain occupies India is but the way the world is. To her, it is something to be overturned. Perhaps not by her, perhaps not even in her lifetime, but she wants that change. And who knows, she may even be working toward it, just not in such a way as could be traced back to her."

"But we were in love and we talked about *everything.*"

"You were in love not long after the Indian Rebellion of 1857."

"I — I see," said Mrs. Watson.

The rebellion of 1857 had mattered little to her while she clawed her way up in the world. But to the maharani it would have been a formative experience.

And when they had met, Mrs. Watson could speak frankly of everything that was important to her, because nothing she said could have got her into trouble — at least, not the sort of trouble that would have bothered a woman who had already been the mistress of three men.

It had not been the same for the maharani,

who, visiting the heart of the empire that controlled her country, had to watch every single word she uttered.

Mrs. Watson squeezed her eyes shut. She had thought her beloved much too sheltered. That her beautiful Sita Devi, raised in the lap of luxury and prestige, had known nothing of the darker underbelly of life.

But as it turned out, Mrs. Watson had been, in her own way, just as divorced from reality. And unlike Sita Devi, who had asked a thousand questions about the world beyond her ken, Mrs. Watson hadn't even known enough to realize the extent of her ignorance.

Lord Ingram was sitting in the library at Hôtel Papillon, sealing a letter to his children, when Mrs. Watson came in.

He rose and smiled at her. "Good morning, ma'am."

She rushed forward and enfolded him in an embrace. After some hesitation, he hugged her back.

"I'm so happy you are all right," she said, her face buried in his lapel. "I kept imagining you dragging Mr. Marbleton toward the inn while thinking desperately of your children."

He didn't know how to tell her that he'd

been thinking of Holmes instead. "Nothing happened to either Mr. Marbleton or myself. As you can see, I'm fit as a fiddle."

She pulled back to have a better look at him. "You *are* looking very well."

He offered her a seat on the chaise longue. "You had a pleasant outing, I hope?"

"The maharani is in town — Miss Holmes and I called on her just now." Mrs. Watson hesitated. "I learned, much to my shock, what the maharani wishes to keep hidden. But I also learned that Miss Holmes made her own deductions concerning the matter and spoke with you about it."

"She did."

"She assured me that the nature of the maharani's secret did not bother you. Are you sure about that?"

Ten years ago, he would have given a very different answer. But now he'd grown wary of the empire. "If an Indian queen reigned as the empress of Britain, and the Subcontinent was in charge of the general direction and development of our country, would you be surprised that our nobles pondered, while among ourselves, on how we might be rid of our colonizers?"

"Pondering is one thing. But what if there were concrete plans?"

So she was still conflicted herself, even

though she had thrown in her lot with the maharani.

"Remington's office keeps track of just that," he assured her. "It might be one of the reasons that the maharani — or was it her son? Holmes thought her son was more likely."

"Her son."

"That might be the reason the young maharaja felt more comfortable writing to someone who appeared to represent a rival European power, because he knew that at his own court there would be someone ready to report on him to the British."

Mrs. Watson needed a moment to digest his words. Her brow furrowed in distress. "I knew nothing of her life. Nothing."

He sat down next to her on the chaise longue and took her hands. "Ma'am, we can none of us know the entire truth of someone else's life."

"I know that," she said sadly, leaning her head on his shoulder. "What I regret is that while I knew nothing of her life, I thought I knew everything."

Charlotte was warming up.

Hôtel Papillon had a ballroom — of course it did — which she decided to appropriate for her *canne de combat* exercises.

Mrs. Watson had taught her a series of movements that the older woman had developed during her theater days, to keep herself loose and limber while waiting to go on. Charlotte circled the room, performing shuffling steps, knee lifts, and lunges. Coming to a stop, she rolled her neck and shoulders. Next, she bent over and set her palms flat on the parquetry floor.

"Holmes —"

The speaker sounded as if he had forgotten whatever else he'd been about to say.

She straightened and turned around. "Hullo, Ash."

She wore a gentleman's sporting suit. This was not the first time she'd dressed as a man before him. But on previous occasions, her goal had been verisimilitude. Which meant that she'd had to glue on a beard and a mustache, use an orthodontic device to change the shape of her face, and don a great deal of padding so that her stomach protruded more than her bosom.

But this suit, and the attendant waistcoat and shirt, had been made for her body. Underneath she wore a half-corset, a merino wool combination, and not much else. The ensemble was intended strictly for swordsmanship practice and not public consumption. She was covered, of course — every inch beneath her chin — and men's trousers did not cling. Still, no feminine garments delineated the shape of a woman's lower body with such blatant clarity, and she might have caused a riot on the street.

Lord Ingram did not appear as if he were about to riot. In fact, he seemed to have wiped his countenance of all expression in the time it took for her to turn around. Dressed in a Harris Tweed sporting suit similar to hers, he looked lithe and remarkably fit.

He picked up one of the Malacca sticks she'd set out. "Shall we begin?"

"Did Mrs. Watson send you in her stead?"

Mrs. Watson had meant to be here to practice *canne de combat* with her.

"I volunteered. My *canne de combat* is a bit rusty."

She raised a brow. He was one of those people who believed modesty to be an actual virtue. For him to consider his grasp of a particular combat technique rusty probably meant that at the moment he could only flatten ten of her, rather than twenty.

"All right," she said. "Let's begin."

She was a far better fighter than she had been in summer, but he proved a far more underhanded opponent than Mrs. Watson.

221

As soon as their weapons met and he slid past her, he swung his cane around to attack her from the back of her arm to the back of her head.

She leaped out of the way and held up a hand, her skin smarting where he'd struck her, however lightly.

Mrs. Watson was an excellent swordswoman. She was also a woman who hadn't lived in dangerous surroundings or used her cane for anything except training and sport for many years. Lord Ingram, on the other hand, sometimes returned from trips abroad with injuries inconsistent with the known risks of archeology.

"I like what you did," said Charlotte. "Teach me how to defend against it. Then teach me how to do it."

"One moment," he said.

He left the ballroom and returned with a stack of broadsheets, which he rolled into two solid cylinders, and secured them with twine. "Let's hope these don't come loose too easily."

The newspaper sticks were softer, but that just meant he pulled back less on his strikes — and moved faster. His footwork was different from Mrs. Watson's, and his aim was also different. Instead of disarming his opponent, he sought to inflict damage.

Clearly he hadn't been fighting London footpads. And clearly he'd been facing multiple assailants, in the sort of melee that didn't allow for the luxury of merely disarming one's opponents, because they would simply pick up their weapons and attack again.

He taught her how to pivot after the initial parry, to avoid exposing her back to an assailant spinning around to whack at her further. Then he showed her what to do when he instead attacked her kneecaps.

"Vile," she said. "Excellent."

"Don't be so open about your perverted tastes," he murmured. "Now see how I move differently when I intend to strike low? I can't lean back at the same time. I must lean in."

"Can I use your own momentum against you here?" she asked. "By the way, my lord, not all of us are as good as you are at hiding perverted tastes."

"You can try, but only if you don't —"

She stepped back, but not before he hit her across the kneecaps.

"And I don't have perverted tastes. I have varied tastes."

She raised a brow. "Is that what they call it these days? Well then, I like how varied your tastes are."

His gaze dropped to a quick sweep of her body. She exploited his momentary distraction with a strike across his chest, which earned her a series of ferocious jabs, forcing her backward, until her retreat was blocked by a pillar.

He pointed his newspaper stick at her. "You've only seen the tip of the iceberg with regard to my varied tastes, Holmes."

She knocked his weapon aside with hers. "I won't believe it until I see the rest of that iceberg in person."

She pivoted, spun, and struck him from his back to the side of his head, much as he'd done to her on their very first pass.

He gave her a dirty look, unbuttoned his jacket, and tossed it aside. She did the same.

He picked up the cane he'd discarded earlier and tossed her hers. "This might hurt a little."

She smiled. "Promises, promises."

It hurt more than a little to be hit left and right. But she also managed some choice strikes of her own.

An hour flew by. Or rather, the first forty-five minutes flew by. The last quarter hour crawled, sobbing a little, to the finish line. The ballroom, like all big, high-ceilinged spaces in winter, was chilly. Still, she perspired freely, her limbs as heavy as cannons and as mobile as clay.

When he at last allowed the session to end, she hobbled to the carafe of mineral water that she'd prepared ahead of time and drank a long draught.

He joined her at the console table and handed her jacket to her.

"Thank you," she said, panting.

He was barely breathing faster.

At least the last time she had panted this hard he had been equally affected.

The console table was near a radiator, genteelly concealed behind a low screen — the house had been outfitted with central heating — so she didn't need to put on the jacket yet.

He was also barely perspiring, but he opened a button on his shirt.

She blinked.

"I have enjoyed looking at you today," he said dryly. "I thought I should return the favor in some measure."

Before she could respond, he poured himself a glass of water and asked, "Did you learn anything new from the maharani?"

"Did Mrs. Watson not tell you?"

"She appeared preoccupied, so I didn't ask."

That was likely the reason he had volunteered to take her place, so that Mrs. Watson could have some time to herself.

"You don't need to do everything for everyone. Mrs. Watson would also have been all right if she fought me for an hour."

"If I didn't do everything for everyone, I wouldn't know what to do with myself."

That was probably God's truth. It was his great weakness, this sometimes-compulsive over-generosity that arose at least partly in response to his doubts about himself and his place in the world.

When she'd been younger, she'd thought of it as only a weakness. But in time she came to understand that it was also his great strength. The doubts did exist, they were deep-seated, and he would always, in one way or another, try to assuage them. But he *was* kind, and he *was* generous, deeply, sincerely so.

And she —

She looked up at his lean, compelling features, his rueful expression, his thick, dark hair, ever so slightly tousled from exertion — and it startled her, how much she liked him.

It unsettled her.

She set aside her water glass. "I learned something new this morning. Earlier the maharani hadn't given us the full picture because she didn't truly believe we would carry through with the task. But today she admitted that there would be no incriminating evidence on or behind the Van Dyck at Château Vaudrieu. That we must exchange the painting for her letters."

He considered her, though it seemed to her that he was thinking as much about her suddenly brisk and businesslike tone as about what she had said. "Well, *retrieval* was always a euphemism for *theft.*"

She didn't think this would surprise him. Lieutenant Atwood had learned of the situation from him, and everything Lieutenant Atwood had said on the topic at dinner the other night had involved the wholesale removal of the painting.

"And then what?" he asked. "What do we do once we have the painting?"

"We will know only then."

He frowned. "I told my children I would be back in a fortnight. Not to mention, invitations have already gone out for a house party I'm giving after Christmas."

"I also don't want to be gone much longer than a fortnight. Mr. Mears mentioned that Bernadine has been faring tolerably since I left, but I'd prefer to be there myself."

They were silent for some time. She allowed her gaze to linger for a moment where his shirt opened to show the hollow at the base of his throat.

"Do you think this is but a clever mastermind using others to steal works of art?" he asked, still frowning.

"I wish I knew. I wish I could be certain of something — anything — about our purpose at Château Vaudrieu." She looked into his eyes. "The only thing I'm certain of is that I don't know enough to judge the situation yet."

The company gathered in the library that afternoon. There was a rich spread of delicacies, both sweet and savory, but only Mr. Marbleton approached it with anything resembling glee. He made a plate for Livia with a few miniature quiches and *gougères,* and brought her a glass of mineral water.

Lord Ingram had fetched punch and cake for Livia on various occasions, but he did that for any wallflower he happened to know. Sympathy, however, did not seem to factor into Mr. Marbleton's motives. He spoiled her because he enjoyed spoiling her, an experience completely novel to Livia, and almost as alarming as it was pleasurable.

She smiled at him. The smile he returned was so brilliant, she immediately wished that they were alone — yet was relieved that they weren't. She looked away, feeling like a train hurtling full bore toward the horizon: The railway was unfinished and she was about to run out of tracks at any moment.

Across from her Mrs. Watson nursed a finger of cognac, looking a little wan. Behind her settee, Lord Ingram stood by the window in a dove-grey lounge suit. Charlotte walked about slowly, examining book spines, sometimes running a finger along the edge of the shelves.

When she reached the door she looked into the corridor outside, closed the door again, then strolled back to stand behind a Louis XIV chair to Livia's left, where she could see everyone in the room.

Mrs. Watson exhaled and set down her cognac. "I have called everyone here because I am an old fool who took on a task that is much too big for me. It has already proved far more perilous than I anticipated and I must hereby release everyone from any further obligation."

"I would like to continue, if you don't mind, ma'am," said Lord Ingram.

"As would I," said Mr. Marbleton, grinning, "for the handsome reward I've been promised."

Livia had been with him earlier, when Mrs. Watson came to apologize, wholly unnecessarily, and to offer to let him go. He'd given the same cheeky answer then.

"I plan to stay with Charlotte," she said.

"And I," said Charlotte, "will stay with you, Mrs. Watson."

Mrs. Watson's throat moved. "In that case, you all have my profound gratitude. Miss Charlotte, would you discuss our next steps?"

Charlotte inclined her head. "I'll be happy to do that, ma'am."

She was in one of the dresses Livia had smuggled out from home, a dusty rose velvet adorned with at least fifteen tiers of scarlet flounce. Despite their sheer yardage, the flounces were narrow enough that the ensemble was almost elegant, considering that this was Charlotte.

"We have learned some things," Charlotte began. "One, I visited a Parisian art dealer yesterday. From speaking to him, I gather that Château Vaudrieu has a reputation of achieving higher prices than elsewhere. Also, that the dealer was personally wary of Château Vaudrieu, for reasons he did not specify but which, to my ears, had nothing to do with art.

"Two, I believe everyone knows that Mrs. Watson and I called on her friend this morning. But you may not know that the

230

friend has revised the description of what she needs from us. Getting to the painting is not the end, but only the beginning. Once we have the painting we will receive further instructions."

Livia hadn't heard this before. Mr. Marbleton raised a brow. Lord Ingram gave no reaction, and Mrs. Watson's expression of general unease did not change.

"This complicates matters, obviously. Earlier it was understood that come the ball, whether we succeeded or we failed, our task would be finished that night. Now, even if we succeed, we will only have succeeded in part.

"But while we must keep that in mind, at the moment what we need to do remains essentially the same: to locate this painting and create enough of a distraction that we can take it out of the château.

"To that end, we must accomplish a number of goals simultaneously. The first is that Lord Ingram's ally and I will attend the reception, two nights hence at the château, for the most likely buyers. We will try to familiarize ourselves with the château, but I fear that the guests will be heavily herded and that we will not be free to move about.

"Our second goal is to get as many of us

231

into the château as possible as temporary staff. Thanks to Lord Ingram and his ally, we now know which agency Madame Desrosiers uses for the extra waiters and maids required for the ball.

"Lord Ingram is not suitable for the task, as his face has been in the papers of late. English papers to be sure, but we don't want anyone at the château to recognize him by some chance. We will also need at least two of us to be among the guests, and it seems to make sense that our ally and I should serve in that capacity, given that we will already be expected to be there, based on our attendance at the reception.

"So that leaves Mrs. Watson, Miss Olivia, and Mr. Marbleton. We are in luck — the staffing agency has dispatched most of its regular roster of personnel to a large house in Paris, for a visit by a foreign dignitary. Which means that they will need to hire extra people very soon. I expect the advertisement to be in the papers by morning. Will you three be willing to try for those positions? Lord Ingram will provide expertly forged letters of character."

"Of course," said Mr. Marbleton. "I can even provide my own forged letter of character, if Lord Ingram is busy."

"It's only right that I do everything I can,"

said Mrs. Watson.

Livia was apprehensive. What if she was the only person whom the service wouldn't take? Or worse, what if she was the only person they did take? "I will do my best."

Charlotte nodded. She took a slice of mille-feuille and set it on her plate. Livia hadn't seen her choose anything so rich since they'd met again — and apparently Charlotte, too, realized her mistake. She gazed at the mille-feuille with a longing that would have been deeply poignant if its object weren't mere pastry, and then she approached Lord Ingram and offered him the plate. "I made a mistake in my selection, my lord. Would you care for it?"

Lord Ingram didn't appear remotely interested. Yet he accepted the plate and, with his attention still squarely on Charlotte, bit into the mille-feuille.

At the sight of his teeth sinking into the dessert, Livia's face heated. She had long believed that Charlotte had no romantic interests. Certainly she'd never mentioned any such inclinations toward Lord Ingram — in fact, Livia had rarely seen them in one setting. But in Lord Ingram's expression there was a certain . . . familiarity. Mr. Marbleton, for all his lively interest in Livia, did not look at her like that.

Good gracious, the boy Charlotte had kissed when she was barely pubescent — Livia had long assumed him to be the very pretty and completely feckless Roger Shrewsbury, but what if it had been Lord Ingram? That made much more sense, didn't it? Mr. Shrewsbury had no discretion at all. And Lord Ingram, other than Charlotte, was the most tight-lipped individual Livia had ever met.

Rather abruptly, Lord Ingram strode across the room, set down his plate, and poured himself a glass of cognac.

"And you, my lord?" Livia heard herself ask. "We haven't heard what you would do yet."

He studied the amber liquid in his glass. "I'm not sure whether what I plan to do has any purpose."

Near the other end of the library, Charlotte ate a slice of orange and made no comment.

"When Mr. Marbleton and I were hiding in the lake, under the bridge, we saw men and dogs running toward the chapel," said Lord Ingram. "I believe they were chasing something. What do you think, Mr. Marbleton?"

"I agree, but reluctantly, since I never saw what or whom they were chasing. Where did

234

they all go when they vanished for several minutes? Did they catch their quarry? They certainly returned tamely enough, those that passed near us."

"Miss Charlotte's opinion was that they all went into the chapel," said Lord Ingram. "I don't dispute that as a possibility. What I want to know is why. Why come running so urgently, in the middle of a wet, freezing night, to a chapel?

"Miss Charlotte then told me what she thought of when she studied the architectural plans for the château. That it did not show another exit, which she believes must be there, as the château had been constructed atop the foundation of a fort.

"She wondered whether, if such an exit indeed existed, it didn't lead out via the chapel. I found the idea plausible, but it still didn't give a reason for the chase. Then she said, what if, since the door of the chapel faced away from us, what we did not see that night was someone running out of the chapel toward the fence? In other words, the dogs weren't chasing an intruder, but someone trying to escape from inside the château."

ELEVEN

Livia had suggested that Mr. Marbleton dress up as a woman for his interview with the staffing company — that way, if they were both hired, they'd be able to work side by side. But he declined.

"Alas, my disguise is good but too casual. For a stroll on a busy street, where everyone's attention is elsewhere, or for an encounter that would only last a few seconds, it might serve. But it wouldn't survive close scrutiny, and I don't know that we won't face such before we are let into the château."

His words proved prescient.

Livia, Mrs. Watson, and Mr. Marbleton all passed the initial round of selection. Livia was surprised, although they looked convincing enough. Mrs. Watson was an expert at staging characters and a quick trip to a less affluent arrondissement's secondhand shops had supplied her with enough clothes and other accoutrements to attire and style them at the correct level of impoverishment: needy enough to stoop to menial labor, but not so destitute as to lack all respectability.

And they sounded convincing enough, Livia with her Alsatian accent, Mr. Marbleton with his slightly throaty inflections of Provence, and Mrs. Watson, the chameleon, now speaking French with a Spanish accent, pretending to be an unhappy widow stranded in Paris.

Still, Livia hadn't believed that they would all make it through to the next round. It would be too much luck, and she, not being accustomed to too much luck, found it unsettling.

But bits of conversation between those who worked at the staffing agency, with the opening and closing of doors, drifted to her ears. And even though they were speaking too fast for her to make out every word, she grasped enough of what they were saying — and of the urgency and franticness of their tone — to realize that the agency was far more short-staffed than they'd let on.

Apparently they had been losing people from their roster either to other agencies or to permanent employment. With the foreign dignitary taking up most of what remained of their personnel, they were scrambling to find suitable servants for the Château Vaudrieu ball. And now, at the very last minute, Château Vaudrieu decided to ask for temporary staff for the reception the next evening, when the agency already had two other functions to man.

But this state of chaos calmed Livia's jitters: It wasn't that they were too lucky, but that the agency was too desperate.

At about eleven in the morning, two hours after they first arrived, those who had been selected for the first round were herded into a room to be looked over by representatives from Château Vaudrieu.

Three men entered and walked among ranks of candidates.

Livia had always thought herself not particularly well respected. And she still believed she was correct in that assessment. But the slights and veiled disdain a not especially popular, not especially agreeable, and not especially solvent woman received on the marriage mart was nothing compared to the open rudeness she'd experienced this morning.

The sense of absolutely replaceability she'd felt, when she'd been interviewed by the staffing agency, along with eleven other women in the room, proved to be again nothing when compared to the humiliation of being stared at by the three men.

Thank goodness that their attention wasn't — as of yet — prurient. All the same, to be looked over as a mere object, unable to tell the men to stop, and instead needing to school her face so as not to betray any discomfort or indignation — this was powerlessness of a sort she'd never tasted.

And to think, she was only playacting. For others this must be an endlessly recurring theme, dignity and self-respect trampled underfoot for the sake of bread and a roof overhead.

Even so, she almost marched over to give the men what for when one of them sneered to a staffing agent, "Why this old hag? You think anyone wants to look at *that*?"

The "old hag" was the beautiful Mrs. Watson!

Livia's nails dug into her palms. She'd often heard the underclass described as prone to violence and had never questioned that assessment. But as her hand itched to grab the nearest umbrella and whack the man, she found herself suddenly understanding that the poor were prone to violence because it was the only tool remaining to them.

She seethed with an impotent rage as the inspection continued.

In the end, she and Mr. Marbleton were among those selected for the reception the next evening. And she could only be grateful, as they remained to listen to their instructions, that Mrs. Watson had already left.

Even though Livia couldn't possibly have tossed aside her pretense to defend her friend, she still felt deeply ashamed that she'd allowed it to happen in front of her, in front of so many strangers, that she couldn't have in any way spared Mrs. Watson this very real humiliation.

Lord Ingram looked up at the woman on the other side of the desk. Leighton Atwood had gone to take possession of a house near but not too near Château Vaudrieu, so he accompanied Holmes to the archives of *Le Temps* — the work proceeded faster with two people, one searching the indexes and locating the articles, the other reading and taking notes.

She worked with a concentration so pure it seemed to form a faint halo around her. She read each article twice in succession, then made her notes without referring back to it again. The notes were in shorthand, not her own modified version but the Pitman system that she learned a year or so after they started corresponding.

One day a letter from her arrived and the only line in normal script was, *I learned shorthand. Rather useful. Can you read this?* It had not been a challenge — he'd understood her enough by then to know that she didn't think in those terms. Rather, she had not yet outgrown the assumption that most others were able to do as she did: pick up a book on the Pitman system and write a letter in perfect shorthand the next day.

It took him longer than usual to reply, also in shorthand, even though she'd never asked him to. As it turned out, shorthand had proved far more useful to him in his various endeavors than it had to her. Still, it didn't change the fact that he first learned it because his pride had been too delicate to withstand the thought that she could now do something he couldn't. Even knowing, a priori, that he was dealing with one of the sharpest and most competent individuals he — or anyone, for that matter — would ever meet.

"Is something the matter?" she asked, without lifting her eyes from her notes.

"Nothing," he said. "I'm just not accustomed to the two of us working together."

In adolescence they'd shared a space while

each pursued a different interest. As adults sometimes they'd worked separately toward the same goal. When he'd been suspected of murder, she'd come to Stern Hollow to dig down to the truth of the matter. He'd very much been involved in the undertaking to clear his own name; but even then, they'd proceeded largely apart, as he couldn't leave his front door without a constable tagging along.

So this was a highly unusual experience. And yet it also didn't feel at all . . . noteworthy, as if this was what they should have been doing all along.

He smiled a little and bent his head to the indexes again. Down the corridor the newspaper's staff ran in and out of offices, the usual organized disarray at a daily publication. But here in the archive room, which was barely larger than a broom cupboard, he and Holmes had the place to themselves and all the relative peace and quiet they could wish for.

"Good find, by the way," she said a minute later. "This article gives the entire history of our Van Dyck, a fairly straightforward history at that. It was commissioned while the artist was in Genoa, a large religious piece for a private chapel. Later a daughter of the family married a Frenchman and brought

242

along the painting as part of her dowry.

"The family fortune went into decline well before the French Revolution. The Van Dyck was sold for the first and only time in 1760 — or rather, it was offered to a creditor to defray expenses. That creditor went on to make a fortune for himself and his heirs and the family has remained prominent since."

"Listen to this: 'The dashing young Monsieur Sylvestre admits that he regularly fields inquiries from art dealers hoping to obtain the piece for Van Dyck admirers willing to part with significant sums. But his response has always been a firm denial. The acquisition of the Van Dyck marked the beginning of the family's rise in the world, and they see it not only as a prized heirloom but as a talisman that safeguards them from life's uncertainties.' "

"Sylvestre? The name sounds familiar." He'd seen it somewhere in conjunction with Château Vaudrieu, but he didn't have her photographic memory and couldn't recall exactly where or in what context.

She flipped back a few pages in her notebook, then slid the notebook to him. "These are my notes from the other day when Lieutenant Atwood and I visited the archives of *Le Temps*."

Ah, now he remembered. He'd seen the name in this exact notebook, one among dozens, of the local luminaries who attended the ball. The dashing young Monsieur Sylvestre, current owner of the Van Dyck, had been a guest at the ball two years before.

"How old is the article you were reading?"

"From a year and a half before young Monsieur Sylvestre first attended the ball."

The family had held on to the Van Dyck for more than a century. Monsieur Sylvestre had clearly expressed a disinclination to ever part ways with it. Yet in a mere few years all that special significance attached to the Van Dyck had evaporated into thin air and the artwork would soon change hands.

"Interesting, no?" said Holmes, her expression unchanged except for a slight gleam deep in her eyes.

"Very interesting," Lord Ingram answered. "Too interesting."

Lieutenant Atwood had his own rooms near Rue de la Paix. When he'd received Lord Ingram's call for help, he did not quit those rooms. Hôtel Papillon was currently on a skeleton staff, given that the family was away. Still, that meant a number of eyes on the premises, and he preferred being able to

244

get in and out of disguises without being seen.

Charlotte had already been to his rooms, to put on her disguise as Mr. Hurst. On the afternoon of the reception, they again headed there, Lieutenant Atwood leaving Hôtel Papillon approximately half an hour before Charlotte.

When she knocked on his door, he was already in his evening attire, holding out a note toward her.

"From Monsieur Sauveterre," he said.

"Finally," said Charlotte.

As it turned out, invitations to the reception were not difficult to come by. Since the occasion was for dedicated art lovers to preview the available collection, one needed only to show proof of a large sum of money on hand at the Banque de Paris to the château's man of business on Boulevard Haussmann.

As soon as he'd obtained the invitations, Lieutenant Atwood, as the very wealthy Mr. Nariman of Bombay, had written Monsieur Sauveterre, the mostly retired art dealer they had called on a few days ago. Given Monsieur Sauveterre's lack of enthusiasm for Château Vaudrieu, both Lieutenant Atwood and Charlotte believed that such a letter would prompt him to object more

245

vociferously. Except Monsieur Sauveterre hadn't responded at all.

Until now.

"I got it on my way in. It's dated today," said Lieutenant Atwood.

Charlotte remembered Monsieur Sauveterre's lean-boned handwriting from their previous exchange. This time, his script was a less elegant scrawl. He'd been out of Paris visiting a friend and returned only this morning. Could he call on Messieurs Nariman and Hurst at their earliest convenience?

"I'll change as quickly as I can," said Charlotte. "Then let's call on him instead."

A meeting with Monsieur Sauveterre now would give them little time to reach the railway station, but she wanted to hear what the art dealer had to say.

Monsieur Sauveterre looked relieved to see them. "Are you on your way to the reception then, gentlemen?"

"Yes. Our train leaves in half an hour, but we thought we could still make a brief call."

The art dealer took a deep breath. "In which case, let me be direct. Gentlemen, I would advise you to have nothing to do with Château Vaudrieu."

"Why not?" asked Mr. Nariman, his expression one of sincere puzzlement. "I assure you, Monsieur, I am in no likelihood

246

of overbidding, as I have very little interest in art. We shall be there strictly as spectators."

"I cannot say more than that, Monsieur Nariman. In fact, I shouldn't even have said what I said. Please promise me that as far as anyone else is concerned, the topic of Château Vaudrieu never crossed my lips."

"Of course not. But I am very touched by your concern."

Monsieur Sauveterre sighed, perhaps recognizing a lost cause when he saw one. "I know that young men seldom turn aside from adventure on the advice of old men. But if you must head to Château Vaudrieu, then be careful."

"Surely, our lives will not be in danger," Charlotte, as Mr. Hurst, said hesitantly.

"No, but be wary and prudent, gentlemen," answered Monsieur Sauveterre, his brow furrowed. "Be wary and prudent, lest you come to regret much."

"Interesting choice of words, do you not think?" said Lieutenant Atwood when they neared the train station.

Charlotte nodded slowly. "Very interesting."

Be wary and prudent, gentlemen. What happened to those who were unwary and imprudent at Château Vaudrieu? They ended up paying more for art? Or did they, like the young scion of the Sylvestre family, suddenly agree to part with treasured art?

After they had made the discovery the day before, she and Lord Ingram had spent hours trying to ferret out whether the Sylvestre clan had fallen on hard times, going so far as to observe their manse from the outside. They unearthed no evidence that the Sylvestre fortune was thinning. That did not prove anything, but added another layer of oddity to the situation.

The countryside outside Paris had its fair share of châteaus, ranging from those hardly bigger than a farmhouse to majestic ruins of former royal palaces, now only stone walls and broken pillars in a slate-blue twilight.

Receptions were usually held later in the evening and ended early in the morning. But since the château was not in town and guests needed to take the last train that stopped at the small village *gare* on its way to Paris, this particular reception started at an earlier time, when Parisian Society would have just started the second course at dinner.

The guests had been instructed to arrive on the same train. They were shown onto four large double-deck omnibuses, each with a seating capacity of about twenty. Unlike most such vehicles, their top decks were enclosed, with braziers placed at regular intervals to keep the space heated.

Charlotte, far more gregarious as her own masculine counterpart, made pleasant small talk in French to those seated near them, a frosty grande dame and a young man who appeared to be her grandson. He was clear-featured, with a ready smile and what must be a handful of rings under his left glove. When he gave his name, she recalled having come across it in an article about the ball — a family of industrialists, with the haughty matriarch the daughter of a duke.

Grandmaman was seriously interested in at least three of the paintings, the young man informed them. But before he could enthuse more, Grandmaman cleared her throat and he stopped, apparently reminded that the kindly looking man he was speaking to was in fact a competitor who might drive up prices.

Inside the gate of the estate, the chestnut-lined boulevard leading to the château was illuminated, not extravagantly, as it would be on the night of the ball, but with only one or two lanterns on each tree. The omnibuses stopped before the bridge. The guests alit and crossed the bridge on foot.

Charlotte dropped a pebble as she strolled over the spot where Lord Ingram and Mr. Marbleton must have trod increasingly icy water, as dogs and men race past. Lieutenant Atwood glanced down and then in the direction of the chapel.

"Sounds deep," he murmured.

"Sounds cold," she replied.

The others who had arrived on the same omnibus had already gone past them, and the minders were busy checking the vehicle to make sure no one had been left behind.

For the moment, they had a measure of privacy.

"The young man isn't related to Grandmaman," said Lieutenant Atwood. "He does a decent imitation of her accent, with overlays of both Paris and Normandy. But I hear the wharfs of Marseille underneath that."

Charlotte didn't have as good an ear for traces of regional French accents, but she also knew that the two were not family.

"Grandmaman, on the other hand, is the genuine article. Makes you wonder, doesn't it?" she murmured. "And by the way, Mr. Nariman, when you were at the architect firm of Balzac & Girault, looking for the architectural plans, did you notice any slack in that particular box or drawer?"

Livia did not enjoy herself.

She, Mr. Marbleton, and ten other temporary servants arrived at the château at noon. They were given a quick meal of stew and bread. She was too nervous to eat but didn't want to appear suspicious by not finishing the contents of her bowl — a maid who didn't have steady employment was not one who would forego any food put down in front of her.

Then the work began.

She had practiced a servant's work with Mr. Marbleton, but she was not prepared for the scale of the reception at Château Vaudrieu. Plates, silverware, glasses by the hundreds, napkins by the gross. Everything had to be taken out of the butlery and carried halfway across the manor to be set up. Ice was delivered at four in the afternoon. She wasn't asked to load large blocks of ice onto handcarts, but she couldn't escape having to squat for an hour, chipping ice with a hammer and a pick.

Once she opened the door of a smaller pantry to find a temporary waiter taking a nap inside. When he'd opened one bloodshot eye to see her standing there, he'd winked lazily and gone back to sleep. She'd never envied anyone so much for sheer impudence.

The servants were given their supper — the exact same food they'd had for lunch. By this time, Livia was no longer nervous, only exhausted, her back aching, her haunches burning. She made herself eat anyway and was grateful for the scalding coffee passed around after the meal. At least now she could stay awake.

Throughout it all, Mr. Marbleton remained close to her as much as he could. They rarely spoke. One time, when they passed each other in a hallway, she with her arms full of a floral arrangement, he carrying empty baskets in which he'd earlier ferried up garlands of spruce and berries, he asked whether she was all right. Another time, after the servants' supper, as they were moving endless platters of canapés into place, she'd snuck a miniature quiche she'd stolen from her platter into his pocket, only to have him immediately hand her a tiny *gougère* he'd saved for her.

It tasted marvelous.

With the endless labor shoved onto the temporary staff, even though she kept her eyes open, she didn't see much of anything except services stairs and passages connecting various pantries and storerooms to the gallery where she'd transferred everything. With the exception of the arrival of a mysterious guest in the afternoon, which made her heart thud with excitement and misgivings.

Half an hour before the guests were to arrive everything was in place, towers of glasses sparkling, wines uncorked and breathing. The temporary staff were sent to wash their hands and change into fresh, spotless uniforms. They were then assigned places for the evening.

Livia had longed for the backbreaking portion of the work to finish. But now that she was standing around, almost immediately she began to worry about Charlotte and Lord Ingram. At least Mr. Marbleton would be near her.

"Did you notice anything?" she asked, when she helped him adjust a garland on the mantel.

He nodded. "You?"

She nodded, too, wondering whether he had also seen the black-swaddled figure slipping into the château like a ghost.

"To your stations!" shouted a member of the permanent staff. "To your stations! The guests will be here any minute."

Livia exhaled, went to her spot, and

looked toward the door, waiting for Charlotte to walk in at any moment.

"You are upset about something," said the maharani. "What is it, Mrs. Watson?"

Mrs. Watson had no idea now why she hadn't immediately thought her beautiful at their reunion. If anything she had become even more striking in the intervening years, with an aura of queenliness to her sculpted features.

This evening she wore a white silk sari edged with borders of cool blue. Mostly Mrs. Watson still found her to be a stranger. Yet other times she would catch glimpses of the young woman she'd once known — like now, with her perceptive question that indicated a willingness to listen.

Thus far on Mrs. Watson's call, they'd already talked about the weather, the maharani's grandchildren, and even the steel tower almost a thousand feet high that would be constructed right on the Champ de Mars, about to break ground in a matter of days.

What Mrs. Watson really wanted to ask was the maharani's stance on the British Raj, but she didn't know how to pose the question gracefully. So she gave her coffee a stir and said, "Two of my companions and I interviewed to be temporary staff at Château Vaudrieu. The young people were selected — they are at the reception now. But I was rejected on the ground of being an old hag, in front of a roomful of people."

The maharani's expression immediately darkened but Mrs. Watson raised a hand to forestall her objection. "The man who said that revealed his own uncouthness than anything else. I know I'm not a young woman anymore. To the sort of men who judge women only on their youth and desirability, I'm about as useful and interesting as a moth to a wolf.

"I was upset not so much for myself, but for the young lady who was with me. She is sensitive. She is afraid of an unsecured old age. And she is facing that dreadful chasm at thirty, beyond which unmarried women become spinsters.

"So what for me was a minor vexation was an ordeal for her. And she's been avoiding me since because she thinks I must have been ten times as devastated as she was as a bystander. I shall need to corner her soon to let her know that I've developed the hide of an elephant over the years and that she mustn't suffer needlessly on my behalf."

The maharani gazed at her a moment. Mrs. Watson's heart thumped. This was the first time they had been alone since the maharani's unannounced call, when they'd both been formal and awkward.

"You've always been wise and perceptive, Mrs. Watson. But what I've appreciated most is the compassion behind your perspicacity." The maharani smiled slightly. "Do you remember when you snuck me around London, to places where my proper escorts would have never allowed me? You understood, without my ever saying it in so many words, that I'd only seen one kind of life and that I longed to know the other facets that had been kept from me."

Mrs. Watson's fingers gripped her skirt. "Then — why did you not do the same for me? Why did you not expose me to other points of view? Why did you not let me see the other facets of your life?"

The château wasn't on the same scale as Chatsworth House or Blenheim Palace, but it was larger than the manor at Stern Hollow. The interior was suitably grand, with marble pillars, ormolu staircases, and huge murals. Velvet ropes guided the guests up a double-returned staircase and down an echoing corridor with a painted ceiling, much as had been described in the article.

Charlotte took note of the men stationed

at regular intervals along the way. They were dressed as footmen, but it must be apparent, even to those without theft in mind, that they served as guards.

The corridor led into a long gallery. A man stood a few steps inside the door and greeted the new arrivals. "You must be Mr. Nariman," he said to Lieutenant Atwood.

"Monsieur Plantier, I presume? *Enchanté.*" said Lieutenant Atwood, in lightly accented French. "My travel companion, Monsieur Hurst."

Monsieur Plantier, a shrewd-looking man in his late thirties, was reputed to be an art connoisseur and the one who curated the private museum at Château Vaudrieu. "We are delighted you could join us tonight. Please have a glass of champagne and savor the beauty of our collection."

"I was hoping to luxuriate in Madame Desrosiers's beauty as well. Is she not here tonight?" asked Lieutenant Atwood.

"Alas, my sister is slightly indisposed this evening, but she very much hopes to be well enough to preside over the ball."

"Our best wishes for her speedy recovery," said Lieutenant Atwood, as they yielded their places to the next guests in line.

A waiter passed by carrying a tray of champagne flutes. They each took one and started a slow promenade down the gallery. There were no Van Dycks, but here, too, there were strategically placed footmen. They didn't pour champagne, circulate with trays of nibbles, or rearrange displays at the buffet to make the remaining oysters look more symmetrical. Instead they kept to their spots, interacted not at all with the guests but studied them with alert and suspicious eyes.

"Oh look, there's Grandmaman's darling," said Charlotte. "Shall we approach?"

Now that he was barehanded, the bulges they'd seen earlier under his left glove proved indeed to be large rings. He was otherwise dressed without undue flare, but those rings . . . Each would have been enough to mark the owner's wealth and importance; four together formed a picture of almost comical pomposity.

"We meet again, Monsieur du Vernay," said Lieutenant Atwood warmly. "Where is your majestic grandmaman?"

"Monsieur du Vernay" made a face. "Away from youth and vitality, obviously."

Grandmaman, from across the gallery, stared at him with a mixture of distaste, anxiety, and yet, also hope.

Charlotte, as Mr. Hurst, nodded sagely. "I find myself admiring, dear sir, your collection of magnificent rings. Are some of them signet rings?"

The young man raised his hand and turned it so that light from the chandeliers — electric chandeliers, so bright as to be harsh — caught and reflected in the rings. "Only one is — this one, which once belonged to Grandmaman's grandfather. Lost his head to the National Razor, alas."

"And the others?"

"This one was the episcopal ring of a cousin of the beheaded. This one, with the amethyst, a favorite of my grandfather's. And this one, with the carnelian cabochon, is *my* favorite, a gift from the Sun King to an even more remote ancestor."

"Marvelous. Absolutely marvelous," enthused Charlotte. "I envy you such connections to the past — and such illustrious forebears! A hundred years ago mine were mere yeoman farmers, without any entrée to the halls of power. But if I may be so blunt, is it not a little inconvenient to wear such large rings side by side all on one hand?"

"Oh certainly, a little. But what's a little inconvenience when such a display could be had?"

Again, he rotated his hand so that everything sparkled.

"I cannot disagree with that at all." Charlotte raised her glass. "To an unmistakable display of pedigree."

The young man grinned. They clinked their champagne glasses and drank.

"You mentioned, Monsieur," said Lieutenant Atwood, "that your grandmother was interested in three paintings here. Do you happen to know which ones?"

Grandmaman had glared at him earlier not because he might betray her interest, but because by speaking too much, those with sharp ears might hear his wharfs-of-Marseille origins. But now Grandmaman was forty feet away, seated on a tufted chaise, her hands gripped rigidly around the head of her cane.

"Oh, this one, of course," the young man pointed at the sentimental Bouguereau tableau before which he stood. "And the Fragonard. And the Watteau."

They circulated away soon afterward but Charlotte kept both the young man and his "grandmother" in sight and noticed that neither paid much attention to the three pictures he'd named, but kept studying a portrait by Jacques-Louis David.

David had been an ardent supporter of Robespierre and sent many to the guillotine. Why would the grande dame want anything to do with the work of the man who might very well have signed her grandfather's death warrant?

There was no rain this time, a very great mercy.

Lord Ingram leaped over the fence and walked quietly but quickly toward the chapel, its dark silhouette haloed by light from the château. He couldn't hear the sounds from the reception, but the air seemed to hum subtly, the difference between being in the vicinity of a nearly empty manor and a fully populated one.

He made his way to the front door of the chapel, which was not visible from the château. He'd brought a pocket lantern. Now he risked opening a panel slightly, letting out a tiny stream of light.

But even without the light, he could smell the new paint on the door frame. He took off one glove. A quick touch showed that the paint still hadn't dried fully. The hasp and the mounting plate both felt smooth, as did the padlock itself, scarcely exposed to the elements. In fact, both the door and the door frame might be new. The painted surfaces did not seem to have ever been subjected to enough violence to unmoor bolts and lock plates.

If Holmes was correct, then the person escaping the château emerged in the chapel, rushed to the door, found it locked from the outside, and with a mighty kick or three, forced it open.

But although the fugitive had come close to freedom, Holmes believed that his attempt had failed. That he'd been caught at the fence and brought back into the chapel. Otherwise Lord Ingram and Mr. Marbleton, under the bridge, should have seen or heard something of the pursuit beyond the fence.

The pocket lantern held between his teeth, Lord Ingram picked the lock. The estate was quiet, the chapel quiet, the goings-on inside the château a barely perceptible vibration. He wondered what Holmes and Leighton Atwood had found out by now.

The padlock clicked, opening. He entered the chapel, closing the door behind himself. Light escaping the château and the grounds brightened the south-facing stained-glass panels slightly, but failed to penetrate beyond. The interior of the chapel was as dark as a nightmare.

There was no carpet in the pews. The floor underfoot was stone, and sounded solid when he tapped it with the heel of his boot.

With the pocket lantern back inside his pocket, he groped his way to the front. The place was too small for a separate vestry, so he turned his attention to the altar, a rather sizable one for this space. It had an antependium of drapery. And behind the drapery, only an empty space.

He crawled under the space, set all the drapes back in place, struck a match, and lit the lantern. He was sitting on a thin rug. And when he'd rolled up the rug, there it was: a trapdoor.

The trapdoor didn't budge when he tried to lift it. But he'd come prepared: not to force it, but to remove its hinges from the other end. Once he had done so, he was able to raise the trapdoor enough to slide a hook into the space underneath and undo the slide bolt.

He screwed the hinges back and stared at the pit before him. A stale odor rose from its unseen depths. The hairs on the back of his neck stood up. He had to force himself to reach in and feel for the ladder.

The ladder went down and down. He didn't dare use the pocket lantern. The darkness seemed infinite, his footsteps on the rungs, as loud as drumbeats.

When he finally reached the bottom, the tunnel that greeted him was scarcely three feet wide and too low for him to stand up straight. Should anyone come from either direction when he was in the tunnel, he would be doomed.

He expelled a shaky breath and took a step forward. At least, if he should disappear tonight, Holmes and Leighton Atwood would know where he was, which was more than he could have said for certain risks he'd taken elsewhere.

The tunnel's interior was brick. For a structure burrowing beneath a lake, it was watertight, no moisture seeping or collecting anywhere. The air was at once thick and somehow not enough. Hunched over, he shuffled along, already regretting his choice. His neck ached, and his calves, too, from proceeding on half-bent knees.

At last he arrived before a door. He risked a little light and saw that it was of heavy oak panels reinforced with ironwork. The wood looked to be hundreds of years old, but the thick bolt and the large padlock that must weigh half a stone were so new they shone, unmarred by rust or scratch.

He frowned. It didn't take a Sherlock Holmes to see that something was wrong with the picture: The two doors at the two ends of the tunnel were both locked from inside.

He frowned some more and turned around. Had he felt any branching along the way? Or a door of some kind? He was certain he hadn't. But then again . . .

Swearing under his breath, he retraced his steps and found what he sought twenty feet away: a small trapdoor on the ceiling.

This one did not have fastenings on either side and lifted at a push of his hand. He hoisted himself up — into another tunnel.

If he wasn't too wrong about the distance he'd covered, then he must already be underneath the island. The tunnel he had been in earlier was probably the original tunnel that had been the fort's escape route. The one he was currently in was much lower and narrower: In the other one he'd proceeded on his feet, however uncomfortably; here there was no choice except to advance on his stomach.

Was this a newer branching, so that those in the château didn't have to go all the way to the basement — the dungeon? — to access the escape route? It was also much more crudely constructed, braced with timber to the side and overhead, but he was crawling over unimproved earth.

It sloped gradually upward. Where would it take him?

He stopped.

Faint thuds.

Was he under a hall and the guests at the reception were walking overhead? No, it was too weak and solitary a sound for that. Wait. Was the tapping in Morse code?

He let out some more light from the pocket lantern, found his notebook, and jotted down what he heard. There were no three-unit gaps to indicate how to break the signal for letters, or seven-unit gaps to show the space between words.

It was not a long message. He recorded for three pages in the small notebook, even though he could see that after the first page, the message began to repeat. He would have kept on documenting for another few pages, but the signal disappeared abruptly.

He waited for it to come back. It didn't.

Ahead the tunnel went on, leading only into darkness. He put away his pencil and notebook, exhaled, and crawled on.

Twelve

The maharani was silent for some time. "You mean, why I did not tell you that I was not and had never been content with the fact that Britain ruled India?"

At last, that question out in the open. Mrs. Watson swallowed. "Yes."

"I suppose one reason was that you were so earnestly unaffected by the currents that governed my life that I was, if not happy, then at least not unwilling, to let you remain in that state of blissful innocence. If you had been somewhat aware or mildly curious, then I might have decided differently."

"I . . . I was unforgivably ignorant."

The maharani sighed. "It is a profitable arrangement for Britain to have colonies. At the heart of the empire, in the homeland, even those without any connection to the colonies benefit from the general prosperity that comes of a ready supply of raw material to feed the fires of industry, and then

267

ready markets for the sale of finished products.

"But the British have convinced themselves that in taking over India, they themselves were the benefactors and the natives of the Subcontinent the beneficiaries. Who would dare tell them otherwise?

"We have met Englishmen and -women of superlative education and refinement, who discuss the philosophies of the Enlightenment and the general human condition with piercing insight and clarity. Those same individuals then prove themselves perfectly willing to regard the people of the Subcontinent as subhuman, far better off as second-class citizens in their own land than as masters of their own destiny.

"By the time I visited Britain, I'd given up on changing British minds. By the time we were . . . part of each other's lives, I was almost glad not to know what you thought on the matter. That way I could pretend that if you knew, you would be sympathetic to my position."

"I would have been. I would!" cried Mrs. Watson.

Now that she thought about it, all those evenings they'd spent together, she *had* asked questions. But the maharani had seemed less interested in talking about herself and her life in India than in learning about the wider world, and Mrs. Watson had been happy to let her guide the direction of their conversation, never guessing that she had intentionally avoided certain subjects.

And then she thought of what the maharani just said with an uncomfortable tightness in her chest. "You said that my lack of insight was one reason your true views never came up. What — what other reasons were there?"

The maharani looked down for a moment and tucked a nonexistent strand of loose hair behind her ear. "There were those around me who worried that your friendship concealed ulterior motives."

Mrs. Watson blinked. What ulterior motives? Had the maharani's underlings thought that she would have swindled her?

"They suspected that you might have been planted by the British government."

Mrs. Watson's jaw dropped. "To spy on you?"

And then, her shock exploded into stupefaction. "Did *you* believe that?"

"For a while I didn't know what to believe: We had no evidence one way or the other. Which was yet another reason that I never brought up my true beliefs on the matter."

Mrs. Watson opened her mouth to argue

her absolute innocence, but the maharani forestalled her with a raised hand. "I did believe you in the end. No spy would waste so much time on me and never get to the point. I especially believed you when you didn't seize the chance to come with me to India.

"Don't misunderstand me. Your refusal devastated me. I'd never been in love before, and it took me a long time to recover from that loss. But at least afterward I knew that you had been with me for me, not playing a role at someone else's directive."

Her eyes were frank and clear, her expression wistful.

Mrs. Watson suddenly felt shy. "It took me a long time to recover, too. I felt the worst sort of mercenary, but I was no spy. I loved every minute of being with you."

The maharani shook her head slowly. "You were not mercenary. What I'd hoped for was the rainbow. But rainbows aren't meant to last. Most beautiful things aren't."

They fell silent.

The past was never quite what one remembered it to be. Mrs. Watson had thought the love between herself and the maharani some of the purest, simplest emotions she'd ever experienced. But for the maharani, it would have been some of the most complicated. All the same, she'd been determined enough to make Mrs. Watson a permanent part of her life, to live with her own and her subordinates' doubts as a price she was willing to pay.

Mrs. Watson swallowed past a lump in her throat. She had better go before she did something embarrassing. She rose to take her leave, and only then remembered that she had not come merely to reminisce with the maharani.

"Your Highness," she said awkwardly, "I need something from you."

Mr. Hurst and Mr. Nariman continued to circle the gallery, stopping from time to time to admire a particular work, savor a new glass of champagne, or replenish their plates with hors d'oeuvres from a table decorated with spruce garlands and olive wreaths.

Not only had they not seen the Van Dyck, they hadn't seen either Livia or Mr. Marbleton.

This was not particularly surprising. No art dealer, not even one who opened for business only once a year, showed his entire stock to all the prospective buyers at once. It was only a matter of whether Mr. Nariman's supposedly fabulous family wealth would let them see the better pieces.

Lieutenant Atwood put on an expression of polite ennui, which almost slid to outright disdain when they passed by a well-dressed young man entertaining a pair of middle-aged ladies with a magic trick. He and Charlotte sat down on a padded bench to sip their champagne and eat caviar on toast, sighing with implied boredom between bites.

"Since ours isn't the only party in attendance with ulterior motives, I'm doubting everyone here," murmured Lieutenant Atwood. "But most of them are probably legitimately interested in the art."

Charlotte had her eye on a pair of good-looking women with their aging uncle. Men of a certain age appeared from time to time with new "nieces." That by itself wasn't particularly notable. But Charlotte had never seen an "uncle" regard his two attractive "nieces" with both a great deal of timidity and almost as much self-reproach.

She had also singled out a solicitor who had been brought along by an aristocrat. She hadn't spent a great deal of time with lawyers but she didn't think the typical lawyer would be that interested in windows and fireplace flues.

"The one that caught your attention." She gestured subtly to the young man playing

272

magic tricks. "Too good?"

"Far too good for someone who isn't a professional," said Lieutenant Atwood from behind his champagne glass. "So good that he can no longer gauge how a dabbler does at these tricks."

Charlotte placed another piece of caviar toast into her mouth. As she chewed meditatively, Monsieur du Vernay walked by and raised his champagne glass in salute. Under the electric lights, his rings twinkled exuberantly.

"I might know who that young man is," said Lieutenant Atwood, speaking softly as Monsieur du Vernay joined his "Grandmaman."

Charlotte knew *what* the young man was, but she had not inferred his exact identity yet. There was no one immediately nearby; still she scooted closer to Lieutenant Atwood. "Go on."

"You yourself aren't an agent of the Crown, but you consulted for Lord Bancroft, when he was still in charge of certain clandestine portfolios."

She nodded.

"I have heard that our French counterparts sometimes use the services of a thief who has made a specialty out of making away with valuable *objets* before a crowd.

In fact, that is the price for his current freedom, that he must come when called. He is said to have spent some time in prison as a juvenile and has *Dieu, ne me quitte pas* tattooed across the fingers of his left hand."

"I see," she said.

She was known for having a pleasantly blank countenance, reputed to be highly unreadable. But Lieutenant Atwood, after a quick glance, said, "You don't agree?"

Before she could answer, she spied Monsieur Plantier, their host, advancing toward them. "Surely, *mes amis,*" he cried heartily, "you have not already tired of champagne and beauty!"

Lieutenant Atwood smiled indulgently. "The champagne is first-rate. The art, well, I will not deny that I am surrounded by beauty. But I must say, I'd hoped to be surrounded by beauty of a far greater caliber."

Monsieur Plantier was not only not offended by his complaint, but he smiled more brilliantly and seemingly with more approval. "Monsieur Nariman is a connoisseur. Please wait a moment. Let me see what I can do."

A few minutes later, a footman discreetly guided them behind a screen at the far end of the gallery. Beyond the screen was a door. Through the door, they were led out to a corridor and then into an ornate *salle,* which still didn't contain the Van Dyck or their companions.

But it did contain the young man and his grandmaman.

Standing under a Frans Hals portrait, Charlotte murmured to Lieutenant Atwood, "Watch the guards. Who are they looking at?"

Lieutenant Atwood turned around nonchalantly to walk to a Bruegel on the opposite side of the *salle.* When he returned, he said, "Our thief."

And then, "Which someone of his caliber should never allow to happen. You think he isn't the thief I mentioned?"

"There are very faint dots of discoloration on the inside corners of his eyes. Very slightly reddish dots."

Lieutenant Atwood's eyes widened. He lowered his voice further. "He's an *actor*?"

Stage performers painted red dots in the inside corners of their eyes to counteract the overbrightness of footlights.

If the apple of Grandmaman's eye was an actor hired to play the part of the thief, the real thief must be walking about the reception, thus far unremarked.

This point no doubt occurred to Lieutenant Atwood. He frowned. Then he turned to Charlotte. "But *you* know which one he is."

"I have a guess. The bit about visible tattoos on his left hand might be a rumor he himself deliberately spread. That way, when he shows up with a perfectly unmarked left hand, no one will suspect him of any intention toward or expertise in theft. And knowing that he had already outsmarted his quarries at the outset, he might even brandish his left hand a little more than the average person."

"The man playing magic tricks in the gallery."

The one Lieutenant Atwood had remarked as being too good. Who happened to have been standing directly under the David portrait.

After a quarter of an hour, during which they diligently studied all the paintings in the *salle,* they were brought back to the gallery.

The solicitor was still there, staring moodily at a window. The "uncle" and his "nieces" were there, all looking bored, as if they also hoped to catch Monsieur Plantier's attention and be brought before greater artistic treasures. Grandmaman and Monsieur du Vernay were still in the other *salle,* but the tattoo-less thief was now at the buffet table, merrily chatting with a pair of very respectable-looking ladies.

Then the ladies screamed, a tower of glasses toppled over, and pandemonium ensued.

THIRTEEN

There was no danger that wasn't made worse by dirt.

Lord Ingram, as a rule, didn't mind dirt. He'd been excavating major, minor, and absolutely trivial archeological sites since he was a child. The careful removal of rock and soil from historical relics was one of his great pleasures in life.

But he sincerely and wholeheartedly deplored dirt, especially the wet, smelly sort, when it was not affixed to historical relics, but to whatever godforsaken task he found himself performing under the guise of archeology.

The only conclusion he could draw was that he was vain enough to want to die a clean man.

Compared to the worst mud he'd experienced, this tunnel was practically luxurious. Still, he longed feverishly for marble, stone, or even brick surfaces, anything that didn't let earthworms wiggle through or a slug fall on his neck.

His picture had been in the papers recently, a merciful excuse to remain behind at Hôtel Papillon. But had he contented himself with a game in the warm, dry, spotless billiard room? No, he'd had to volunteer for the worst task of the night, one that no one had asked him to do.

You don't need to do everything for everyone, Holmes had said.

One of these days he ought to listen to her.

But his wiser future self obviously dwelled too far in the future to save him tonight.

The tunnel itself, steadily climbing, didn't have any obvious turns, but his compass indicated that he'd proceed in a semi-spiral. He'd been facing west earlier; now he was facing near south.

A few feet farther along he came to a half door set directly before him, rather than above. He listened for a long time, wary of meeting any oncoming guards as he stepped into the château. But when he opened the door, he encountered not a room or corridor, but more darkness.

After some hesitation, he let light out of his lantern and looked around.

It was not so much a passage as a narrow,

rectangular well, with stones protruding an inch or two out of the walls to provide footholds. The floor, too, was stone, what he had been praying for, but he almost wished he had some more by-now familiar dank earthen passages to crawl through. In the stillness, his breaths echoed against the walls.

He took off his dirt-soiled outer layer of oversized garments. Those, along with his shoes, he stowed on the other side of the half door. In his stocking feet, the lantern again lit and clasped between his teeth, he climbed up until he reached another trap-door.

Above the trapdoor was yet another passage. He examined the floor. There wasn't much dust. In such an enclosed space, without ready changes of air, the supply of dust was limited. But the distribution was what one would see in a normal corridor that wasn't cleaned frequently: a layer of encrusted dirt near the edges of the walls, the center of the passage clear from foot traffic.

He bent his face almost to the floor. Too clear. The passage had been used recently. Within days.

Now the choice of whether to keep his small, dim lantern lit. In the end, he did not close the front panel, though he did close it as much as possible, while still letting out a sliver of light. He was counting on being the only intruder in this space tonight. Hoping that even if someone else came in, it would be a customary user, walking with a bright light and heavy footfalls, who would give him enough notice to darken his lantern and get away.

Twenty feet out he was glad he'd left the lantern on, or he might have knocked over the item placed directly in his path, even if he'd been feeling his way with his hands. The lantern emitted so little light that at first he thought he'd encountered a barrier. Only when he opened the lantern's front panel a little more could he make it out as a tripod. A surveyor's tripod, the sort that could easily support the weight of a theodolite, or some other optical instrument.

As an archeologist, he'd done his share of land surveys and always shipped a few such tripods in crates as part of his equipment. But what was a surveyor's tripod doing in a secret passage concealed inside the walls of a château?

Of course.

He lifted the tripod carefully, moved it eighteen inches out of the way, and took its place. But the spot where a camera would have aimed was nothing but wall. He pushed, tapped, and even ran his fingers up and down lines of mortar, but nothing at all happened.

Unless . . . the one he thought to be the inner wall was actually the outer wall?

He turned around 180 degrees and pressed and prodded the opposite wall — and almost leaped back when a panel slid open. Beyond the panel was a pane of something cool and smooth.

Glass.

And beyond the glass, darkness.

His fingertips tingling, he shut the panel. Had the light from his lantern been seen? His heart pounding, he stood and listened, but heard nothing. After a while he dimmed the lantern and slid open the panel again.

The same unrelieved darkness beyond the glass pane. Seconds ticked by. A minute. The darkness didn't change at all. He set his ear against the cold, slick glass: still nothing, except for a faint din that could be either reverberations from the reception or merely blood pumping through his own veins.

He drew back and wiped a handkerchief across the glass pane, removing any trace of oil or dirt his skin might have left behind. Then he closed the panel, put the tripod back, and walked on.

About twenty-five feet out, he encountered another such tripod — and another hidden panel in the wall, with another glass pane behind it.

Another twenty feet or so, yet another tripod. Altogether he counted five tripods before the tunnel ended. He felt around but couldn't get any part of the wall to move or even recess. He retraced his steps.

The trapdoor he'd come through was somewhere in the middle of the long passage. The five tripods he'd encountered were all west of it. There were more tripods on the other side of the trapdoor.

The process had become familiar to him by now: Move aside the tripod, peer behind the wall panel, see nothing, and move on. He fully expected the same result to keep repeating, but the second wall panel east of the trapdoor opened to reveal an illuminated room beyond.

Not only illuminated, occupied: Two women were walking out of the luxuriously appointed bedroom. Instinctively he moved to the side, afraid that there might be others in the room and his silhouette would be seen.

When he risked another peek, however, the room was empty, though the door was left open to the passage outside. The peephole was oddly placed, perhaps two feet from the floor, implying that the secret passage itself straddled two floors. Which made sense. Walls were punctuated with windows, and the passage must be placed higher than the tops of the windows below and lower than the sills of the windows above.

Other than its rather low vantage point, the peephole gave a clear panorama of the room, as if the furnishing had been placed just so to avoid obstructing the view.

He was about to pull out Mr. Marbleton's detective camera and take a picture when a grinding sound came from the middle of the passage: a secret door being opened.

There wasn't enough time for him to reach the trapdoor, get through, *and* put it back in place behind himself. He broke out in a cold sweat, shoved back the detective camera, and moved toward the eastern end of the passage, holding out an unsteady hand to feel for any more tripods.

His fingers touched one. He took care to go around it without making any sounds and continued his retreat. Light — too much light — spilled in from the secret door. He moved faster, praying that he would not pay for his speed by bumping into the next tripod.

But there were no more tripods; only the end of the tunnel. And luckily, there was a protuberance, built to accommodate either pipes or a chimney flue, with just enough space behind for him to hide.

He flattened himself against the wall as a bright lantern swung. His heart raced. He'd come to this level in clean clothes and his stockinged feet and shouldn't have left any traces of dirt that would cause suspicion.

But one never knew in these situations.

The lantern swung a few more times before a woman said, in lilting French, "This way, please."

Footsteps. The slight scrape of the tripod being lifted out of the way.

Then the woman spoke again. "You see, Madame, it is not that we are not treating you as an esteemed guest, it is only that the rooms in this château that qualify as estimable all have such peepholes. I do not know your preferences, but me, I cannot abide such intrusion into my privacy. Even if I cover up the peephole I will still know it's there."

The other woman — if those two were the same two people who had walked out of the room he was peeking into earlier — did not say anything.

But the first woman appeared satisfied.

"Let us go," she said. "I have something that will prove my sincerity much better."

Perhaps the other woman made a questioning face. The first one went on to say, "Let's just say it involves a syringe and a choice of injectable solutions."

If it weren't for Mr. Marbleton's steadying presence, and the Van Dyck that hung directly opposite her station, Livia would have gone completely out of her mind.

Well, maybe the Van Dyck was also a reason she was partly out of her mind. It was much bigger than she had thought it would be. Not the sort of painting that took up an entire wall, but still, much, much too big to carry. Much too big to even cut out of the frame without a solid five minutes, unless one wished to lessen its value considerably.

And how would anyone get five minutes alone with it, when there were at least twenty-five people in the gallery, guards, waiters, and maids combined, even without a single guest?

Where *were* the guests? The servants had been told to take their stations at least an hour and a half ago. And not a single person had come through the still-closed doors.

Not even one who wandered in by mistake

looking for the cloakroom.

What was everyone doing here, then? Why had they carried up all the heavy plates and glasses? Why had Livia bothered to crush so much ice — her back still hurt — for the oysters and the mousses? Were all those platters upon platters of hors d'oeuvres to be carted off at the end of the night, without even having been looked over?

And the worst part was that she couldn't say anything or ask any questions. She could only stand quietly, as did everyone else, the gallery silent except for an occasional shuffle of feet and a clearing of throat — and even those got warning looks from the members of the permanent staff.

When the screams came she almost screamed, too, out of relief, if nothing else. At least now someone had to come and explain why the château sounded like an abattoir.

Still nothing happened. The temporary staff glanced at one another. The permanent staff seemed to have turned entirely mute.

Then screams subsided and footsteps approached. The doors were thrown open and guests poured in. They marveled at the pristine spread of food and rushed to be the first in line for wine and champagne. There was excitement, loud chatter, and even trills

287

of overwrought laughter.

Livia at last saw Charlotte, in a masculine disguise reminiscent of the one she had deployed at Stern Hollow, but pared down and without unnecessary flourishes. They did not exchange any communication, not even a nod. Still, she was so happy to see her sister.

And to glean from the sometimes-incoherent conversations that the guests had been at the other gallery in the manor and that a trio of ferrets — though some insisted they were huge sewer rats — had sprung out of nowhere and run amok among the guests, causing many of the ladies to shriek and a cross section of the gentlemen to match them in both pitch and volume.

Guests shoved one another to get out of the way. Plates and champagne flutes shattered. Entire tables overturned, dumping ice and foie gras all over the marble floor. All of a sudden, like a herd of wildebeests that had caught the scent of a lion, everyone rushed toward the door in a near stampede.

But at just the right moment, the double doors were thrown wide, the guests drained out, and in the cordoned corridor, they were corralled by a smiling but firm Monsieur Plantier, along with a phalanx of footmen.

Monsieur Plantier extended his deep apologies to the guests but reminded them that his sister was indisposed and needed her rest. Would *mesdames* and *messieurs* please take a second to collect themselves and follow him?

And now here they were, thirsty for champagne and oh, why not have a few éclairs and petits fours to calm the jitters? Livia didn't know how the atmosphere had been in the other gallery, but the gobbling, guzzling guests in front of her were becoming more convivial by the moment, and there was, whether natural or intentional, a rising sense of fellowship, of having experienced and survived a remarkable event together, even if that event was only an attack of rats.

Or ferrets.

Charlotte, as Mr. Hurst, flitted from group to group, talking to everyone, laughing merrily. But she seldom looked in Livia's or Mr. Marbleton's direction and most certainly never at the prominently displayed Van Dyck.

Lord Ingram cursed himself.

He should be out of the tunnels, over the fence, and far away from Château Vaudrieu — by any measure he'd made enough discoveries this night.

But no, because the woman, who was most likely Madame Desrosiers, said that all the rooms that served as dignified accommodation had spy holes, after he returned to the main tunnel, the one that was locked on either end, he'd looked for yet another trapdoor overhead, and unfortunately he'd found it, too.

So here he was crawling out of another branch tunnel, scaling another well, and hauling himself through yet another trapdoor, praying fervently that nobody would think to step into this one.

No one did.

Alas, when he thought there was nothing else left to explore, at the far end of this passage he discovered more footholds on the wall, which led up through yet another trapdoor, into a tunnel that was only four feet high.

Here he encountered no tripods, but he did find spy ports. Ten of them, far closer together than the ones on the level below.

The fourth one he opened gave onto a room lit by a single lamp, a much smaller, less opulent room than the one he'd peeped into earlier. There was no one inside, but a battered trunk sat against one wall. The trunk had been unlocked but not too many items taken out. A few unremarkable dresses hung in the wardrobe, a book and a note-book sat on the table, an indifferent water-color hung over it.

The room of a governess, if he had to take his guess. But apparently whoever had been placed here had complained, and had been taken seriously enough to be shown the secret passage. To be assured that she was important enough to merit privacy at least, except there was no true privacy here either.

Then again, he was making assumptions. This could very well be the room of another woman, and not the one in the secret pas-sage Madame Desrosiers was trying to re-assure.

He waited for some time for the room's occupant to come back. But he couldn't wait too long: Ideally he wanted to time his departure with the guests', so that the guards' attention would be on them, and not on a furtive shadow slipping out of the chapel.

As he was closing the panel, he spied a framed page of pressed flowers on the night-stand. This peephole was also set low to the ground, and the bulk of the bed concealed most of the frame, but he could see that the top flower seemed purple and vibrant, caught in the peak of its brief bloom.

He thought of Lucinda and the pressed

flowers she wanted to make for her mother — and missed his children with an acute pain in his heart.

Sliding the panel closed, he went on with his task.

FOURTEEN

Somehow Livia had forgotten that the end of the reception did not mean the end of the evening for the staff. Hard work began anew. Everything that had been hauled up to the gallery needed to be returned to the pantries and butleries below. The tablecloths and napkins were bundled up to be sent out for laundering, but all the other service items had to be scraped, cleaned, washed up, and then put back in perfect order.

Charlotte had reviewed the dishwashing process with Livia, Charlotte who had read household management books from end to end and warned her that it would be hard work. Livia, tired from carrying heavy trays up and down, was in fact relieved to be able to stand in one spot for some time. Only to learn what hard work meant, to be stuck in place, her legs, back, and shoulders aching, up to her elbows in hot water and washing soda for hours on end.

She was near tears when they were at last allowed to leave the scullery, in the small hours of the morning. The château did not house its temporary staff, but put them on an omnibus and drove them fifteen miles to the door of the staffing agency. She didn't even know that she'd fallen asleep with her head on Mr. Marbleton's shoulder until he shook her awake for them to alight.

The staffing agency offered some lodging, but not enough to accommodate everyone on its roster, and certainly not its newest hires. The huddle of servants who stumbled off the omnibus shook hands with one another and dispersed amidst a chorus of "Bonne Nuit!"

Livia clutched the money she received, her work-dulled brain trying to convert it into pound sterling, scarcely believing the pittance that she'd earned for all her back-breaking labor. She didn't have a clear idea of how much things cost in Paris, but in London she wasn't sure this would be enough to pay for both room and board.

Her own life had never been easy. Yet it was both luxurious and carefree, compared to that of the woman she was pretending to be.

She and Mr. Marbleton walked for nearly a quarter of an hour before a carriage drove by them and came to a stop beyond the next intersection.

"There's no one else nearby?" she asked, her voice half-hoarse.

"Everyone who got off with us has gone in different directions," he said.

They nodded at the coachman, Lord Ingram, and got into the carriage. Lord Ingram's ally had secured an idle farmhouse two villages over from Château Vaudrieu. Lord Ingram had driven there the previous day, so as not to make another appearance at the Mouret train station.

She was glad he was safe.

And she was asleep again within seconds.

Livia had a vague impression of being helped out of the carriage by Charlotte and Mrs. Watson and half carried into her room. She woke up late. And she, who usually had very little appetite upon rising, wolfed down the copious breakfast that had been prepared for her, leaving barely a crumb on the tray.

Breakfast was followed by a long hot bath to soak away the aches and cramps of the previous day. Even as she sighed, her muscles unknotting, her mind still remained on the woman she was pretending to be. That woman, who lacked steady employment, wouldn't have the luxury of sitting in a deep claw-footed bath in the middle of the day. She'd have gone out at dawn to find work. And if she had anyone depending on her . . .

Livia had long rued her lack of independence. But independence without funds was like immortality without eternal youth, a proposition that became untenable over time. Was that why Charlotte always analyzed the world the way she did? Because in the end, when all the niceties were stripped away, everything was all about how many resources any given person had at her command?

Charlotte's greatest resource was her mind. What was Livia's?

She had just finished dressing when a knock came at the door. "May we come in, Miss Olivia?"

Mrs. Watson.

Livia flushed with the memory of her secondhand mortification, but she had no choice but to open the door. Mrs. Watson swept past in a faint cloud of attar of jasmine, followed by Charlotte, in another one of the dresses Livia had brought for her from home, an explosion of silk rosettes on green brocade that even Madame de Pompadour would have thought overwrought.

"Oh, you look much better, my dear," said

Mrs. Watson, with great empathy in her eyes. "It was terribly hard work, wasn't it?"

"Much harder for those who must do it day after day."

"There is that. Now shall I help you coif your hair?"

Livia allowed Mrs. Watson to lead her to the vanity table. "Is everyone waiting for me to confer about last night?"

"No," said Charlotte, taking a seat near the door. "Last I heard, Mr. Marbleton just climbed out of his bath."

Livia exhaled. Some people loved to make a late, grand entrance. She never could withstand the sort of attention that generated. Being the last to arrive made her want to crawl under the carpet, certain that she had inconvenienced everyone present and that they all secretly despised her.

Mrs. Watson combed Livia's hair, her hands sure but gentle.

"You are an expert," marveled Livia.

"In my younger days, I traded on my appearance. I was conversant with just about every skill and trick there existed to make a woman more beautiful. And my hair, of course, was never neglected."

"I can only imagine how stunning you were," said Livia sincerely.

And of course, at the peak of her beauty,

no one would have denigrated her.

"Oh, I rather thought so myself — I was always a cheeky one." Mrs. Watson started plaiting Livia's hair. "But not everyone agreed. You should have heard men passing opinions on my looks. One day someone would think my arms lacked all voluptuousness. The next day a different someone would opine that my waist was too thick. I've heard my nose called too large, my eyes too close-set, my hands too knobby, and my neck nowhere near swanlike enough. And when I was twenty-five I was already called too old by gentlemen who liked their companions barely grown."

"I — That's —"

"Since I always intended to profit from my physical appeal, I grew a thick skin early. But I came to realize that most women, even respectable ones who would never think of taking a protector in exchange for money, have their appearance judged the same way, except perhaps less overtly. Everyone is imperfect to someone. And even the impossibly beautiful ones grow old and are pitied for not being as beautiful as they once were."

Satisfied with the plaits to either side of Livia's ears, Mrs. Watson formed the rest of her hair into a chignon. "For that reason, I learned to heed my own opinion of myself more than anyone else's," she said, sliding pins into the chignon with such smoothness that Livia barely felt any pressure on her scalp. "A woman who allows the disdain and casual callousness of strangers to make her feel less worthy can have nothing but a difficult time, and I am well past that phase in my life."

This was Mrs. Watson letting Livia know, without saying it in so many words, that the comment of the stupid man from the other day had not affected her — or at least hadn't affected her anywhere to the extent that it had affected Livia.

She would be more embarrassed at having been so overwrought that Mrs. Watson felt the need to console her, if she didn't feel such relief. And such overwhelming admiration for the indomitable Mrs. Watson.

Charlotte, sitting to the side, was reading a French newspaper, seemingly absorbed in its contents. Livia waited for her to say something. When she didn't, Livia asked, "What do you think, Charlotte?"

"Of course Mrs. Watson is right," said her sister, her head still bent toward the paper. "But fundamentally, this is about the imbalance of power between the sexes. As long as women's primary access to power is via access to men, and as long as men value women primarily as either carriers of their bloodline or vessels for their carnal desires, both men and women will be commenting on women's youth and beauty — or the lack thereof — ad nauseum, the former group as they would appraise any other interchangeable commodity, and the latter as assessment of competitive advantages and disadvantages.

"Certainly it's admirable for any given woman to learn to appreciate her own worth, despite all the countervailing forces. But it cannot be enough for those who are treated as lesser to feel better about themselves. That they are treated as lesser is an injustice. And that injustice itself must be rooted out and eradicated."

Instead of the library, the company met in the dining room. The dishes for luncheon were served *à la française,* everything placed on the table at the same time. The servants filed out and the diners helped themselves.

Livia, still full from her late breakfast, only took some carrot salad and a few mussels that had been steamed in white wine.

"Before we begin our discussion," said Mrs. Watson from the head of the table, "please allow me to thank each and every

300

one of you. And know that I will never be able to thank you enough."

Lord Ingram, seated to her left, briefly placed his hand over hers. Livia, Charlotte, and Mr. Marbleton all inclined their heads.

Mrs. Watson gave Lord Ingram a tremulous smile. Then she turned to her right and said, "Miss Charlotte, will you summarize your findings?"

"Certainly," said Charlotte, looking up from her soup. "The longer we have been at this task, the more our situation strikes me as odd. Let me begin with the staffing agency.

"Ever since I heard that the roster at the staffing agency had been stretched to the breaking point because some foreign dignitary needed a large house manned, I've wondered whether we were the only party trying to get into Château Vaudrieu for illicit reasons. Recall also that Mrs. Watson's friend mentioned that her contacts in Paris couldn't find any French thieves both able and willing to take on the project.

"At the time I thought that implied some sort of criminal underbelly to Château Vaudrieu — it very well still could. But the unavailability of professional burglars could also serve as further evidence that Mrs. Watson's friend isn't the only one being pressured to steal art from the yuletide masquerade ball. That she, coming from abroad, had a later start than everyone else and therefore could only resort to English thieves, after all the good French ones had been pledged elsewhere."

Livia hadn't thought of it at all. She glanced at Mr. Marbleton. He winked at her and touched a hand to his hair. He'd sent her a lovely bouquet to thank her for caring for him after his near-brush with hypothermia. And today, before leaving her room, she'd tucked a single stephanotis blossom from the bouquet into her coiffure.

She hesitated a moment and winked back.

"Last night Mrs. Watson called on her friend and obtained the actual blackmail letter her friend received," Charlotte went on, and passed a photograph to Livia, who sat next to her.

A *photograph?*

The words of the letter that had been photographed were clear and readable. But still, how odd. She studied it a bit longer, then handed it to Mr. Marbleton across the table from her. Their fingers brushed at the moment of transition, a lovely sensation.

When the photograph reached Lord Ingram, Charlotte said, "I believe that this photograph was sent, rather than the letter in the photograph, because that letter had not been handwritten, but produced via a Cyclostyle."

"What's that?" Livia and Mrs. Watson asked at the same time.

"A stencil duplicator. You write with a special stylus on wax-coated paper. The tip of the stylus breaks through the wax coating and leaves you with a stencil of the text you want. And then you can push an ink roller over the stencil and end up with a decent copy of the original. It's very useful for businesses. Suppose you need ten copies of something. It's too small a run to take to a printer, yet it's tedious work copying by hand, not to mention prone to errors."

Livia didn't know about the Cyclostyle because she had never worked in an office, nor needed ten exact copies of anything. She supposed that must be the case for Mrs. Watson also. Charlotte, likewise, had never worked in an office. But Charlotte read Patent Office catalogues and was conversant with any number of new inventions she'd never used or even seen in her life.

"If you'll notice," said Charlotte, "in this photographed letter, where the artist and the title of the artwork are mentioned, these words, '*Deposition* by Van Dyck,' are noticeably more stretched out than the others, and still there seems to be extra space before and after that particular phrase."

Livia hadn't noticed that particular detail at all. The photograph was still going around the table, and when it came back to her, she saw that Charlotte was right.

She glanced up at Charlotte. "So . . . you're saying that the extortionist came up with a general template of a blackmail letter, made a number of exact copies via a Cyclostyle, and specified a different painting on each copy."

Charlotte nodded. "Precisely. Each copy would have the exact same amount of space reserved for that purpose but '*Deposition* by Van Dyck' needs a great deal less room than, for example, '*Saint Francis of Assisi in Ecstasy* by Caravaggio.'

"And of course all of these deductions would be pure speculation if at Château Vaudrieu I hadn't come across multiple unrelated parties who seemed to have ulterior purposes similar to ours. I believe it is a member of one of those parties who released the ferrets that caused the chaos in the first gallery."

Livia sucked in a breath. She looked again at Mr. Marbleton. His face had become grave.

"So you believe, Miss Charlotte," he said

slowly, "that although the various parties at the château were unrelated, they were all, including us, there because of a common mastermind."

Livia had arrived at the same conclusion. But hearing those words spoken aloud felt as if someone had kicked her chair.

Unhurriedly, Charlotte took a spoonful of her soup. "At the moment, that is my interpretation of the evidence. Here's something else: When our ally went to steal a copy of Château Vaudrieu's architectural plans, there was some extra room in the drawer in which the architectural plans were located. That by itself might not mean anything, but if I may make so bold a conjecture, what if this mastermind had placed multiple copies of the plans at the architectural firm? And that the other parties, arriving earlier on the scene, took most of the copies, resulting in the space in the drawer our ally noticed?"

Livia barely had a moment to chew over this idea before Charlotte said, "Lord Ingram, will you speak of your discoveries?"

Lord Ingram gave a concise account of his evening, in particular the two branching tunnels that led to secret passages, with tripods set before spy holes that peered into bedrooms.

"It's my opinion that the tripods are meant to support cameras. And the cameras are meant to photograph unsuspecting guests in private moments. The ball at Château Vaudrieu is a masquerade ball. Such occasions are not necessarily less than respectable, but attendees, believing in their anonymity for the night, might feel a little bolder in indulging in conduct they normally wouldn't engage in."

Livia didn't know where to look — certainly not at Mr. Marbleton this time. They were verging on topics that, in polite society at least, did not come up in mixed company, certainly not when there were unmarried young women present.

"Quite so," said Charlotte, who appeared to feel none of Livia's discomfort. She was finished with her soup and served herself some carrot salad. "I mentioned at our previous conference that the art dealer I visited, Monsieur Sauveterre, seemed wary of Château Vaudrieu. We met again before the reception, and this time his warning was unambiguous. He said if I was determined to see the château for myself, then I must be 'wary and prudent.' In light of what Lord Ingram discovered, M. Sauveterre's strenuous advice makes much more sense. Those who are unwary and imprudent have their unwise acts photographed.

"Artworks have been known to exchange hands at Château Vaudrieu, on the night of the ball, for twice as much as similar pieces fetch elsewhere. What if this is how Château Vaudrieu profits from the evidence it has in stock? A gentleman caught in the embrace of another gentleman last December? Well, this December he must pay double what a painting is worth on the open market.

"And even with those paintings available for sale, we don't know whether they come from willing sellers — some owners could very well be forced to give up family heirlooms to avoid scandalous photographs surfacing." Charlotte looked around the table. "The beauty of this scheme is that there are most likely legitimate transactions at Château Vaudrieu as well, and the market for art is known for its occasional outliers, both of which help to disguise the irregularities."

"So . . . . this entire masquerade ball is a racket," whispered Livia, her fingers tight around her knife and fork.

"That would be putting it mildly," said Charlotte.

"But if it's the people at the château carrying out these dastardly deeds," asked Mr. Marbleton, puzzled, "then why would they

307

want the targets of their blackmail to disrupt this year's ball? Or is there more than one set of blackmailers?"

"That perplexes me, too, and I have no good answer for you," answered Charlotte. "It's possible that there is some sort of internal schism. Will you talk a little of the tapping in code, my lord?"

"When I was in the first branch tunnel, I heard some very faint tapping." Lord Ingram set down his cutlery, pulled out a piece of paper from his pocket, and passed it to Mrs. Watson. "I recorded it as best as I could but haven't been able to make sense of it."

Everyone examined it, but Livia sensed that they were all waiting for the code to reach Charlotte, who was eating her carrot salad in a terribly refined and ladylike manner, while eyeing the potato *au gratin* in its *chauffe-plat,* kept hot above a bain-marie.

But Charlotte, when the piece of paper came to her, passed it on with barely a glance. "I don't know what it says either, not without taking some time and effort to decipher it."

Lord Ingram tucked away the code carefully. "I wonder whether the tapper is the same person as the one who tried to run away the first time Mr. Marbleton and I visited the château."

"A prisoner," murmured Mrs. Watson, pushing around the food on her plate.

"I hope there won't be another," said Lord Ingram. "There is a female guest at the castle. The hostess, possibly Madame Desrosiers, led her into a secret tunnel to show her the peepholes, as a way of explaining why she hasn't been given more luxurious lodgings. But later I saw a room that might be hers — of that I have no assurance — but that one, too, can be spied upon."

"I saw her arrive in the afternoon," said Livia, relieved to be able to add something, at last, to the discussion. "When ice was delivered, I happened to look out as a woman stepped down from a hired carriage. She had a hooded cloak and held the hood low with her hand, so I didn't get a good look at her face. But I did see that it was Monsieur Plantier who welcomed her."

She'd seen Monsieur Plantier again, when he came into the gallery where she'd waited an eternity to see a single guest, and she'd easily inferred his status as the host.

"What's this woman's purpose at Château Vaudrieu?" asked Mrs. Watson. "Is she at all related to the ball and the trap it sets for the attendees?"

Lord Ingram frowned and slowly shook

his head. "If the guest Miss Olivia saw arriving was the same person who was shown the secret passage, well, the way they spoke, it sounded as if she and Madame Desrosiers barely knew each other. The guest was prickly and Madame Desrosiers was careful to reassure her — but nevertheless didn't entirely trust her.

"And yet Madame Desrosiers also appeared keen to prove her sincerity. Her last words to the guest, concerning how she would achieve that, was 'Let's just say it involves a syringe and a choice of injectable solutions.' "

The dining room was silent as everyone pondered the cryptic sentence.

"What else did you observe?" Charlotte asked Livia.

Alas, Livia's usefulness as a spy had been severely limited not only by the amount of work heaped on the temporary staff, but also by the general watchfulness of the permanent staff. "There were guards stationed along the routes the temporary staff used to carry food and other things back and forth. I can mark those places on the architectural plans, but I think the guards were just there to keep an eye on us.

"I did learn that most of the food at the reception was catered by an establishment in Paris. Usually they deliver the food in the afternoon, but this time, men from the château went to Paris in the morning and brought everything back. The cooks at the château did some final baking, assembly, and garnishing — I heard them grumbling over this additional work."

"Thank you, Miss Olivia," said Charlotte, a note of approval in her voice. She placed a beef paupiette on her plate and turned to Mr. Marbleton. "Did you notice anything interesting, sir?"

He thought for a moment. "Several things, though I don't know whether they are of any use or not. First, I overheard some permanent staff complain to one another. They don't like outsiders at the château. For the ball temporary staff is considered unavoidable, but usually the permanent staff takes care of the reception, and those I heard didn't care for the last-minute decision to hire extra help for the occasion.

"Which makes me wonder if this 'servant problem' isn't related to the attempted escape that Lord Ingram and I didn't quite witness the other night. Maybe more guards were needed for the prisoner. Maybe some were let go because they let him get as far as he did. Maybe that was why the château suddenly found itself shorthanded even for the reception."

He loved his little jokes and moments of lightheartedness, but now he spoke with an assurance beyond his years. Livia's heart skipped a beat. This moment she found him rather . . . manly.

"Second," he went on, "I'm almost certain that a few other members of the temporary staff from last night were also there under false pretenses. But I can't be sure that they were interested in art or ways of stealing art. In fact, I couldn't understand what they were doing until just now, when Lord Ingram mentioned the code that he heard someone tap, in the bowels of the château.

"I don't know whether Miss Olivia noticed, but several of the waiters in the gallery with us, during the time we waited for guests to appear, seemed to be always tying their shoes, straightening a corner of the tablecloth, or wiping away stains on the floor. But then I'd notice that they still hadn't stood up. One time I crossed the room for more napkins at my station and saw that a waiter had disappeared altogether.

"After a minute, he was back. The floor was solid — he couldn't have gone anywhere so he must have been under his station, concealed by the tablecloth. And it stands to reason that he was there listening for the code, though I'm not sure whether he or his cohorts would have heard anything."

"Wait!" Livia exclaimed. "Was this the fellow with the thinning blond hair and a small mole next to his nose?"

"Yes, it was."

"Good gracious, I caught him in a pantry on the floor. I thought he was taking a nap. He must have been listening there, too — he even had the audacity to wink at me. I thought he was some cheeky bloke happy to be paid to do nothing."

A chill ran down Livia's back. She'd stood in that gallery, doling out champagne, without the least idea of the undercurrents raging all around her. She glanced up to see Mr. Marbleton looking at her, his expression clearly conveying the question, *Are you all right?*

After a moment, she gave him a small nod. She'd been fine the night before at the château; there was no reason for her not to be fine now.

Beside Mr. Marbleton, Lord Ingram took a sip from his water goblet. "Do you think those men were there for the code?"

The question was for Charlotte.

"They could have been, provided the code is a code and is meant to be overheard —

and not, for example, someone merely tapping along to a piece of hummed music." Charlotte raised a hand to forestall the collective objection from around the table. "I am not denying the likelihood, merely considering all possibilities."

"So what do we do now?" asked Mrs. Watson, pushing away her plate with its largely untouched food. "The situation has become more complicated at every turn."

"We prepare, as best as we can, for the night of the ball — and beyond," said Charlotte calmly.

Despite foregoing puddings and rich French desserts, she still remained plumper than usual, her face ever more cherubic. All the same, no one questioned her authority, least of all Livia.

Charlotte looked around the table, stopped when her gaze reached Mr. Marbleton, then glanced at Livia. "By the way, did anyone pay attention to the Van Dyck?"

FIFTEEN

To prepare for the night of the ball, Mr. Marbleton and Leighton Atwood remained in France; everyone else returned to England. Their journey was uneventful. When they reached London, Lord Ingram bid the ladies good-bye and continued on to his brother's country estate.

He arrived under a darkening sky and was shown to the duchess's solarium. His sister-in-law rose with her arms extended. "Ash, my dear!"

The Duchess of Wycliffe was a handsome woman of forty, with a wide smile that showed a great many teeth. She enjoyed poking fun at her own slightly sharklike expression and loved boasting that she had the finest enamel among the entire Upper Ten Thousand.

"We thought you'd be away for another week at least," she said, taking both of his hands in her own.

315

"I missed my children. And everyone at Eastleigh Park, of course."

The duchess shook her head. "Come, let's have a cup of tea. Then you can go up to the nursery."

She didn't ask him what he'd been up to, but told him a bit about herself and his brother, and a great deal about his children and hers, who'd had a grand time pretending to be Romans and druids — and sometimes Yorks and Lancasters.

"What children their age playact the War of the Roses?" asked the duchess, a note of indulgent accusation in her tone.

"Such are the bedtime stories Lucinda prefers," answered Lord Ingram with a smile. "I've left out the bloodiest and the most salacious bits."

"History, the ultimate gossip," said the duchess authoritatively, and shooed him off to see his children.

Outside the nursery, however, he came across Miss Yarmouth, the children's governess, hovering in the corridor, obviously waiting for him.

"Miss Yarmouth." He stopped.

"My lord, there is something I need to tell you before you see the children," said Miss Yarmouth, her expression anxious.

She was presumably embarrassed to be

standing before the man to whom she'd proposed a marriage of convenience, but her demeanor made it obvious that her anxiety was, for the moment at least, not related to the success of her suit.

He waited.

She bit her lower lip. "Miss Lucinda — Miss Lucinda insists that Lady Ingram visited her three nights ago."

He stared at her, his ears ringing.

"Children can be fanciful, but Miss Lucinda has never made up stories," said Miss Yarmouth in a low whisper, even though there was no one else in the corridor. "So I asked her to tell me all the details of Lady Ingram's visit.

"She said that it must have been late at night. She woke up, opened her eyes, and Lady Ingram was sitting by her bedside. She was thrilled to see her mother, of course. Lady Ingram said that she couldn't stay for long, so Miss Lucinda made her lie down on the bed with her and then proceeded to tell Lady Ingram everything that had happened since they last saw each other.

"And then Lady Ingram told her that she should go back to sleep. Miss Lucinda asked if she could tell me about the visit. Lady Ingram said that she could and that she might as well tell you, too, but that she should probably not tell her brother, because he didn't wake up and would be sad to know that he'd missed her visit."

Miss Yarmouth stopped and peered at him, looking apprehensive. He realized that he was scowling. How had Lady Ingram managed to waltz into and out of the nursery without alerting a soul at Eastleigh Park? What had she wanted with the children?

He forced his features to relax even as his hands balled into fists behind his back. "I see," he said. "You are sure about the timing of Lady Ingram's visit, Miss Yarmouth?"

Three nights ago. Why had Lady Ingram come at that specific moment?

"I'm sure," said Miss Yarmouth, nodding. "Miss Lucinda told me the next morning, while Master Carlyle was playing with His Grace's heir — I can't ever forget how stunned I was.

"Yesterday when I was alone with her I asked her again to tell me about Lady Ingram's visit. She added some details and didn't mention some other details from the first telling, but overall it was the same account. You weren't expected back for a while and I thought of letting Their Graces know. But I kept hesitating. I thought you should learn first, before Their Graces."

He exhaled. "Thank you, Miss Yarmouth. You made the correct decision to tell me first."

"Thank you, my lord." She flushed with pleasure.

He inclined his head. "If you'll excuse me."

Lord Ingram spent the rest of the afternoon with his children, until they were led to their bath. He had an early dinner with his brother and sister-in-law, then returned to the nursery to put the children to bed.

Carlisle, after a long, full day, dropped off soon. Lucinda, who had obviously been waiting for that moment, clutched Lord Ingram's hand. "Papa, Mamma came to see us."

Her eyes shone. Lord Ingram's heart pinched. He brushed away a strand of hair from her face. "Miss Yarmouth told me. You must have been happy to see her."

"I told her all about our visit to the Natural History Museum when we were in London. And about me playing Margaret of Anjou in a game of Yorks and Lancasters."

Despite his mounting unease, he smiled. "Margaret of Anjou, eh?"

Not exactly the most beloved figure of her time.

"She was busy — I like that," said Lucinda. "But I had to remind Mamma who Margaret of Anjou was — Mamma said she couldn't tell those kings and queens from four hundred years ago apart. I think she was sad when I got to the part about Margaret of Anjou being exiled to France so I told her that later Margaret became queen again."

He did not want Lady Ingram to return from her exile to hold court in their lives again. Then again, even Margaret of Anjou couldn't hold on to her reclaimed throne for very long.

"Did Mamma say how she is?"

"She said she was fine."

He did not doubt that. "Did she mention why she came to visit you?"

Lucinda knocked him gently on the forehead. "Silly, of course it was because she missed us."

His temples throbbed. He didn't know why he believed he'd be able to find out something by talking to Lucinda. As precocious as she could be at times, she was still a child. "You're right. Of course."

Lucinda sank a little deeper under the covers and yawned. "She cried when I gave her the page of pressed flowers I made for her."

When Lucinda had told him about making pressed flowers, he'd thought it would be years before mother and daughter reunited, not mere days.

In fact —

Something gonged loudly in the back of his head. "Pansies," he said weakly. "You were going to make pressed pansies."

"Yes, purple pansies. A whole page of them. The duchess even gave me a frame for it." Lucinda smiled dreamily, her eyes closing. "It looked so pretty. Mamma said she'd take it with her everywhere she went and look at it every day."

Charlotte considered herself skilled enough as a cryptographer, but she didn't always enjoy a cryptographer's work. Decoding a Vigenère cipher, for example, was analogous to hitting herself repeatedly on the head with a mallet. She could only hope that the code Lord Ingram had obtained from the bowels of Château Vaudrieu would not prove quite as trying.

She had memorized the code on the rail journey back to London and could see the entire sequence of dots and dashes in her mind's eye. The problem was, without any indications on how to group the symbols, there were too many possibilities — too many futile paths to follow.

A light knock came at her door. It was Livia, in her dressing gown, her hair in one long plait. "Are you working on the cipher, Charlotte?"

"Reluctantly." Charlotte extended the paper on which she'd copied the code. "You can help me."

"Me?"

"Why not you? You were the one who first taught me about coding and decoding messages."

Livia scoffed. "Caesar ciphers that every five-year-old can do."

"When I was a five-year-old, yes. But don't forget you also learned about and constructed all the subsequent ciphers I decoded, too, all the way up to the Vigenère cipher."

Old habits were hard to break. Their mother had always put Livia down, and Livia, in turn, had learned to put herself down even faster.

For a moment Livia looked as if she might argue further, but then she came forward, took the code from Charlotte, and sat down on the spare chair.

Charlotte put a kettle in the grate. "Some tea?"

Livia looked up. "You must be missing hot

cocoa. That's what you prefer for long winter nights, isn't it?"

"I miss hot cocoa with a burning passion," Charlotte sighed. "Every time I approach Maximum Tolerable Chins, I make solemn resolutions to be more moderate in my cake intake. And then a year passes and I'm at Maximum Tolerable Chins again."

This made Livia chortle.

She had a lovely laugh, but she didn't laugh very often. Maybe, Charlotte thought, her sister would laugh more if Mr. Marbleton were a permanent part of her life.

"Did you want to speak to me about something?" Charlotte asked.

Livia nodded, sliding her fingertips along the edge of Charlotte's desk.

Charlotte waited.

After a few seconds, Livia said, "I'm almost done with my Sherlock Holmes story — and I'm stuck."

"Stuck in what way?" Charlotte was not familiar with the process by which fiction was produced, but she understood it to be closer to handicraft than to manufacturing and might not turn out as specified.

"In a strange way." Livia bit her lower lip. "I was making decent progress until I realized that I had much less to write than I thought I did, only a few thousand words left. Almost immediately I couldn't write anymore. I knew exactly what I wanted the next sentence to say. And the next paragraph. But somehow putting pen to paper became impossible. I kept jumping up from my chair. I couldn't do anything useful at all.

"I thought that was an anomaly. I thought it was just a fit of nerves. But I haven't been able to write since either. Granted, that was the day you and Mrs. Watson came back and said you needed to go to France and we'd had plenty to do since. But I hadn't been *that* busy that I couldn't have written a single word. Just now I sat for a while with Bernadine and didn't make any progress. I sat for a while in my own room and still didn't make any progress."

Livia pressed her fingers against her temples. "I've been in worse surroundings, worse moods, worse company, and I've managed to write. I would think that maybe Mrs. Watson's house doesn't agree with me, except I wrote just fine here after I came, before I realized that I was near 'the end.' "

The kettle whistled. Charlotte put two cups of tea to steep and asked, "What would have happened had you finished your story?"

Livia looked at her in puzzlement. "I . . .

would have finished it?"

"When Mr. Marbleton called on me to deliver the letter you wanted forged in his mother's handwriting, he told me, with great delight and even greater details, of his meetings with you during his family's visit to ours. I believe, when the two of you went for a walk, you promised him he would be the first to read your finished story."

Livia's jaw dropped. "You think I don't want him to read my story?"

Charlotte tilted her head. "I think you would be ecstatic if he loved your story and devastated if he didn't. If I didn't like your story, you would still be crestfallen, but you would be able to tell yourself that we have very different taste in fiction. That, in fact, I have no taste for fiction at all.

"But Mr. Marbleton is a reader of fiction. And he enjoys the same books you do. If he didn't like it, you wouldn't know what to tell yourself."

Livia picked up her teacup and held it with both hands. "What should I do then?"

"Do you like your story?"

"I . . ."

"Don't think about everything that needs improvement. Do you *like* your story?"

Livia breathed in and out heavily, almost as if she were panting. "I do."

"Then you finish it. As much as Mr. Marbleton's views matter to you, your own should matter still more."

Livia was silent for some time, looking down into her tea. "Do you think I'll ever manage that?"

"Maybe," said Charlotte, "but only after a great deal of practice."

Livia snorted. Charlotte allowed herself a small smile. "Now come help me with the code."

Around midnight Livia asked whether the code should be interpreted as numbers, rather than letters. Charlotte had always kept that in mind as a possibility, but numbers presented the same problem as letters: too many possibilities, and too many paths to nonsense. Not to mention, in Morse code, some digits were represented by four or more consecutive dots or dashes, but the cipher did not feature any such easily noticeable strings.

Charlotte had already been looking for encoded dividers. She decided to see whether there were small strings of dots and dashes breaking apart long strands of only dots or only dashes. There weren't.

"What if the divider is bigger than the thing it divides?" mused Livia, whose mind was often livelier after midnight.

That seemed counterintuitive, but that would be precisely the reason to use it, to confound unauthorized code breakers. It took Charlotte and Livia another two hours, but in the end they found a string of eight dots and dashes that changed order every time they appeared — the first item in the string becoming the last item in the next iteration.

And when they had accounted for these mutating dividers, they were indeed left with an assortment of digits, twelve to be exact.

"What are they?" asked Livia, her eyes wide.

Charlotte waved her out. "We'll worry about that in the morning. Now go rest."

Unlike Livia, Charlotte's ability to think reduced sharply after midnight. She'd already exhausted herself solving the code, and now her brain wasn't much more useful than a turnip.

She climbed into bed and was almost immediately awakened by loud and insistent knocking on her door. "Miss Charlotte, Lord Ingram is here to see you."

She opened a bleary eye and glanced at her bedside clock. It had been at most four hours since she laid down, and if Mr. Mears would stop knocking, she could easily go back to sleep in the next moment, Lord Ingram's presence notwithstanding.

She forced herself to sit up. His brother's estate was not on a main branch of the railway. Even if Lord Ingram had caught the earliest train out that morning, he still wouldn't have arrived in London in time to call on Charlotte before the crack of dawn.

So he had to have left the previous evening, at the latest, mere hours after arriving.

What could have torn him away so abruptly from his reunion with his children?

"I'll be there in a second," said Charlotte to Mr. Mears, on the other side of the door.

A second was, naturally, a euphemism. Even with Livia and Mrs. Watson's help, a good ten minutes passed before she was sufficiently dressed and coiffed to receive a gentleman to whom she was not related.

"I'm sorry to disturb your rest," said Lord Ingram, rising.

His clothes were travel-rumpled, his face dark with stubble. Looking as he did now, had he disturbed her rest in certain other ways, she wouldn't have minded at all.

She waved a hand and indicated that he should retake his seat.

Mr. Mears, entering the afternoon parlor behind her, set down the tea tray, poured, and left.

"What happened?" she asked, her voice still raspy from sleep.

"The woman who arrived at Château Vaudrieu the afternoon of the reception, the one I almost ran into in the secret passage . . . I have reason to believe she might be Lady Ingram."

Charlotte narrowed her eyes. "Why do you think so?"

She'd thought about the mysterious guest but had decided that as long as she wasn't the maharani, they didn't need to worry about her identity. But if she was Lady Ingram, then that changed things.

"I didn't mention this earlier because it seemed barely worthy of attention, but in the woman's room at Château Vaudrieu — or at least in the one I assumed to be her room — there was a frame of pressed flowers on the nightstand. I saw only a corner of it, but I had the impression that the one visible pressed flower was purple.

"Yesterday I learned from my daughter that several days ago, Lady Ingram had visited Eastleigh Park at night. And that she left with a gift from Lucinda, a frame of pressed purple pansies."

His jaw was clenched, his entire person tense. Charlotte extended a cup of tea

329

toward him, but he shook his head.

"Ash, the connection you made seems fl . . ."

Her voice trailed off. On its own, the connection *was* flimsy. But less so when one considered what Lord Ingram had overheard between the two women.

Let's just say it involves a syringe and a choice of injectable solutions.

Lady Ingram had left Moriarty's fold when she learned that Moriarty's underlings had murdered a close relative of hers with little pity and no remorse. The woman had died from alcohol poisoning caused by an injection of absolute alcohol.

If Madame Desrosiers was helping Lady Ingram achieve vengeance, then from Lady Ingram's point of view, an injection of poison into the killers — an overdose of perhaps none other than absolute alcohol — must be poetic justice.

Charlotte passed a hand over her face. She was awake now, but her brain was still dull from a lack of sleep. "From your description of the two women's conversation, it sounded as if they did not know each other well, or even at all. Why would Lady Ingram go to a stranger's place?"

Lord Ingram rubbed his bloodshot eyes. "I wonder if Madame Desrosiers's people found Lady Ingram and, to demonstrate their goodwill, arranged for her to get into Eastleigh Park to see the children. Left to her own devices, she couldn't have achieved that without alerting anyone at all."

Eastleigh Park was no bastion. Still, it was far from other dwellings and had a full complement of staff and gates that were locked and watched. For Lady Ingram to infiltrate the children's nursery, then to depart without leaving a trace, she must have had extremely competent help.

Which wasn't something a woman who no longer had any backing could count on, normally.

"Why would anyone take such trouble for her?"

Lord Ingram raised a brow. "During the investigation at Stern Hollow, weren't you the one who said that she would be an asset in many situations?"

"I was arguing that it made no sense for Moriarty to kill her — and I was proved correct on that account. But Lady Ingram is no longer in the same position she was then. She's made accusations against Moriarty in front of both Scotland Yard and the biggest gossips in London, and brought notoriety to the doorstep of the man who's always preferred to operate in shadows. In short she's declared herself an implacable enemy."

"Moriarty must have other implacable enemies. Perhaps Madame Desrosiers is one, too. Perhaps she and Lady Ingram wish to band together and capitalize on that shared enmity."

"Perhaps."

The Marbletons were also implacable enemies of Moriarty, but while they could keep themselves safe, would they have expended so much energy to aid Lady Ingram?

Lord Ingram rose. "I have to set a few things into motion, and then I plan to return to Eastleigh Park. I'll be back in London tomorrow."

Charlotte got to her feet. "I'll see you out."

At the door of the parlor he turned around and took her hand. "Be careful, Holmes."

She gave his hand a squeeze. "You too, Ash."

She expected him to let go of her hand and open the door. Instead he enfolded her in an embrace. A brief one. Before she understood what was happening, he was already descending the stairs in the direction of the breakfast parlor.

Only his scent of wool and sandalwood

lingered.

She inhaled deeply, and sighed.

Mrs. Watson half-heartedly stirred her tea. Livia spread more butter on her muffin, without intending to consume either. They glanced at each other again, wondering what had brought Lord Ingram to confer with Charlotte at this unexpected hour.

"Mrs. Watson, Miss Holmes," said Lord Ingram from the door of the breakfast parlor.

They rose hurriedly. "Is everything all right?" asked Mrs. Watson.

"Nothing is amiss," said Lord Ingram. "I learned something yesterday evening that Miss Charlotte needed to know without delay."

Without taking a seat, he asked them about their doings since they parted ways and then took his leave. Livia and Mrs. Watson saw him out, then climbed up to the afternoon parlor, where Charlotte told them about Lord Ingram's suspicions.

"Lady Ingram!" Mrs. Watson cried. The next second she covered her mouth and looked around, as if someone might be spying on her in her own home.

When she spoke again, her volume was much lower. "Do you think he's right, Miss

Charlotte?"

Charlotte tapped the pad of her index finger against her chin. "I have no way of verifying anything — I wasn't in the secret passage, and I wasn't there during Lady Ingram's visit to Eastleigh Park. But Lord Ingram isn't the sort to jump to conclusions. For him to rush over here like this, at least *he* is convinced."

"But you aren't?" asked Livia.

"I'm not sure whether my belief matters one way or the other. Does the identity of a guest at Château Vaudrieu change anything for us, as far as our task and the Van Dyck painting are concerned?"

Livia blinked. The news that Lady Ingram might be lurking about Château Vaudrieu was so sensational that she hadn't even once considered that it might *not* make any difference.

"If everything Lord Ingram reported was accurate, then Lady Ingram doesn't know and doesn't entirely trust her hostess — and the feeling is very much reciprocated. When she still moved in Society Lady Ingram disliked balls and considered them a chore. I doubt she would take part in the masquerade ball, let alone participate in any of Château Vaudrieu's schemes. If her presence doesn't change what we need to do, then why do we need to know with complete certainty whether it's her in the château?"

"So we are to completely disregard her presence at Château Vaudrieu? To think of it as altogether tangential to our plans?" asked Mrs. Watson, sounding incredulous.

"I can't think what else to do," said Charlotte, "unless . . ."

Her expression changed.

A barely perceptible flicker, such a tiny ripple, smaller than that caused by the landing of a dragonfly on the surface of a pond. But to Livia, long accustomed to subtle variations in Charlotte's expression, it was as if Charlotte's jaw had fallen all the way to her lap.

"Unless I've read the situation entirely backward."

"How?" cried Livia.

"Lord Ingram and I both assumed that since Lady Ingram had become an implacable enemy to Moriarty, whoever was helping her must share that enmity to some extent. What if we were wrong about that? What if this isn't a 'the enemy of my enemy is my friend' alliance? What if this is simply Moriarty bringing Lady Ingram back into the fold?"

"What?" Livia and Mrs. Watson exclaimed in unison.

"But Moriarty killed her twin sister!" Mrs. Watson went on. "And Lady Ingram gave his name to the police. Why would Moriarty seek a reconciliation?"

"Moriarty didn't personally kill her sister," Charlotte pointed out. "In England de Lacy is Moriarty's deputy, and I very much doubt de Lacy soiled his own hands in the matter. That would have been done by some minions of de Lacy's.

"All Moriarty had to do was to kill de Lacy and the minions in front of Lady Ingram — or maybe even let her do the deed herself, by injecting them with poisonous substances. Not an act beyond her ability or temperament — not if those about to meet their end were already subdued."

"But why would Moriarty do that for Lady Ingram?" Mrs. Watson pressed her hand into her heart, as if her courage needed bolstering amidst all this talk of wanton killings.

Charlotte, on the other hand, was back to her imperturbable self. "Perhaps he already meant to get rid of de Lacy and decided to kill two birds with one stone. Lady Ingram is still too inexperienced and too brittle. But she is a beautiful, intelligent woman burning to prove to herself and everyone else that even though she is now without a friend in the world, she can still make something of her life. Something remarkable, even."

Livia looked from her sister to Mrs. Watson and back again. "Charlotte, if you are even remotely correct in your line of reasoning, does that mean" — she swallowed — "does that mean we are about to enter Moriarty's lair?"

SIXTEEN

"Moriarty," said Lord Ingram, slowly. "You think Château Vaudrieu is Moriarty's stronghold?"

It was evening the next day. He'd just returned to London again. The invitation to dine at Mrs. Watson's was most welcome, but he'd wondered why Holmes had sent along a note for him to arrive half an hour early. Now he knew. While Mrs. Watson and Miss Olivia were in their rooms, finishing their toilette, Holmes sat him down in Mrs. Watson's afternoon parlor and gave him a general outline of her hypothesis concerning Château Vaudrieu and Moriarty.

"It's possible," replied Holmes, "but it's hard to estimate the actual likelihood. Suppose that the likelihood of you being correct about Lady Ingram visiting Château Vaudrieu is eighty percent. Then my hypothesis about Moriarty, which depends on yours being correct, not to mention a host of other assumptions, can't be more than fifty percent likely to be correct. In fact, even pegging the likelihood at forty percent is generous.

"Which makes the next hypothesis I'm mulling less than ten percent likely to be proven right."

"Your *next* hypothesis?"

"Remember how unlikely it is, but if the château belongs to Moriarty, then I must wonder whether the prisoner in its bowels isn't my brother Mr. Finch."

She handed him a piece of paper. "Livia and I broke the code. It's a rather ornate code. And you remember that Mr. Finch was Moriarty's cryptographer."

He studied the solution — and remained silent for another two minutes. "If that's the case, we must think about how to get him out."

Holmes regarded him steadily. "No."

"*No?* But you just said —"

"I said that idea is highly, highly unlikely to be correct. It is a possibility I have thought of, not something I will act on."

"You would let Mr. Finch remain a prisoner at Château Vaudrieu?"

"When I am less than ten percent confident that the prisoner is Mr. Finch? Of course. We have scant manpower, scant opportunity, and only a vague idea where Château Vaudrieu keeps its prisoners. Even if I were far more sure that Mr. Finch is at Château Vaudrieu, I would still hesitate to devise, let alone execute, a plan based on what little we know."

Logically he knew she was right, but the idea of her brother locked away far underground gnawed at him. "What if his life is at stake?"

"A cryptographer good enough for Moriarty must be one of the best cryptographers in the world. Were I Moriarty, I would put him to use, rather than summarily execute him."

"You can't be sure of that."

"No, yet I'm surer of that than I am of Mr. Finch being at Château Vaudrieu at all." She studied him some more. "Who would risk his life to infiltrate the dungeons of Château Vaudrieu, if such a place exists, to rescue Mr. Finch? I take it you would consider it your obligation?"

He didn't say anything. But yes, he would.

Her eyes bored into his. "Who taught you that your life was so cheap? And why did you allow yourself to be sent on missions where you had only your wits to keep you alive? You are not a tool to be deployed at the whim of some reckless master, and you

340

don't have to prove your worth by leaping at every task other people are too afraid to do."

He flinched. "I don't know."

But perhaps he did know. His irregular parentage, his failed marriage, his opportunistic and cold-blooded brother — everything contributed. But they would all have been irrelevant if he hadn't burned with the desire to be not only above reproach, but indispensable.

He needed to be needed.

Looking back, more than Lady Ingram's beauty, it had been her seeming vulnerability that had drawn him to her. How he'd loved being her knight in shining armor. And when that had turned to dust, he'd become a willing instrument for Bancroft: Bancroft might have needed only a brave fool, and he'd often felt worse for letting himself be used, but still, he'd been needed.

Holmes sighed. "Keep Mrs. Watson in mind, will you? We can't afford to divert resources to a different objective on the night of the ball. She needs all of us, including you, to stay on task."

He studied her once-again smooth and composed countenance. Surely she knew that if she said *she* needed him, he would . . .

Pledge his devotion the way a knight of yore would to his liege lady, ready to slay dragons. Alas that he should be born in the wrong age and his liege lady preferred to confine him to her bed and direct her own artillery unit, should firedrakes appear in the sky.

Not that she wouldn't be the first to remind him that the ladies of yesteryear, whose fathers, husbands, and brothers were often away for years at the Crusades, had been they themselves as tough as dragon hide and accustomed to command.

He looked down for moment at his lap. "I'll speak no more on Mr. Finch. And I'll concentrate on the task at hand."

"Thank you," she said softly. "We couldn't possibly do this without you."

And just like that, he was ready to build her a French bakery brick by brick with his own hands.

Mrs. Watson poked her head into the parlor. "Ah, there you two are. Shall we to dinner?"

At dinner Lord Ingram learned that the ladies had been busy. In the day and a half since they had returned to London, not only had they cracked the cipher, they had also visited an art expert, a stage magician's *in-*

génieur, and not one but two stage costumers. In addition, Mrs. Watson and Miss Olivia had attended to various needlework and alterations and Holmes had spent time with Mr. Lawson, Mrs. Watson's groom, from whom she learned lock picking this past autumn.

"You've done the bulk of the work," he said in admiration and with a measure of self-reproach. "I'm afraid I've spent my time playing either a Roman legionnaire or Margaret of Anjou's favorite adviser."

"And that's as it should be," said Holmes. "You can't — and shouldn't — always do the bulk of the work."

"But if this is Moriarty, then we can never prepare enough."

"And since we can't, whatever we can do will have to suffice."

She was right. They could never do everything. He exhaled. "Does Mr. Marbleton know that we might be entering a Moriarty lair?"

Holmes glanced at her sister. "Not yet — that's something better relayed in person. But I did cable him today and ask him to take another look at Château Vaudrieu. And our ally already paid a visit to Monsieur Sylvestre."

Monsieur Sylvestre, the young scion and

current owner of the Van Dyck piece they'd been tasked to steal, who might have put it up for sale most reluctantly.

"Did he get the response he wanted from Monsieur Sylvestre?"

"No, but he did tell Monsieur Sylvestre that we will wait until the day after the ball and not a minute longer."

Lord Ingram looked toward Miss Olivia, who was eating her peas slowly, one by one, and said to Holmes, "I'm looking forward to that day, when this will be behind us."

Now Miss Olivia was only moving the peas around her plate. No doubt she also longed to be done with their task, but that would also mark the day she must start for home.

"Mr. Marbleton, I believe, has plans for all of us to meet again, now that we know a forged letter from Mrs. 'Openshaw' works to extract Miss Olivia from home," he went on. "He was speaking very enthusiastically about Andalusia in southern Spain."

Some color came into Miss Livia's pale cheeks. "Andalusia — is that where the Alhambra is?"

"Among many other beautiful sights, yes."

"That is a marvelous idea," enthused Mrs. Watson. "You devised a magnificent scheme, Miss Olivia, to come and visit, but we haven't been able to show you a proper good time. Let us make it all up to you next time."

"My goodness, no one around this table owes me anything. I came to spend time with you all and I have done exactly that. But the south of Spain does sound so very enticing." Miss Olivia placed a hand over her heart. "And so very sunny."

Lord Ingram glanced at Holmes. Maybe this could be the beginning of their tour around the world, it if was meant to be a real trip.

Holmes, on the other hand, seemed not to be thinking of warm, bright Spain at all. "My lord, after dinner, we will need to consult with you on the architectural plans."

He sighed inwardly but was already looking forward to poring over the plans with her.

Yes, m'dear. He tried the phrase in his head — and shuddered. No, that would not do at all.

"Over port or cigars?" he asked instead.

And that, at least, got a very slight smile from her. She turned to Mrs. Watson. "You have both, I believe, ma'am?"

When they adjourned to the late Dr. Watson's study, Mrs. Watson was the only one to take a cigar, from her fine Cuban collection. Livia imbibed a little port. Lord Ingram, probably too long accustomed to not doing either in mixed company, abstained. Charlotte, too, refrained.

Her vice was the consumption of sweet, delicious foodstuff that was, alas, largely unnecessary for the sustenance of the body. Perhaps because of the current lack of sweet, delicious foodstuff in her life, she found herself more aware of Lord Ingram's nearness. Of the brush of his knuckle against the architectural plan as he traced a line in thought, the neat, close crop of his hair around his ear, and the set of his chin in the valley between his thumb and forefinger as he considered the locations of fireplaces and chimneys.

Livia and Mrs. Watson, as if by unspoken agreement, slipped out. He appeared not to have noticed their departures, but he must realize that they were now alone.

He did not take advantage of the situation, but moved to where a globe stood and frowned at it. The numbers she'd decoded, if read as longitudes and latitudes, landed them in the middle of the Atlantic Ocean, halfway between Cape Verde and the Lesser Antilles, not exactly a useful locale for anyone.

Which was why she had decided that they were not coordinates.

At last he glanced in her direction — and considered her. *Would he?* she wondered rather idly. Would her dear stick-in-the-mud friend overcome his many scruples to consort with her on this fine night, with a fog rolling in and the outside world disappearing beyond the windows?

There was no lust in his eyes. A slight bemusement, perhaps, as if he were regarding an artifact he'd unearthed, something that seemed to share a surface resemblance to other objects he'd come across, only to turn out, on closer examination, to be utterly different.

No lust, but a greater and starker intensity to his gaze, that of someone who has lost sleep over his artifact, who pondered its mysteries in every spare moment.

"Do you think . . ." he said slowly. "Do you think I could meet Miss Holmes?"

He was speaking of Bernadine.

"Yes," she said. "Come with me."

Bernadine, who had no obligations that she must fulfill, did not keep particularly early hours. Charlotte brought Lord Ingram to her door and went in first. Livia was there and she was surprised to see Charlotte.

"She's fine," said Livia. "She's better here

347

than she was at home."

"That is not saying much," answered Charlotte. "Lord Ingram wishes to meet Bernadine. Is it all right if he enters?"

"Yes, of course," said Livia, though she sounded a little befuddled. It wasn't every day — in fact, it was exactly never — that anyone had sought an introduction to Bernadine.

Charlotte admitted Lord Ingram, who glanced toward Bernadine, seated at her usual spot before the rack of spinnable objects, and immediately looked back at Charlotte.

She had told him that she and Bernadine shared a great resemblance, but still he seemed stunned to see this alternate version of her, the same hair, the same features, but rail thin, and in a world that contained only herself.

"Bernadine, this is our good friend Lord Ingram, who has come to pay his respects. My lord, my sister."

Bernadine did not look at either Charlotte or her visitor, but Lord Ingram inclined his head. "A pleasure, Miss Holmes. I've heard a great deal about you."

And then, as if he often met with those who didn't even return his greeting, he turned to Charlotte and said, "Shall we leave Miss Holmes to her occupation?"

Livia came out with them into the hall. "She really is doing much better. She looks . . . more settled."

"Even though we've been away," said Charlotte.

Even though they'd been away, this was a calm household, with a noticeable undercurrent of cheerfulness. Bernadine responded well to a lack of acrimony in the air.

Livia said her good-byes to Lord Ingram. Charlotte accompanied him to the front door. "The fog seems horrid. I'm sure Mrs. Watson wouldn't mind if you stayed in a guest room — or at 18 Upper Baker Street."

"I'll be all right," he said. Then, after a moment, "Miss Olivia tends to be anxious. At least now Miss Holmes will be a lesser source of anxiety for her."

They were talking around the matter — talking about everything but themselves. She was used to not talking about what was and wasn't between the two of them, but she couldn't help but feel that there was something he wanted to say to her.

And she wanted to hear what it was.

"When Mr. Marbleton was waxing poetic about the south of Spain, what did you think, Ash?"

Her question seemed to startle him. "I'm

afraid I wasn't thinking of Spain then," he said quickly. "Mr. Marbleton was on the verge of hypothermia, and my only concern was getting both of us back to the inn."

She sighed inwardly. "I see. Good night then, my lord. Be careful out there."

Stephen Marbleton was thinking ardently of Andalusia, as he often did when he was cold. It had been home to him in the spring and early summer of the year he turned twelve — or at least in the year his family celebrated his twelfth birthday — one of the few times in his life his family remained in one place for longer than a few weeks.

They'd stayed in a slightly run-down farmhouse, near a vineyard on the outskirts of Jerez de la Frontera. He used to walk between rows of vines under a cloudless sky, hoping, knowing that it was futile, that he would still be there for the grape harvest.

He'd never gone back, afraid that the place had changed or that his memories would prove inaccurate. But with Miss Olivia he wouldn't have such fears, and he would be happy to squire her to the most lavish Moorish palaces, or the least remarkable remote village.

God, it was cold. He took a gulp of the hot ginger tea in his canteen. Château

Vaudrieu had become much more tightly secured since the first night he and Lord Ingram ventured onto the grounds. The chapel was now guarded. The château and all the outbuildings were brightly lit on the outside. And at least four sets of guard dogs circled just inside the fence, making an unauthorized entry a much more harrowing proposition.

Fortunately, Miss Charlotte Holmes had specifically asked him to refrain from unlawful entries. So he had staked out a good elevated spot nearby and put his most powerful pair of binoculars to use. And since he wasn't trespassing, the illumination around the château made his work easier.

In fact, he had already made a thorough study of the chimneys, as Miss Charlotte had asked him to, and could theoretically slip off to the country house several miles away that was now their secondary base and sit in front of a large stove to warm up. But since it wasn't raining and his misery wasn't intolerable, he'd remained in place, in case he came across anything else useful.

The night wore on, growing chillier by the quarter hour, and nothing beyond dogs and their handlers stirred. Even the guards in front of the chapel seemed to be sleeping on their feet. He thought again of the potbellied stove and decided that he'd been away from it long enough.

The lights around the château went out. He blinked in the sudden darkness.

It wasn't absolute. The lights outside the chapel, the distant dairy, and some other outbuildings were still lit. Once he became accustomed to the relative dimness, he saw that a horse-drawn cart approached the château.

From inside the château came men carrying large, long bundles. He sucked in a breath. The size of those bundles, around six feet in length, and their apparent weight — two bundles each took two men to carry, a third needed three . . .

They were bodies, wrapped in cloth, now being tossed onto the cart. The cart pulled away at a sedate pace, escorted by a phalanx of men. Cart and men did not head in the direction of the gate but turned after they crossed the bridge and were soon lost behind the bulk of the château.

He gave up any further thought of the potbellied stove.

Three days before the ball, the ladies and Lord Ingram returned to Paris. The moment they stepped on French soil, Livia's pulse became irregular. Sometimes her heart raced, sometimes it thudded, sometimes she could barely feel it beat beneath the intense pressure on her chest.

The first time she visited Château Vaudrieu, as a matter of general reconnaissance, it had felt like a holiday, or at least a rather lighthearted excursion. The second time she'd been nervous, but too overworked to fall victim to such things as dry mouth or sweaty palms. But now, knowing she could very well be stepping into Moriarty's lair — or one of his lairs — she could not stop her body from reacting as if she were already in certain danger.

She didn't say anything to anyone, but Mrs. Watson patted her on the back from time to time. And Charlotte brought her a glass of *vin chaud* as everyone gathered to confer again in the library at Hôtel Papillon.

"Should I imbibe when no one else is?" asked Livia. "And isn't it a bit too early to have wine?"

It was only three o'clock in the afternoon.

"You are among friends — and this is France. Not to mention" — Charlotte tilted her head in the direction of Mr. Marbleton, who raised his own glass of *vin chaud* to them — "you won't be drinking alone."

Livia smiled at Mr. Marbleton and took a

grateful sip, already feeling less jittery.

"Our original objective was to obtain Van Dyck's *Deposition.*" Charlotte, standing behind a Louis XIV chair, began. "Obviously, as we were dealing with blackmailers, the situation was never simple. Now, however, it has become considerably more complicated.

"The most important thing to understand is that in the overall scheme, we are but a distraction — not even the stage magician's skimpily attired assistant, only the rhinestones on her bodice. I don't think the mastermind behind our forced incursion into Château Vaudrieu cares in the least whether we succeed or fail. There are a number of other paintings that are smaller, easier to steal, and just as valuable. The only reason to assign a seven-foot-by-five-foot work to be pinched in the midst of a crowded function is to ensure that we would resort to the most desperate measures and thereby cause maximum disruption.

"If we, and three or four other parties like ours, are to provide a large-scale distraction, it behooves us to ask its purpose. Why does the mastermind want the chaos?"

Mr. Marbleton seemed to be perfectly at ease, listening attentively, but without any sense of premonition. Livia, however, was already bracing herself, as if they sailed rough seas and at any moment the floor might dip sideways. Her heart thudded. It thudded even harder when Lord Ingram looked first at him, then at her.

"Incidentally, or perhaps not incidentally at all," continued Charlotte, "remember the woman Miss Olivia saw enter Château Vaudrieu on the afternoon of the reception? During our trip to England, Lord Ingram unearthed certain facts that lead him to believe that the woman is Lady Ingram. Given that Lady Ingram has very few people she can turn to for help, there is a possibility that she has reconciled with Moriarty and that the host of the ball at Château Vaudrieu is none other than Moriarty."

Mr. Marbleton had been about to raise his glass to his lips — and stopped mid-motion. Livia held her breath. When he spoke, however, his voice was calm. "That makes a great deal of sense. Blackmail has long been a bread-and-butter method of income for Moriarty."

Had it? A chill spread at the back of Livia's neck.

"Those who want to disrupt the ball at Château Vaudrieu seem equally comfortable with extortion," Charlotte went on. "It doesn't seem farfetched to suppose that they learned from the same book, that they are, perhaps, former colleagues."

Mr. Marbleton took a sip of his *vin chaud.* "You are saying we are caught in the middle of a factional dispute?"

Charlotte's expression remained bland. "*Dispute* might be too mild a word. I'd say we are caught in the middle of a factional struggle. Obviously, the side occupying the château currently has the upper hand and the side that has to rely on the shenanigans of art thieves is at a disadvantage, but perhaps things might change at the ball, depending on whether the insurgents succeed."

"What do they want?" asked Mr. Marbleton, turning his glass between his fingers.

"The code Lord Ingram recorded in the tunnel, when deciphered, becomes a series of digits. The numbers are not coordinates of a point on the map. At the moment I'm inclined to think that they are the combination to a safe."

Mr. Marbleton frowned. "Why would anyone transmit code this way?"

"Perhaps our transmitter had no choice. Perhaps the unsuccessful escapee the other night should have been the one to carry out the code. We have no way of knowing."

"No, I mean, obviously if there is a prisoner and there are people mounting a rescue, then this person has loyalists. Yet none of them knows the combination to the safe?"

Since the discussion began, only Charlotte and Mr. Marbleton had spoken. Now Lord Ingram joined in for the first time. "Perhaps those who have spent enough time around Moriarty become as suspicious as he and prefer to keep friends close and secrets closer."

A trace of sorrow came into Mr. Marbleton's eyes. "I think I might have some idea who this prisoner is."

"You do?" cried Livia and Mrs. Watson at the same time.

Mr. Marbleton set aside his glass. "Most people who choose to escape Moriarty's orbit do not last long in the outside world, but my family has managed to remain safe and whole for two decades. We believe we have someone on the inside. My mother insists that she and my father never looked for a friend there but they had one anyway, someone from whom we received warnings, who also helped us spread misinformation about our whereabouts."

"And you think Moriarty finally found out?" Livia asked. Her stomach felt as if it was being twisted like a rope.

If that was the case, then the Marbletons' safety — *his* safety . . . She clutched at the glass in her hand.

"I can't be sure. Do you remember sending me to check the chimneys at Château Vaudrieu, Miss Charlotte?"

Charlotte nodded.

"I saw something that night that I didn't think was a good idea to convey by either post or cable: I saw three bodies being carried out of the château. Out of the château, but not away from the grounds, which led me to believe that they were interred on the property itself."

Livia could hear her own voice rising steeply. "And you think that this person or persons who had helped your family are now dead and buried?"

"I am of the opinion that those were not the Marbleton family's benefactors," Charlotte said quietly. "Remember what Lord Ingram overheard the hostess say to the female guest? 'Let's just say it involves a syringe and a choice of injectable solutions.'

"Lady Ingram's twin sister was killed by an injection of absolute alcohol. Moriarty bringing her back into the fold by sacrificing de Lacy and a couple of de Lacy's minions would easily have resulted in three dead bodies on the property, a separate matter from the tapping of the coded numbers that Lord Ingram overheard."

"So that person is still alive?" asked Lord Ingram, looking intently at Charlotte.

"I have no idea. Château Vaudrieu might be full of prisoners and executing a batch nightly, for all we know."

Livia recoiled. Mrs. Watson, too, turned pale.

"Don't worry," said Charlotte to Lord Ingram. "I still don't believe the prisoner is Mr. Finch."

Charlotte had mentioned that she hadn't heard from their half-brother in months, but she'd said that he was most likely on a voyage to Australia and Livia had been happy to believe her. Now her heart pounded again.

Mr. Marbleton picked up his glass of *vin chaud* and came and sat down in the chair nearest hers. At first she thought he'd come to bolster her courage. But perhaps Mrs. Watson and Charlotte's repeated counsel on not thinking so little of herself was finally having some effect. He also needed his own courage bolstered, she thought.

And I will do that for you.

They were not alone in the room, but she briefly laid her hand over his. They nodded at each other.

I'm all right.
I'm all right, too.

"Then who do you think the prisoner is, Holmes?" asked Lord Ingram.

"If I must guess now, Madame Desrosiers," mused Charlotte. "Mr. Finch told me at one point that Moriarty is believed to be thrice a widower — obviously incorrect, as Mrs. Marbleton, his second wife, is still living — and that since his third wife died, he's chosen not to marry again. But he is said to have a mistress of whom he is very fond. It's likely that Madame Desrosiers is that long-term mistress; she would also have been in position to have helped Mr. Marbleton's family over the years."

Mrs. Watson walked across the library to the decanter of cognac. "Then who was that woman who acted the part of the hostess the other night, to the woman we now presume to be Lady Ingram?"

Charlotte shrugged. "Another woman in Moriarty's employ, possibly. Remember Madame Desrosiers was said to be indisposed the night of the reception."

Mrs. Watson brought back two glasses of cognac, one for herself and one for Lord Ingram. Lord Ingram accepted his, thanked her, and returned his attention to Charlotte. "And Moriarty is this Herr Albretcht, the mysterious Swiss manufacturer who owns the château?"

"Maybe. Or maybe he is Monsieur Plantier, although Monsieur Plantier seems a bit young to be Moriarty." Charlotte poured herself a cup of coffee. "In any case, we do not have the luxury of involving ourselves in this dispute. We are there to help Mrs. Watson's friend, and we will restrict ourselves to that capacity.

"However, I have racked my brains and even consulted an *ingénieur,* but the fact remains that we cannot work magic tricks on the Van Dyck when we won't have the gallery to ourselves for any length of time. So I have no choice but to recommend that instead of the Van Dyck, we make the contents of this safe to which we now hold the combination our priority."

This was news only to Mr. Marbleton — Charlotte had already discussed her plans, in depth, with everyone else who had returned to England. Livia had fretted over whether this mythical safe in fact existed, Lord Ingram had demanded to know its exact location, and Mrs. Watson had been deeply concerned on how such a significant course change would affect her friend.

In the end Charlotte had convinced them not only that the safe existed and that she knew where it was, but also that the contents of the safe, and not any artworks for sale on the night of the yuletide masquerade ball, were the true aim of the mastermind who blackmailed Mrs. Watson's friend.

As it stands we have no chance of making away with the Van Dyck. But we do have some chance with the contents of this safe. Should we extract it, we would have more than enough with which to bargain for your friend's letters, Mrs. Watson.

Mr. Marbleton took some time to consider Charlotte's proposal. "Your words carry weight with me, Miss Charlotte. If you think that we should concentrate our efforts on the safe, then I trust that you have thought the matter through.

"Still, I have to ask about the residents of the château. Don't they know where the safe is?"

"I think not," answered Charlotte without any hurry. Or any hesitation. "I think if they did, then our insurgents wouldn't be interested in it anymore."

"But wouldn't those insurgents stand in our way?"

"I would rather face a few fellow burglars than try to get the Van Dyck off the wall and out of the château."

Mr. Marbleton thought for some more

362

time, then nodded his assent.

Livia exhaled.

When no one else spoke, Charlotte said, "I have asked Mrs. Watson's friend to join us today. She should hear from me directly about our change of directions. And also because I shall require her participation, since we are shorthanded.

"She will be here at" — Charlotte glanced at the grandfather clock — "well, she should have arrived three minutes ago. Forêt should be announcing her any moment now."

As if she'd summoned him, a knock came at the door, followed by Forêt's gentle voice. "Mesdames et Messieurs, a visitor to see you."

Forêt showed in a woman in a black dress and a widow's veil. She took a seat next to Mrs. Watson on the chaise longue.

"This is Madame, my friend," said Mrs. Watson, as if it were quite normal to welcome a covered-up stranger into the midst of a clandestine, possibly criminal discussion — and to divulge nothing of the stranger's identity.

Then again, they all knew this was the friend for whom Mrs. Watson had taken on this Herculean task.

Forêt served cake and coffee to Madame,

even though a woman in a veil was hardly going to expose her face to snack. When he had departed, Charlotte gave a highly condensed version of their earlier discussion, leaving out all references by name to Moriarty and Lady Ingram.

Madame listened intently. At the end of Charlotte's explanations she asked, "What if this safe isn't there? Do you have any contingency plan, with regard to the Van Dyck?"

She spoke in French, her accent subtle enough and unfamiliar enough that Livia couldn't place it.

"Our ally has arranged for something," said Charlotte. "But we don't know how likely it is to happen and cannot count on it."

"So we proceed without any guarantees."

"We proceed without any guarantees."

Madame hesitated. "Very well, then. Let's proceed however we may."

"Excellent," said Charlotte. "Now it's time we discuss the specifics of the plan, which will involve some loverly conduct. Miss Olivia and Mr. Marbleton are excused from said conduct. The participation of everyone else, including Madame, will be required."

Livia blinked. If Charlotte was to partner with Lord Ingram, then who would Mrs.

Watson and Madame partner with? Surely not each other?

Madame glanced at Mrs. Watson. Some kind of unspoken communication passed between them. Then she nodded, the gesture extraordinarily regal.

Charlotte inclined her head. "Very well. Let us all change into appropriate attire and proceed to our first rehearsal."

In Charlotte's bedroom, Livia helped her sister with the most important part of her costume. Charlotte's disguise as a man required a substantial stomach to hide her generous bosom. Usually a lot of padding was used to achieve that bulk, but this time a paunch had been made specifically for the ball.

"You are going to have Mrs. Watson and her friend do 'loverly' things together?" asked Livia, tightening the straps that secured the paunch to Charlotte's person.

"The camera is stationary. They will be able to angle themselves so that they will only *appear* to be intimate," answered Charlotte with her usual detachment.

"But even if they position themselves with one person's back to the camera, they will still need to remain in an embrace. How awkward it will be for them."

A knock came at the door.

"Come in," said Charlotte.

Mrs. Watson.

Livia's face heated. She hoped Mrs. Watson hadn't overheard anything.

"Oh, Miss Charlotte," said Mrs. Watson, shaking her head, "what a thing to make two old ladies do."

"Extraordinary times call for extraordinary measures," replied Charlotte, sounding not at all chastised, not that Mrs. Watson appeared at all interested in chastising anyone.

Mrs. Watson sighed. "It will be awkward, since we have been apart and out of touch for so many years. But at least we won't be doing anything we haven't done before."

A buckle fell out of Livia's hand. She didn't know where to look. Did Mrs. Watson mean to imply that . . . that . . .

Mrs. Watson chuckled. "If you have any questions, Miss Olivia, you can ask me directly. I'm standing right here."

"Ummm . . ." Livia finished with the straps and pulled on them to make sure they were tight enough but not so tight that they would cause Charlotte discomfort. "I take it you and your friend enjoyed a romantic friendship, like the Ladies of Llangollen?"

Lady Eleanor Butler and Miss Sarah Ponsonby had run away from their homes in County Kilkenny, possibly to escape unwanted marriages, settled down in Wales, and maintained a household together for fifty years.

"Well, the Ladies of Llangollen strenuously protested any characterization of their friendship as other than pure and chaste. I, on the other hand, can make no such protests."

Livia's jaw fell. Mrs. Watson and her friend had been . . . sapphic lovers? Didn't some German Herr Doktor just publish a book on sexual pathology and classify lesbianism as a type of neurological disease?

"Anyway," said Mrs. Watson, "I've been tasked by my friend to tell you that you are a cheeky young lady, Miss Charlotte, for making us old ladies engage in possibly lewd exhibitions. But between you and me, I think *cheeky,* coming from her lips, is a compliment."

She was gone the next minute, because she still needed to change.

Livia turned to Charlotte. "I don't know what to think about any of this."

Charlotte gave her a blank look. "What's there to think about? What Mrs. Watson and her friend do and don't do with each other doesn't affect you to any extent."

But the problem seemed blindingly obvious to Livia. "Well, if Mrs. Watson is inclined toward ladies, don't you worry that she might feel something other than friendship for you?"

Charlotte's look remained blank. "No more than Lord Ingram worries that she might feel something other than friendship for him. She did have a younger husband once. Who is to say that she can't have an even younger one?"

Livia's lips flapped a few times. "But he doesn't live with her."

"Most men and women engaged in illicit affairs do not live together."

Charlotte's expression still hadn't changed, nor had her tone. But Livia suddenly felt silly. She adored Mrs. Watson. She'd adored Mrs. Watson from the very beginning as the mother she never had. Nothing about Mrs. Watson had changed. Why should Livia now establish hurdles that Mrs. Watson must jump over, when she had never needed to prove anything to Livia in the first place?

When she looked back at Charlotte, she said, "I think your austerity measures are working. You're visibly farther from Maximum Tolerable Chins than you were a few days ago."

Charlotte patted herself under her jaw. "I

will not bore you with tales of hardship, but it has been dreadful. The things I do in service to my vanity."

Livia smiled. In the corridor, Mr. Marbleton was calling for the rehearsal to begin. She tapped Charlotte on the shoulder. "Let's go."

Hôtel Papillon sat on a large but irregular plot of land and had its own sizable garden. In the middle of the lawn, the gentlemen who had stayed behind in Paris had installed an eight-foot-wide section of wrought iron fence.

It wasn't identical to the periphery fence at Château Vaudrieu, but it was of the same height and the same design, with similar sharp finials on top, pickets the same width apart, and, as was the case at Château Vaudrieu, no crossbars except at the very bottom and the very top.

The garden was shielded from view by high walls. The servants had been sent out for various tasks. The ladies, for whom the practice session had been arranged, arrived wearing bloomers. The strategy was clear. Charlotte must always be the first person to be sent over the fence, as she, along with the contraband that would be strapped to her person, made for the heaviest escapee and benefitted from having all the other three women helping her up.

Lord Ingram and Mr. Marbleton were on the scene to lend a hand, if need be. But mostly Mrs. Watson coordinated the ladies. It took Mrs. Watson, the maharani, and Livia some time to work out how to best arrange themselves, so that they gave the greatest upward boost to Charlotte.

The first time Charlotte got both of her feet on the top crossbar, she became petrified. She was too high for anyone to reach up and steady her. The fence, which had felt firmly planted while she was on her way up, now seemed to sway to and fro. She was sure that if she swung her leg over, she would bring the whole thing crashing down.

Lord Ingram was already reaching for the ladder that had been brought for just this purpose, but Mr. Marbleton stopped him. "Miss Charlotte, I promise you this fence is solid as a rock. Whatever you do, it will not tilt over. You have my word on it."

With that, he scaled the fence in a single motion and shook it from the top. Charlotte didn't scream, but she did let out an audible gasp. But as Mr. Marbleton promised, the fence held. Very well, too.

Charlotte exhaled and swung her leg over, only to then become sincerely stuck on the

370

finials, which hooked onto the voluminous fabric of her bloomers. She sighed. She'd never been fond of bloomers, which did not flatter her figure, but now their uselessness was confirmed.

The ladder was brought. Livia climbed up and freed Charlotte's bloomers. Mr. Marbleton now demonstrated for her how she was to hold on to the top crossbar and gently lower herself, and then finally to let go and drop the remaining distance to the ground.

Or rather, to the mattress that had been placed on the other side.

She landed on shaky legs. Her arms too felt sore from exertion. And of course she was the weakest one among the ladies, the maharani proving herself surprisingly agile, Mrs. Watson strong and determined, and Livia as scrappy as any street urchin who needed to scramble up a wall to escape a bobby.

Charlotte dearly wished to settle down in a comfortable padded chair with a cup of hot tea, a slice of heavenly cake, and a Patent Office catalogue or two. But there was nothing for it. She took a deep breath, rubbed her hands together, and said, "Let's try that again?"

■ ■ ■ ■

The day before the ball, Livia and Mr. Marbleton took a walk in the Jardin des Tuileries.

They'd strolled from one end of the Grand Allée to the other and taken in the sweeping view from the Louvre to the Place de la Concorde. Now they were in a slightly more intimate area, walking past stone sculptures and old Parisian women seated in clusters. It wasn't the best time to be in the garden — the trees had lost their foliage and stood naked underneath a grey sky. Still, Livia loved a large, well-kept park at the heart of a city.

And Mr. Marbleton's company.

She'd been worried about him going into Moriarty's stronghold. He, far less concerned than she, pointed out that it was a masquerade ball, and that no one would see his, or anyone else's, face. And so she had allowed herself to relax a little.

There were still preparations to make and rehearsals to hold for their undertaking at the ball, but he'd insisted that she couldn't come to Paris without having experienced a little of the city. After the park they would browse in his favorite Parisian bookshop and then have a meal at a neighborhood brasserie, before returning to Hôtel Papillon for the home stretch.

"I have finished my Sherlock Holmes story!" she blurted out, as they rounded a faded garden bed.

He stopped in his tracks. "Congratulations!"

She wanted to laugh and cry all at once. "Thank you. I got to the end on the rail journey from Dieppe to Paris."

The day she, Charlotte, Mrs. Watson, and Lord Ingram returned to France.

"You reached this monumental milestone two days ago and you didn't say anything in the forty-eight hours since?" He threw up his hands in mock outrage.

"I — I wasn't ready for anyone to read it yet. And I'm still not. But since I promised you that you would be the first, here it is." She pulled out the stack of three notebooks from her reticule. They were tied together with a dark blue ribbon, the bow now half-crushed. "I'll need to leave for home very soon after the ball. You can read it after I leave."

He accepted the notebooks with both hands and held them as if she had placed a flower in his palms. "Thank you. I have never read anyone's manuscript." He looked up, his gaze clear and sincere. "I will guard your manuscript with my life and make sure it returns safely to you."

Her heart had never felt so . . . permeable, yet so spacious and all-encompassing. She laughed. "And now, after I have made my grand gesture, I will need to put these notebooks back in my reticule so that you won't need to walk all around Paris with them."

He pushed her hand away and gave her a brilliant smile. "Absolutely not. I insist on walking around with them, as the proudest man in Paris."

When Charlotte arrived in the ballroom, Lord Ingram and Lieutenant Atwood were still at their *canne de combat* practice.

She'd very much enjoyed it when Mrs. Watson and Miss Redmayne had demonstrated maneuvers for her — they moved with such lightness and dancerly grace. The men before her fought not with dancerly grace, but with an animal ferocity. She studied their footwork, the rapid steps and turns; she studied how their offense and defense seemed apiece, attacking and safeguarding in the same flowing motion.

She was no expert, but if anything, Lieutenant Atwood seemed the superior combatant. When the two stopped, it was because Lord Ingram asked him to demonstrate a particular stance. Lieutenant Atwood explained, then the two men reengaged, but at a much slower speed, for Lord Ingram to see how Lieutenant Atwood pulled off his maneuver.

She didn't consider Lord Ingram a humble man, but he'd shed a good bit of unnecessary pride over the years. Ten years ago, he would not have had the confidence and humility to ask for instruction. Would probably have been displeased, even vexed, that he'd come across a greater opponent.

Everyone changed. But it was rare to meet anyone who could be relied upon to change for the better.

The men looked in her direction at almost the same time. Lieutenant Atwood inclined his head and left from a different door. Charlotte advanced toward Lord Ingram.

"That was an impressive display of prowess."

"More so on Lieutenant Atwood's part than mine," he said.

"He is better, but you are also very good."

He smiled.

She raised a brow. "Are you thinking that another woman would have assured you that you are at least his equal?"

"Where you are concerned, I am well past that. I am simply delighted that you think I am very good," he said, patting at his forehead with a handkerchief. His shirt, open at the collar, displayed a few enticing inches of sternum, also covered with a faint sheen of perspiration.

She might prove a more regular practitioner of *canne de combat* if her practice partner always looked like this.

"Shall we start?" she asked.

They still had a great deal left to do, but with Livia and Mr. Marbleton at the Jardin des Tuileries, Mrs. Watson at the maharani's hotel for the final fitting of the maharani's ballgown, Charlotte thought a little exercise would be helpful for her well-being and her concentration, not to mention her figure.

He did not answer immediately.

"What's the matter?" she asked.

He seemed to be debating with himself concerning his answer. The debate lasted several more seconds. "You asked me the same question a while ago."

She had. They had been in a hansom cab, talking about the maharani and her possible interest in removing the British from the Subcontinent. Later that evening she'd set out with Livia, Mrs. Watson, and Mr. Marbleton across the English Channel, to begin their French adventure.

Or misadventure, as it could still become.

At the time she'd decreed that something was bothering him; he had made no response. "So something *is* bothering you?"

He tapped his fingertips against the head of his cane. "My children's governess is thinking of emigrating to Australia — she has a cousin who has done very well there."

Aha! She'd seen the governess once or twice over the years, trailing behind Lady Ingram and the children. It would seem that the rather mousy Miss Yarmouth had grown bold in Lady Ingram's absence.

But why was he telling her this? Did he mean to — no, he had no intention of applying any kind of pressure to Charlotte. He was simply asking a good friend for advice.

"Australia has better marital prospects, I've heard," she said. "For women, that is."

"A very important consideration for Miss Yarmouth. She is, however, willing to forego the trip if I would espouse her myself, after the official dissolution of my current marriage."

He spoke so somberly. The corners of her lips almost quirked. "My goodness, since when is one English divorcé worth a continentful of rich, virile bachelors? Miss Yarmouth is shortchanging herself."

He snorted, then laughed outright.

"Is she in love with you or does she really hate ocean voyages?"

"I have no intelligence on the latter. And we all know I am terrible at judging how women truly feel about me."

Strictly speaking, he had only been terrible at judging how *one* woman felt about him. By using the plural, did he mean to say that he also had no idea how Charlotte felt about him?

"Did Miss Yarmouth offer inducements?"

"Besides not abandoning my children? Just that she will be content with a marriage of convenience." He looked at her. "Any advice on how I ought to proceed?"

Given that the current impasse between them could partly be attributed to the imminent demise of his marriage, and that with great freedom came great likelihood of regrettable choices, did she want him to go back to being a married man?

And for nothing else to ever come of their friendship?

"You can find better candidates for a marriage of convenience right here at Hôtel Papillon," she heard herself say. "My sister, for one. She is desperate to leave my parents' household and adores Stern Hollow.

She would be no trouble at all as Lady Ingram."

"Good God!"

"You are excused for your language, sir. But you know who would be even better? Mrs. Watson. She also adores Stern Hollow, and she loves children. She would make for the world's best stepmother."

He glared at her — and laughed again. "Be serious, Holmes."

Fine, if she must. She sighed. "I think you deserve better than a marriage of convenience."

His expression turned solemn. "What do I deserve then?"

She had no good answer.

After a few moments, he said, "Shall we start our practice?"

SEVENTEEN

Livia hadn't danced with Charlotte in ten years, not since they'd been girls preparing for their first season. Charlotte had been slightly uncoordinated as a child. Livia, worried that she would step on gentlemen's feet, had made Charlotte practice at home, with Livia as the gentleman.

But now Charlotte was the gentleman. She did not wear a wig, but sported her own still quite short hair. Her full beard was correspondingly blond, hiding the otherwise too-smooth skin of her face. Behind a black-and-white harlequin-patterned mask accented with bright teal, her eyes were kind and cordial.

All the space between them was taken up with Charlotte's stomach, the most protuberant it had ever been. Livia was afraid to bump into it, afraid that she might accidentally nudge it out of place. She leaned back as Charlotte swept her into a turn, even as her hand tightened on the sleeve of Charlotte's formal jacket, made of a bright teal satin to match her mask.

"You look very lovely tonight," said Charlotte.

Livia had absolutely no idea how she looked — not that it mattered, with her own gold and blue mask on. She was sick to her stomach, her palms perspiring freely inside her ball gloves. "Thank you," she managed.

All around them, other dancers whirled and gamboled. So many brilliantly hued masks, wild with feathers and rhinestones, so many diamond necklaces, sparkling in every direction, so many daringly attired ladies, jewel-toned gowns plunging front and back, spinning endlessly on the black-and-white marble floor.

Livia could not look too long at her surroundings — it made her dizzy. So she stared at Charlotte's right ear, just visible behind her mask. Charlotte hummed to the music. Livia could *hear* the music, but it was only indistinct sound above an underlayer of chatter and laughter and nowhere as audible as the thudding of her heart and the whooshing of blood in her veins.

She didn't even know whether they were in the midst of a waltz or a schottische. Her body followed along to Charlotte's lead, while her mind cowered and whimpered somewhere in a dark room.

Charlotte, as ever, seemed immune to the strain that threatened to both crush Livia and cause her to explode. She steered Livia clear of other twirling couples, while scanning the entire ballroom with every turn.

"Mrs. Watson's friend and Mr. Marbleton aren't far behind us. She seems taken with him — and I'm sure she's not easily charmed," she murmured.

Livia didn't look for their colleagues. Beyond their immediate vicinity, everything was a kaleidoscopic blur. So much color, so much gaiety. But to her nerve-stricken senses, the gaiety seemed forced, a great deal of froth without any true effervescence.

Perhaps she was correct.

Over the years a number of guests would have gone upstairs to those bedrooms, in search of forbidden pleasures. Knowing what she knew of how Château Vaudrieu operated, those unfortunate guests, already threatened with exposure, were probably also compelled to return year after year, lest attendance from the best Parisian Society seemed to wane over time.

She glanced at the couples spinning past. How many of them had to force themselves to dance and make merry? How many whirled in the midst of a place they loathed, gritting their teeth to convey good humor and high spirits?

All at once she couldn't wait to be gone from this accursed manor.

But not until they'd done what they needed to do.

Every minute lasted an hour. Yet somehow she felt that they were behind schedule. Lord Ingram and Mrs. Watson, according to the plan, should be strolling arm in arm on the balcony above, alert for any guests exiting toward the bedrooms. And Lord Ingram's ally was watching the galleries where those who'd attended the reception and received special personalized tickets were to place those tickets, on which they'd hand-written their offers, into glass jars marked with the names of the paintings.

They were also on the lookout for a third signal. Charlotte was certain that at least one group of art thieves would try to sabotage the supply of electricity. She was also sure that the château must have a second electrical plant and that the outage would not last very long.

But when that moment of sudden darkness came, the guests, some of whom were already a little tipsy, might become amorous in their conduct. Which meant that after the light was restored, there would be a steady exodus of guests searching for privacy.

Charlotte and co. were to make their move after Lord Ingram's ally had put in his bids, but before the stampede toward the bedrooms.

"Haven't we danced enough? Shouldn't we be at the next stage of the plan by now?" Livia whispered, as the music came to an end.

Charlotte glanced toward the balcony. "Maybe we already are."

Lord Ingram and Mrs. Watson were nowhere to be seen, but a man in a distinctive black horned mask stood with an elbow braced on the balustrade. Charlotte offered her arm to Livia, and together they climbed up.

"Mr. Nariman," said Charlotte in a jolly tone, "did you put in your bids?"

Was this man Lord Ingram's mysterious ally?

"I did," he said in slightly accented English. "But there were only glass jars for incoming offers in the galleries, and no artworks at all. I spoke to the staff stationed near the glass jars and they couldn't — or wouldn't — tell me anything."

Livia's stomach rolled. They knew that the château had taken a number of defensive measures, including guarding the chapel against unauthorized entry and going to a different agency for the temporary staff required for the night of the ball. But removing the artworks altogether when the ball was also a celebrated occasion for transactions in art?

What was going on?

It was difficult to gauge Charlotte's reaction with her mask on. She was silent for some time, and when she spoke, it was only to say, softly, "Here are Madame and Mr. Marbleton."

Everyone addressed Mrs. Watson's friend as simply Madame. Her black ballgown was modestly cut and revealed a Mediterranean skin tone. Mr. Marbleton had on the usual black formal attire. They wore matching gold masks with enormous purple plumes that nodded from above their heads.

"What does this mean?" asked Madame tightly, in French, when she and Mr. Marbleton had been informed of the latest development.

The five of them stood shoulder-to-shoulder along the parapet of the gallery. Below, the dancers eddied and swirled. For a moment Livia had the disconcerting sensation that she might fall into this human tide and be carried away.

"The château must have decided to neutralize all the would-be art thieves tonight," said Charlotte. "All their plans of disruption would have been contingent on the paintings being within reach. Remove the paintings altogether and there is no point in any of the plans being put into motion."

"You have been prescient, Miss Charlotte, in bypassing the Van Dyck in your preparations," said Madame.

"Not this prescient." Charlotte smoothed a gloved hand on the parapet. "Let's not wait for any other signals. We will proceed to the bedrooms now."

She placed Livia's hand on Mr. Marbleton's arm. Then she offered her own arm to Madame. Lord Ingram's ally tucked Madame's other hand into the crook of his elbow. A lone man wandering the hallways might make the guards suspicious, but a couple, or better yet a ménage à trois, would pass for revelers feeling a little too frisky for their own good.

Livia didn't feel frisky. She barely felt the ground beneath her feet. Only Mr. Marbleton's arm seemed real and solid. She clung on, trying not to double over in panic.

As they neared their destination, they encountered Lord Ingram and Mrs. Watson, who had been directing traffic. "Only two parties came up so far, and they went to the other corridor. But there is a guard stationed outside the linen closet."

They needed to access the first secret passage Lord Ingram explored, the one in which he had to hide from the two women who entered, one of whom being possibly his wife. From studying the architectural plans, which did not show any of the secret passages, Charlotte had deduced that that the women must have used a hidden door in the back of a linen closet.

And now the linen closet was guarded.

Livia's heart beat so hard her chest hurt.

"This is not unforeseen," said Charlotte coolly. "We've rehearsed for it. Let's proceed."

On the night of the reception, as Lord Ingram had explored the château's hidden passages and looked through the spy ports, he had seen the interior of two rooms. One, small and utilitarian, was on the other side of the château. Charlotte now stood before the door of the other.

She exhaled deeply, inhaled, exhaled again. Lord Ingram had already entered the room a minute ago. The guard at the linen closet, two doors down, pressed his lips together in contempt upon realizing that it was a man rendezvousing with another man. Charlotte pretended to be ashamed.

Once inside, she leaned against the back of the door and bit her lower lip, giving every impression of hesitancy. Lord Ingram, who seemed to have been pacing back and forth in the room before her arrival, stood still for a moment, looking at her from behind his glittering yellow-and-green mask — the better to convey his surprised and tremulous happiness that she, or the man she was pretending to be, had showed up after all.

He closed the distance between them and braced a hand by the side of her head.

"Lieutenant Atwood didn't laugh," she said softly. The watchers inside the secret passage most likely couldn't hear them, but she didn't want to take the chance.

He grinned. "Lieutenant Atwood is a better man than I."

He ran his fingers lightly along her beard, and then just as lightly over her paunch. Heat skittered along her nerves, even though he'd yet to touch her skin.

"All right." His expression turned more somber. "In this position, the watcher can see only my back and the bits of you that I don't entirely obscure. Once we leave this spot, be more careful."

"Where is the spy port?"

"Concealed by the ornamental sunburst under the window seat with the books. You ready?"

He turned her and maneuvered her so that her back was against the nearest bedpost. To avoid dislodging her stomach, he stood to her side rather than directly in front. And now he traced the outline of her mask, his cool fingertip leaving a scalding trail.

"Lie with me," he said in French, in case the watcher could read lips.

He should say things like that more often. She gripped the edge of the bed to show her trepidation. "Monsieur, that is . . . that is . . . I don't know . . ."

"Do you doubt what I feel for you, *chéri*?"

Perhaps on the inside he still wished to laugh, but she no longer did. His tone was deeply serious and perhaps a little afraid. As an actor he could not do better. And if he were in any way channeling his own sentiments . . .

He had said that he loved her, under questioning by the chief inspector who'd suspected him of murder. Dressed as Sherrinford Holmes, she'd been in the same carriage when that happened. But he'd made the admission with his head turned away from her and had never mentioned it again.

Certainly not like this, gazing directly into her eyes, his expression open and vulnerable, his yearning naked.

Her voice caught. "My dear sir, so much stands between us and any possibility of happiness."

"Yet where the possibility of happiness exists, do we not owe it to ourselves to try?"

Her breaths turned shallow. "I — my life is tidy and contained, sir. I don't know whether anything will remain tidy and contained anymore, after we . . . try."

He set his hand against her cheek. "Perhaps our lives will become more complicated. But that we will be together, does that not mean anything to you, *chéri*? Does that not make up for some difficulties here and there?"

Her skin scalded at his touch. She set her hand on his wrist. Beneath her fingertips, his pulse raced. Her heart, too, was racing. "What will happen to our friendship? Love can easily dissipate. Should our hearts founder, will we still be friends — or will we become strangers?"

For the first time since she had entered the room, he looked away from her. His hand left her face. Silence, their old companion, returned once again.

A strange melancholy settled over her. In

playacting, had they been more truthful with each other than they had ever been in real life?

He turned toward the door. "That may be my wife."

This, too, was part of the script. She mentally shook herself. They still had their difficult and dangerous task ahead; she could not afford any distractions.

He went to the door, walking without his usual animal grace, but with his shoulders hunched, his gait almost shuffling. He listened, glanced back at her, and said, "You stay here, my friend."

That was her signal that it was indeed Mrs. Watson and the maharani outside. After he closed the door behind himself, she set her ear to the keyhole and could just make out the sound of Mrs. Watson giggling. "But why, Monsieur *le garde,* why should we go into a bedchamber? We are not doing anything that requires a bed, are we, *mon choux?*"

The maharani giggled, too, a rather shocking thing to hear. "*Non, mon petit choux doux.* And we like how you look at us, don't we?" she said, now with a distinct Russian accent to her French.

"Please, Mesdames —"

The guard's request was cut short. There

was a brief scuffling. When it was silent in the corridor again, Charlotte opened the door a crack, then went to stand directly before the spy port.

A short while later, Lord Ingram and Lieutenant Atwood pulled the guard, already bound and gagged, into the room. Lieutenant Atwood pulled out a handkerchief, soaked it in chloroform, and secured it over the man's nose and mouth.

Livia had asked them earlier whether they planned to use chloroform to remove the guards. All the gentlemen sighed sadly: Alas, it would take several minutes of holding a chloroform-drenched cloth over someone's face for them to become unconscious. But they could use it after the guards were incapacitated, so that they didn't wake up too soon to make trouble.

They stowed the man under the bed, where he wouldn't be visible from the spy port. Lieutenant Atwood left, raising a finger to indicate that they had one minute. Lord Ingram went to stand near the door, closing it as if he'd just come in.

Only then did Charlotte leave the spot before the spy port. "Was it your wife?" she asked.

"No, just some other women."

He took her hands. They did not say

anything. The clock on the mantel ticked. When there were fifteen seconds left, she said, "I — I had better go."

"Please don't," he said. Again he sounded as if he meant it.

She dropped her gaze. She found herself reluctant to continue with the script, but now she must. "I think it would be best if we kept things as they are."

He dropped her hands, took a step back, and turned his face away. "I know why you think as you do, my dearest friend. But if you change your mind in the next hour or so, you'll find me here."

Charlotte needed a moment outside the door to collect herself. Then she strode toward the linen closet.

Mr. Marbleton had taken the guard's place. His mask had been taken off; his jacket, which they'd had specially made in London, turned inside out to closely resemble the château's livery. Mrs. Watson and the maharani had gone into the bedroom immediately to the other side of the linen closet, and Livia should be in the room farthest down the hall — that the company had kept others from coming into this corridor meant that they themselves must now be the ones to distract the watchers.

When Mr. Marbleton was certain no one else was in the corridor, he let Charlotte into the linen closet. Lieutenant Atwood, already inside, had found the mechanism that opened a secret door at the back of the linen closet.

"Watch out for steps," Charlotte whispered.

The secret passage was located between floors. Lord Ingram had not come across any steps in the passage itself, so the change in elevation must happen somewhere between the linen closet and the passage.

Lieutenant Atwood went in alone. Seconds passed. There came the soft, slow grinding of stone on stone.

Light from the corridor seeped in from underneath the front door of the linen closet. But it penetrated only a few inches before dissipating into the shadows. Where Charlotte stood, she could barely see her own hand held in front of her eyes. Where Lieutenant Atwood had disappeared, the darkness was stygian, a thick impenetrability that seemed only to grow blacker as he opened the door to the secret passage where the cameras were.

The grinding sound stopped.

"You at the western end, anyone in your rooms?" said Lieutenant Atwood, sounding uncannily like Monsieur Plantier.

"Oui, monsieur," came the reply. *"Une dame."*

That would be Livia, sitting in a room at the far end of the corridor, nervously playing with the buttons on her gloves, as if she were waiting for someone else to show up.

"You in the middle?"

"Two women in the yellow room."

"You at the eastern end, what about you?"

"Two men in the blue room earlier, but they left one after another just now. So I've no one."

This was the configuration they intended. Artworks in the galleries or not, at least so far their plan had held.

"Then you come with me," said Lieutenant Atwood. "We need more men below."

"Oui, monsieur."

More careful grinding of stone on stone. Footsteps in the dark. An almost noiseless scuffle. An interval during which Lieutenant Atwood must be tying up the unfortunate watcher. A soft grunt of exertion as he dragged the latter into the linen closet.

A strong odor of cigarette smoke clung to the unconscious man.

"You are very good at this," Charlotte murmured.

"I've seen someone who can disarm multiple men at a distance while barely lifting her fingers — compared to that, I'm nothing."

And you saw her in Chinese Turkestan?

She didn't ask that, but only put her ear to the linen closet's door.

Almost immediately someone spoke on the other side. "Why are you standing there?"

The tone was icy, the French a little stiff, but the voice was indisputably lovely. Lady Ingram.

"I'm here at Monsieur Plantier's orders, Madame," said Mr. Marbleton, in his capacity as the counterfeit guard.

"Step aside."

"Alas, Madame, I can't let anyone in unless Monsieur Plantier says so."

Charlotte whispered in Lieutenant Atwood's ear for him to move himself and the guard so that they wouldn't be visible with the opening of the linen closet's door. Then she slipped out, inclined her head at an astonished Mr. Marbleton, and said, "My lady, I was rather hoping to run into you. Shall we take a round?"

Lady Ingram stared at her in suspicious distaste. Charlotte smiled. Of course Lady Ingram would object to a man in a teal evening jacket and matching mask. She herself was in a deadening grey gown that absorbed light without giving anything back, and her mask was equally dull.

"You know me, my lady," said Charlotte in her own voice. "A little promenade?"

Lady Ingram recoiled with shock. Her brow furrowed. But she eventually settled her hand on Charlotte's arm.

"What are you doing here?" she hissed.

Charlotte walked her out of the corridor. "Long story. But you may be sure I didn't come for you."

Elsewhere on this floor, card rooms had been set up for the gentlemen and lounges for the ladies where they may rest on chaises or have seamstresses repair hems that had been damaged by vigorous dancing. As Charlotte and Lady Ingram moved away from the bedrooms, more guests milled about, chatting, some obviously flirting. A faint music floated in the air: In the ballroom below it was another energetic waltz.

Lady Ingram removed her hand from Charlotte's arm. "Is my husband here?"

Charlotte raised a brow. In her exile, was Lady Ingram becoming somewhat fonder of the man about to divorce her? "Yes."

Lady Ingram inhaled audibly. "Are you sleeping together?"

"Would he do that to you?" Charlotte

retorted lightly.

Lady Ingram's grimace was obvious, even with the mask covering half her face.

"But I didn't come to speak of Lord Ingram, but of Moriarty," continued Charlotte. "I take it you and he have reconciled?"

"What do you mean?"

"You are here at his château. Did he sacrifice de Lacy to win back your good favor?"

Lady Ingram smiled grimly. "De Lacy is dead. I emptied the syringe of absolute alcohol into him myself. But Moriarty had nothing to do with it. He has been deposed."

Charlotte stopped in her tracks. *"Deposed?"*

"Madame Desrosiers is in charge of the organization now." Lady Ingram almost sounded as if she was proud to know the woman.

Charlotte's fingertips tingled. "Is she? Where is Moriarty then?"

Lady Ingram shrugged. "She never told me. Besides, he's been deposed for months. So why does it matter anymore where he is?"

"It would matter if he were here," said Charlotte, a chill slithering up her spine. "Have you not felt it? The château has been preparing for something."

Lady Ingram had stopped when Charlotte had, but now she resumed walking. "Art thieves — they've been preparing for art thieves. There is an overabundance of them this year."

Charlotte caught up with her. "I hope they have prepared for more than that. If Moriarty is held here at the château, then there will be an attempt to rescue him tonight."

Everything made sense now. Moriarty still had loyalists, but they were at a disadvantage. Even before the coup, Madame Desrosiers must have made sure that the château was populated by her own most stalwart supporters, let alone afterward. She would have also made sure that he had no way of communicating with his own followers.

They, on the other hand, would have done their best to infiltrate the château. Charlotte would lay good money that the person caught escaping the night Lord Ingram and Mr. Marbleton first trespassed on the grounds was not Moriarty but an infiltrator who had given himself away by getting too close to Moriarty's cell.

What was to have been his mission? To get the combination to the safe from Moriarty? Or the location of the safe? No, Moriarty would not have given away the location of the safe. That was his bargaining chip, both with Madame Desrosiers, if she suspected the existence of such a thing, and with his own rescuers: If they knew the location of the safe, who was to say they wouldn't concentrate their efforts on liberating the safe, rather than him?

Now they were coming for him — both the true loyalists and the hired guns.

Did Madame Desrosiers and Monsieur Plantier know what they would be facing tonight?

"This place is hardly undefended," said Lady Ingram, perhaps echoing the attitude of her hosts.

She was not wrong. Château Vaudrieu was braced for more than an onslaught of art thieves this night. It had to have been preparing, for a while, for trouble from Moriarty's followers.

The reason the château had been short-handed for the reception? A purge of its own roster, following the discovery of the infiltrator who had run out from the chapel but hadn't made it over the fence.

The reason Livia, Mrs. Watson, Mr. Marbleton had been subject to inspection by men from the château while they were still at the staffing agency? To prevent Moriarty's known followers from coming

400

back inside.

In fact, Charlotte thought as they rounded a corner, if it weren't so expensive to stage coups and defend against Moriarty's followers, Madame Desrosiers and Monsieur Plantier might not have held the ball this year at all. But they needed the cash from the art sales and the future income generated by photographic evidence of fresh indiscretions. So they took a risk in carrying on as if nothing had changed.

And in securing the château as best as they could, they had reason to be confident. Charlotte had seen firsthand the aplomb with which host and staff had handled the disruption on the night of the reception.

But perhaps, with that very competence, they had sown the seeds of their own downfall. Moriarty's followers, knowing that they faced a wary and capable defense, had had time to revise their plan of attack.

Charlotte would not want to be on the receiving end of it.

She took a deep breath. "You are right that the château is defended. But defended doesn't mean impregnable. I would recommend that you seek refuge tonight at the village inn. If all is well, you can return tomorrow."

Lady Ingram looked insulted. "You think

I feel so little loyalty to the woman who helped me avenge my sister that I would run at the first sign of trouble?"

Charlotte gave her a look. Lady Ingram had an odd sense of loyalty; still, she couldn't say the woman didn't have one. "If you wish to help Madame Desrosiers, please do. I only ask that you do not mention my name. Or Lord Ingram's."

"Of course not. I need him alive and well to look after my children. And I still owe you a debt for finding out what happened to my sister," said Lady Ingram, sounding unhappy about both.

Considering that Charlotte's investigations were also responsible for Lady Ingram's exile, Charlotte would not have said Lady Ingram owed her anything. But she inclined her head. "Thank you, my lady. Good luck to you."

She turned to leave.

"Wait. Why were you in that linen closet? Were you trying to take photographs of anyone at their indiscretions?"

Charlotte turned back around. "Were *you*?"

"I wanted to see what sort of indiscretions people get up to." Lady Ingram laughed rather dryly. "It astonishes me that they would come to a ball and . . . do such things. All I want when I'm at a ball is to go home and be alone."

"I was not taking anyone's photographs," said Charlotte, folding her hands primly before her.

Lady Ingram's lips thinned. She turned around and walked away, perhaps understanding that she was better off not knowing anymore.

EIGHTEEN

When Charlotte returned to the corridor, Lord Ingram and Lieutenant Atwood emerged from the easternmost bedroom. They looked disappointed.

"No safe that we could find," said Lord Ingram. "You might be right after all, that one needs to access it from the secret passage itself."

Charlotte nodded. "By the way, I spoke to Lady Ingram just now."

Lord Ingram had first suggested that his wife might be at the château. But judging by his reaction, one would have thought the idea had never occurred to him.

He mastered himself quickly. "Did you learn anything from her about Moriarty?"

"Yes, that he's been deposed and Madame Desrosiers is in charge now."

The men stared at her, then looked at each other, then back at her again.

"Does this mean —" Lord Ingram began.

"Yes and I don't think the château is prepared for what is going to happen."

"They handled the ferret attack with perfect aplomb," said Lieutenant Atwood. "Are you sure they will be unequal to tonight's travails?"

"I'm afraid Moriarty's people have seen that nonchalance and realized that the château could handle any distractions dreamed up by art thieves. And I'm afraid that they will now try devices and methods that art thieves couldn't even conceive of."

"Such as?" ask Lord Ingram, his expression tense.

She shrugged. "Whatever it will be, let's finish what we need to do and get out. I'm going into the passage."

Lord Ingram gripped her arm. "You realize that you mean to empty the contents of *Moriarty's* safe?"

"I can't prevent his return. But I do believe I can make it a little less triumphant."

For Mr. Marbleton's sake, if nothing else.

She glanced at the young man who had become so important to her sister. From his post outside the linen closet he watched them, his face solemn. They'd been speaking in low voices. She didn't think he had overheard anything, but their demeanor would have been enough to indicate the gravity of the situation.

"Tell Mr. Marbleton for me," she said to Lord Ingram.

"Tell him yourself. Let me go into the passage instead?"

He could. But all she had were twelve digits, not a fixed combination for the safe. She trusted that she could do the trials faster.

"I'll be fine." She lifted Lord Ingram's hand from her sleeve and held it for a moment. "And now more than ever, I need you gentlemen to keep an eye on things. Give me all the cigarettes you are carrying, by the way."

The request was met with a look, but Lord Ingram extracted a cigarette case from his jacket and handed it to her. There were three cigarettes inside. "Do you have any?" she asked Lieutenant Atwood.

He did, adding four more to her collection. She thanked them and went on her way.

As she passed Mr. Marbleton, he looked at her inquiringly. But she could only give him a quick pat on the shoulder.

Time to go into the belly of the beast.

The guard in the linen closet had been removed. Charlotte reversed her jacket and

406

put it back on — the material was ordinary black wool on this side.

The walk from the linen closet to the stone door of the secret passage felt like squeezing down the esophagus of some very large beast, especially as she went down the steep steps. The descent was greater than she expected, from the position of the spy port in the room where she and Lord Ingram had acted out their little scene. It was possible periscopes had been built into the spy ports, so that the watchers wouldn't have the tops of their heads bump up against the ceiling of the secret passage.

The walk space widened a little toward the end. She kept close to the left wall — Lieutenant Atwood, while giving her the cigarettes, had warned her about the piss bucket to the right, though of course he had not called it that.

The mechanism, too, was on the left, a lever that would swing a portion of the wall open. There was a bolt that would keep the door shut — as always, Château Vaudrieu worried about infiltrators — but now it was unbolted.

She took a deep breath and inhaled cigarette smoke. When she opened the door, even in the dark, she could see a cloud of smoke billowing her way, overwhelmingly pungent.

"You already back, Mercier?" said a man not far to her right, startling her.

She gave a deep grunt of assent and turned left to head to her spot.

"What did you do down below?" the same man asked. "They never tell us anything. Just do this, do that."

She tensed.

"No talking in here, Poulaine, you know that," said another man.

She looked back. This man was farther away from her than Poulaine, at the western end of the passage, his profile momentarily lit as his cigarette glowed with a pull of breath.

"Ah là là, Barre," grumbled Poulaine, "talking to you is like pissing in a violin. Can you be any more of a stick-in-the-mud?"

All the same, he shut up.

Charlotte exhaled.

She walked carefully — it wasn't easy to get around the camera stands with her paunch. When she reached the last camera stand, she unbuttoned her jacket, her waist-coat, and her shirt and reached into the great space created by her prosthetic stomach to pull out a large piece of thin woolen cloth. This she draped over the stand.

408

With Livia in the westernmost room in the corridor and Mrs. Watson and the maharani in the room just west of the linen closet, Barre and Poulaine were both west of the stone door and Charlotte had the eastern section of the passage to herself. She hoped that in the dark, with the distance, the draped camera stand would appear to the two men as the silhouette of a person with his eyes fixed to the camera

Then she tiptoed to the spot where Lord Ingram had hidden when Madame Desrosiers and Lady Ingram had come into the secret passage, behind what he'd thought to be a flue.

The passage was directly over a gallery Charlotte had visited on the night of the reception and there had indeed been a large fireplace at roughly this spot. And according to the pictures Mr. Marbleton had taken with his detective camera, there was a chimney on top of the roof also at this spot.

Except on the night of the reception, both arriving and leaving, Charlotte had not seen any smoke rising from that particular spot on the roof, when all the while a fire had burned merrily in that grate.

Whatever the contents of the safe, Moriarty wanted them. Charlotte could be sure then that Madame Desrosiers also wanted them. And she would have searched the house thoroughly. Where could this safe be that she had likely not found it?

Charlotte did not consider hers a particularly good deduction — there was so much of the house they hadn't seen. But it was worth a try.

She struck a match, to light a cigarette and to study the "flue." Brick and mortar. Brick and mortar. The scalding heat at her fingertips forced her to extinguish the match. She used the lit cigarette to light another one, walked back to the camera stand, and placed one of the cigarettes next to the camera, away from the draped blanket so that it wouldn't catch fire, but would be visible to the other men in the passage.

She hoped that it would be enough to disguise the second cigarette, which she would be putting to use behind the flue. But no matter how she prodded and pried, she couldn't find any loose bricks.

The back of her head throbbed. Was she wrong about the location of the safe? About the existence of the safe altogether? She tried the "front" of the flue, even thought there was barely room for her to fit between the flue and the wall. Again nothing.

Surely Moriarty couldn't have set the opening panel of the safe on the side facing the rest of the passage. Then again, if he'd never expected to be in here except by himself, then perhaps it made sense to have it open to the side where there was the most space for him to maneuver.

She put out the cigarette still in her hand and felt this side of the flue, examining the bricks row by row. At last, where it was almost too high for her to reach, a brick moved slightly at her touch. And it had just enough space around it for her to pull it out.

She set the brick down carefully. Standing on her toes, she put her hand through the space vacated by the brick and felt for the mechanism, activating it as gently as she could. She braced for a loud pop, but a part of the flue swung forward almost noiselessly.

She let out a breath, went to the camera stand, and used the cigarette there to light yet another one, taking care not to let anyone see two points of light. She adjusted the blanket she'd draped earlier over the camera stand. It should obscure the safe behind it.

When she was done, she sat down before the safe that had been revealed. It was twice as large as she'd anticipated. And the combination lock itself was massive, almost the size of a ship's wheel.

411

The combination locks she'd seen in her lock-picking practice all had a wheel that went from zero to ninety-nine. But this one went up to one hundred ninety-nine.

Ah, now it made sense. The code had deciphered to be twelve digits, which was too many numbers for a three-number combination. But if she was dealing with a safe that had a four-number or five-number combination, some of them triple digits, then the total number of digits worked.

Which meant that the first number was either one, fourteen, or one hundred and forty-nine. Fortunately, she could put her ear to the safe and hear the tumbler pin fall into place. Still, trials lay ahead of her.

She set to work.

Mrs. Watson felt as if she were in a dream. She knew that she was under surveillance. She knew that elsewhere in the château her companions were taking enormous risks. Yet here she and Sita Devi were, sitting on a sheepskin rug in their ballgowns, drinking wine and talking, while a fire crackled in the grate.

Were they young women again? Had time flown backward?

Sita Devi had described, in some detail, her yearlong pilgrimage to many of India's holy sites — the trip might have been undertaken to avoid being her son's adversary at court, but she'd come to appreciate the experience deeply.

Then she had made Mrs. Watson tell her all about her own years in India and Mrs. Watson had obliged.

"But I guess everything I experienced was from the colonial perspective," she said after a while. Her husband had been, after all, an army physician. And his presence in India, and consequently her own, had been a direct expression of colonial power and control.

"Maybe," said her old friend. "But it was also from your perspective and I've always enjoyed your perspective."

Mrs. Watson unclenched somewhere inside. "Thank you."

Sita Devi inclined her head. She looked like a very regal, very beautiful bird, with her gleaming black gown, golden mask, and tall purple plumes rising from that mask. Mrs. Watson gave an inner sigh of sheer aesthetic appreciation.

"I —" she began, and stopped.

"Yes?"

"Nothing," said Mrs. Watson, a little embarrassed. "Just that when I was in India I remembered you often."

She'd been happily married, but she'd worried, especially when she was happy, about Sita Devi.

"I —" She looked as embarrassed as Mrs. Watson felt. "I used to have violent thoughts about your duke."

She meant the late Duke of Wycliffe, the first person Mrs. Watson took up with after the maharani returned to India — and also her very last protector.

Mrs. Watson's eyes widened in surprise. She couldn't help giggling a little. "You did?"

Sita Devi sat cross-legged, one elbow on her knee, her chin in her palm. She turned her face to gaze into the flames leaping in the fireplace. "I loved to imagine him walking into doors. And then I would imagine you feeling a terrible revulsion for that clumsy dolt — and missing me very desperately."

"I did miss you desperately — I tormented myself with thoughts of the life we could have had, especially in the early years." Mrs. Watson's fingers knotted together. "Did . . . did you ever find anyone?"

She'd prayed fervently for Sita Devi's happiness. But she found herself growing ambivalent even as she asked the question.

If there was no one in Sita Devi's heart now, if . . .

"It took many years but" — her lips curved with a smile — "she did at last come into my life."

Disappointment stung Mrs. Watson. But it was a flash as brief as it was ferocious. A great big grin on her face, she leaned forward and took Sita Devi's hands. "Tell me all about her. Who is she, and how did you meet?"

Sita Devi drew back her hands, but only to cover her mouth as she laughed. "You wouldn't believe it."

"Then tell me faster."

"She is my daughter-in-law's aunt. She raised the girl so I've taken up with the woman who is more or less my son's mother-in-law!"

Mrs. Watson laughed, too. "Strengthening family ties, are we?"

"I try. Oh, that woman. What a temper." She shook her head, but the smile on her face was fondly indulgent.

"I'm so happy for you," said Mrs. Watson, meaning every word even as her heart again pinched a little.

"Thank you." This time, it was Sita Devi who took her hands. "Whatever happens tonight, Joanna, thank you for everything."

"Will these women do something? All they do is talk and talk," grumbled Poulaine.

When no one answered him, he grumbled some more and moved to the camera set up for what Charlotte thought of as room 5, one farther away from room 4, where Mrs. Watson and the maharani were.

"Now look at these two," he said with long-denied satisfaction. "They've just closed the door and already he's got her skirts up."

Charlotte exhaled and hoped that would hold his attention solidly.

"Shhh," hissed Barre from the far end.

Charlotte gave thanks for the blessed silence and turned the well-oiled dial. The final pin tumbled into place. She wiped away a bead of perspiration from the tip of her nose and opened the safe door.

A stack of gold bullions greeted her, so bright she was afraid they'd magnify the light from her cigarette tenfold. Above the bullions were pouches of gems. Charlotte enjoyed a good bauble, but alas, she was not that sort of thief, even though this must be misbegotten wealth.

A number of envelopes crowded the top

rack. She put back those filled with currencies and deeds. At last she came to three padded envelopes filled with photographic plates. Next to it, another envelope bulging with what appeared to be letters. There were two other envelopes, both dark in color, the contents of which she couldn't immediately judge. She removed another blanket, a pocket lantern, and a bobby's nightstick from her false stomach and stuffed all the envelopes in, cinching tight the belts that held the stomach shell in place.

Her loot stowed, she closed the safe and the panel and slid the single brick back in its place. They'd discussed blowing up the safe to avoid anyone guessing that it had been opened by someone who knew the combination. It was not terribly difficult to do: All she needed was to leave a suitable quantity of powder inside the safe and close the safe door with putty except for one tiny space through which threaded a slow-burning fuse. Then light the fuse, leave, and half an hour later, *kabloom.*

But if she didn't, Moriarty's suspicions would fall not on Charlotte Holmes, but on Madame Desrosiers, his former mistress, who had every opportunity to find and open the safe during the time he'd been held captive. So Charlotte didn't need to cover her tracks quite that thoroughly.

The blankets from her paunch she folded and set on the floor. The specially made pocket lantern, hardly bigger than a matchbox, she stuffed into her pocket, next to Lord Ingram's cigarette case. It would be perfect if Poulaine was still watching room 5, but he was back at room 4, which was closer to the exit. She weighed her choices and decided not to wait for him to move farther away: The sooner she got out of the passage, the sooner everyone could leave the premises.

Stubbing out a still-lit cigarette, the nightstick in hand, she sauntered toward the exit, the piss bucket on the other side an excellent excuse for stepping out.

As she neared the secret door, Poulaine struck a match to light a cigarette. In that flare of light, he glanced at her.

She held her breath.

"*Merde.* You are not Mercier. Who are you? What are you doing here?"

He charged toward her. She struck him across the cheek with her baton, then kicked him in the solar plexus. He stumbled back, crashing into the camera stand behind him.

Now where was the exit, exactly? But Poulaine was back on his feet. Another match flared — Barre, too, was coming.

"Drop your weapon or I'll shoot," growled Poulaine.

She fired her derringer first, at his hand. Poulaine howled as his revolver clattered to the floor. She rammed her shoulder into the exit. As soon as she and her stomach were through, she started to shove it shut. But Barre had reached the door and was pushing it open.

She wouldn't be able to hold it against him for much longer. Should she run? Or let the door go and shoot him as he crashed through?

All at once the door moved in her favor, closing. Her colleagues had joined her, Lord Ingram and Lieutenant Atwood, most likely. Together they pushed back against Barre, the door closing, closing.

And wouldn't close anymore.

Barre must have blocked it with something.

"Back!" Lord Ingram ordered in a fierce undertone.

As one they leaped back.

Barre fell through. Lord Ingram kicked him hard. Barre staggered back and hit the wall of the secret passage. They all three pushed the door shut and threw the bolt in place.

A hand settled on Charlotte's shoulder.

"Are you all right?" whispered Lord Ingram urgently. "Are you hurt?"

"I'm fine, perf—"

The floor shook. For a moment Charlotte thought it was because Barre had thrown himself at the door. But it was not that. Lieutenant Atwood struck a match. In the flare of light he, Lord Ingram, and Charlotte glanced at one another.

"So the rescue has started in earnest," said Lord Ingram, his voice tight. "They brought explosives."

Charlotte put a hand under her stomach to help with the weight. "We have to get out of here. Please have all the ladies come to room two."

They already knew where the spy port was in room 2. Charlotte went in and set a chair before it, and then yanked the cover from the bed to drape over the chair, blocking the spy port's view.

Mrs. Watson and the maharani arrived first. Without a word, they helped Charlotte remove her jacket, waistcoat, and shirt. And then, with greater care, her now-heavy false stomach. The false stomach was not simply a shell, but was lined with thick canvas where it rested against her torso, to prevent anything inside from falling out, and also because they'd always intend to take it —

420

and its contents — off her.

And to then turn it around and reattach it to her, so that it served as a bustle, albeit an unwieldy one that exerted considerable pressure on her lower back and abdomen, where the women tightened the straps hard, to prevent it from falling off.

Livia came into the room then. She opened her mouth. Charlotte immediately placed a finger before her own lips, shushing her sister. Under the bed, hidden from view by the blue silk bedskirt, the two guards who'd been blindfolded and stowed there were coming to, groaning softly behind their gags, and she didn't want them to overhear anything.

Mrs. Watson waved Livia toward Charlotte. Outside the window the sky glowed: Fireworks shot up and burst noisily into showers of brilliance.

The ball always concluded with a display of fireworks. But this was too early in the evening. Moriarty's people must have set off their own fireworks, to distract the guests from the real explosions.

Another tremor came from underfoot. Fear flashed in Livia's eyes, but she worked quickly to help Charlotte pull out the skirt of the ball gown that had been rolled up and tucked into the waistband of her trousers, along with two layers of petticoats. As Livia smoothed out the skirts in the back, Charlotte refastened the trousers that she still wore so that they wouldn't fall off her now-much-slimmer waist.

Meanwhile, Mrs. Watson had her own skirts up and the maharani was on her knees, fastening Charlotte's discarded items of men's clothing to the ribs of Mrs. Watson's reinforced bustle: They didn't want to leave behind any of Charlotte's menswear. If the guards were questioned, they wanted Moriarty's men to be looking for a portly young man, preferably a portly young man in a bright teal jacket.

That way they wouldn't look too closely at a woman in an unremarkable beige gown.

Charlotte signaled Mrs. Watson and the maharani, who were done secreting Charlotte's garments, to leave. She didn't want them all to rush back to the ballroom at the same time.

She took off her mask. Livia set a wig on Charlotte's head, covering up Charlotte's very short hair. Charlotte put on her mask again, this time reversing it, so that it was a solid and unexciting blue-grey, instead of teal on black-and-white.

She gestured at Livia, who nodded and slipped out of the door. She waited one minute and stepped out herself. Lord Ingram was waiting for her.

They had just stepped back into the ballroom when the ground shook. Chandeliers jerked and swung, crystal drops clinking together like a sudden rainstorm striking the windows. The guests, congregated near the windows for the best view of fireworks, looked up and around.

Unsettled murmurs rose.

"How much dynamite are they using?" wondered Charlotte.

If she were planning this rescue, she would have started in the chapel, which, according to Mr. Marbleton, had been guarded by two men when he last reconnoitered. Even if there were four men guarding it, it would still be possible to get them out of the way without too much trouble.

From there, all the way to the reinforced and heavily locked door before which Lord Ingram had turned back, there had been nothing that needed explosives, not even that very door. They must be trying to destroy something made of pure steel.

Charlotte glanced around at the gallery. Livia and Mr. Marbleton, who was again in proper evening attire, stood fifteen feet away. Lieutenant Atwood, Mrs. Watson, and the maharani were twenty feet away in a different direction. Everyone looked different. The horns on Lieutenant Atwood's mask was gone, as were the prominent purple plumes on Mr. Marbleton and the maharani's masks. And their masks, like Charlotte's, were now worn on the reverse, their former splendor exchanged for black and grey nondescriptness.

Lord Ingram leaned an elbow on the parapet. Even with his mask on, it was obvious he was frowning. "I don't understand why Moriarty would give away the combination to the safe."

Charlotte had been wondering about that, too. "Demolition isn't Moriarty's usual method. These people coming to rescuing him aren't his loyalists, but people they have hired. But what did they have to hire them with? Moriarty probably kept a tight control of his organization's finances and Madame Desrosiers certainly wouldn't help fund his rescue.

She should have realized that there was something ramshackle about the plan to blackmail the maharani, and others like her, into theft. The maharani did not make for the best candidate, if one wanted an art thief — nor did the aristocratic Grandmaman. Knowing what she did now, she could see that Moriarty's loyalists didn't have much to go on. It was difficult to get messages to or from a locked-up Moriarty. All the blackmail evidence was in a safe to which no one had access. And given the secretive nature of the organization, even the loyalists probably only knew a handful of quarries to whom they could apply pressure, cases they had worked on personally.

"While the loyalists still had infiltrators in the château, it's possible they got Moriarty to agree to give the combination to the dynamiters," she went on. "But I doubt he was happy about that. He could have given them a false combination, but I think it pleased him far more to give the correct one, but in such a way that he was sure no one would be able to use. Even if the dynamiters heard him tapping everything out on the day of the reception, it was in code — and in a code that he judged to be far beyond their ability to solve."

Outside the fireworks continued to go off. They were louder here, producing long, sinuous whistles as they shot up and solid bangs upon bursting. But they could no longer hold the full attention of the guests, who were looking around and talking uneasily with one another.

"And the dynamiters were happy with that?" asked Lord Ingram. "Some tapping they might or might not have heard and couldn't make heads or tails of?"

"His loyalists probably had to cough up everything they had and it's possible they aren't terribly pleased with him at the moment. But enough about Moriarty," said Charlotte. "When I spoke to Lady Ingram, I told her to leave. But she insisted that she owes Madame Desrosiers more loyalty than that."

Lord Ingram pulled his lips. He, obviously, did not care for Lady Ingram's concept of loyalty. But in this, Charlotte did have some sympathy for Lady Ingram, who had probably thought she needed to pretend to love him for only a short time, and that he'd then lose interest in her and start confessing his devotion to other women.

In Lady Ingram's shoes Charlotte, too, would have found that sort of devotion suffocating.

But Lord Ingram didn't let his opinion of his wife get in the way of his gallantry. "Do we need to help Madame Desrosiers against Moriarty?"

Charlotte shook her head inwardly. "I dropped my nightstick during the scuffle. I have only one bullet left in my derringer and a heavy weight hanging on my hindquarters. Maybe the other ladies are in bet-

426

ter condition to fight, but my sister has no training or experience with dangerous scenarios. I need to get her out as soon as possible."

The château shook again. Crystal beads fell from the chandeliers. Fortunately, most of the guests were still at the windows, and no one was struck from above. But the floor glittered with broken shards.

"There's an anarchist attack!" shouted a man.

"*Mon Dieu,* bombs, bombs!" yelled another.

Cries of panic ricocheted in the ballroom. Livia came running. Charlotte took her hand. "Remember, we expected chaos."

"Not this much chaos!"

Charlotte squeezed her sister's fingers. "But our response must be the same. Don't succumb to it. And don't add to it."

The ballroom was on the ground floor, but because the château was set on an island, it didn't have French doors leading to a terrace outside. On the balcony above the ballroom, they were at an advantage, as the rest of the guests must first come up the steps.

"Let's go," said Charlotte.

All the electric lights blinked out. Livia gasped aloud.

"Keep walking. You studied the architectural plans. You know the way. We are already along the wall, and there aren't any major obstacles in our way."

The art thieves currently on the premises had no reason to cut the electricity — greater chaos did them no favor when they didn't even know where the paintings were. She couldn't think of a reason Moriarty's people wanted the lights gone — they were already using explosives; too late for any subtlety to their endeavor.

This would be Madame Desrosiers's loyalists then, trying to slow down Moriarty's progress. There wasn't much else they could do when faced with invaders who deployed bombs as if they were throwing rice at a wedding.

The entire company headed for the coat check. The night was bitterly cold and they were all dressed for a heated interior, with hundreds of vigorously dancing guests. Unlike the night of the reception, for which the château had provided omnibuses to and from the nearest railway station, the ball had too many guests and its hours were too inconvenient for public transportation.

The guests, most of whom had arrived in private carriages, had been dropped off by the bridge, where their coaches turned

428

around to find a place outside the château. She'd heard from late-arriving guests that the line of carriages stretched more than half a mile either way along the country lane.

Had the ball proceeded normally, they would now be just done with supper, with much more dancing to come. In other words, it was too early for any carriages to have come back onto the grounds. And they would need to walk for least fifteen to twenty minutes in the frigid December air, if not more, before they reached their carriages.

Coats and cloaks, then, were an exceedingly good idea, especially for ladies with exposed shoulders and bosoms.

The fireworks were still going off, providing flashes of light for them to see their way down the grand staircase. The coat-checkers weren't at their stations. The gentlemen of the company kicked down the door and grabbed mantles for everyone.

Mr. Marbleton handed one to Livia and smiled at her. Charlotte, watching them, was filled with an unhappy premonition. She had told Livia — and Mrs. Watson and Lord Ingram — that Stephen Marbleton could be Moriarty's son. But when she had asked him, point-blank, about his parentage during the past summer he'd answered with ease and certainty that his father was Mr. Crispin Marbleton.

Then, she'd assumed that he preferred not to speak of the truth. But he'd since turned out to be the sort of man who did speak the truth, often at the cost of convenience, at least to those important to him. And yet he'd never mentioned to Livia that he was Moriarty's son.

And now they were on the same premises as Moriarty, albeit alongside hundreds of others, and in the middle of pandemonium.

The fireworks ended abruptly. Charlotte exhaled, feeling cold in the greater darkness.

The bulk of the guests, having made it out of the ballroom, were now coming down the grand staircase to the entry hall. They struck matches to light their way. Shouts of *Be careful!* and *Don't push! Don't push!* echoed against marble walls.

"Why are we just standing here?" whispered Livia vehemently. "People will get ahead of us!"

"Stay close to the walls," Charlotte warned. "And stay where you are."

The tide of guests flowed past them. The front hall, a wide, cavernous space, was now packed to the gills. Those with matches must be conserving them; the place was almost unnaturally dark.

Light appeared, causing a stir among the guests. At least a dozen men, holding torches, came down double-returned the staircase. They were not in evening attire, and their suits were covered with dust. Except for the man at the very center, surrounded by torchbearers. His clothes, while worn and too informal, were at least clean.

And his face — his face was so similar to Mr. Marbleton's that Charlotte had to look away.

Mr. Marbleton had turned his body in such a way that he blocked Livia's view of Moriarty. Or was he shielding her from the latter's gaze?

He'd already seen Moriarty, hadn't he?

The guests were loudly complaining that at last someone had thought of torches. For God's sake, why had it taken them so long? And what was the matter with the electrical plant, anyway?

But they fell silent as the men approached and parted them like the Red Sea. Charlotte had the sense that Moriarty was looking for someone. Madame Desrosiers? Or the thieves who had opened his safe and taken his hard-gathered hoard of evidence?

Cold air rushed in — someone had

431

opened the front doors.

"What's this? Why is this gate locked?" came the angry shouts of the would-be escapees in the courtyard, at the very front.

"We are looking for a portly blond man with a full beard. He may be wearing a teal jacket."

Ah, so it would seem that the guards upstairs had already been questioned.

"Do any of us look portly to you?"

"You may be slim, Monsieur, but please remain put for a minute or go back inside the château, where you'll be warmer."

"And what, be struck by falling chandeliers? Who are you, and why are you keeping us at this dangerous place?"

"I'm sorry, Monsieur, but you must stand back from the gate. I have my orders — and a loaded revolver."

"How dare you? My uncle is the president of the Third Republic. Get out of my way."

"Stand back!"

Charlotte, despite her warnings to Livia to stay near the wall, tiptoed so that she could see out of a window.

The guard, who had set his torch in a cresset by the wrought iron gate, raised his revolver. But the guests pressed forward, led by the irate nephew of the president. The guard fired his revolver at the sky. And while he still had his arm raised, half a dozen guests fell upon him, wrestled the revolver from his grip, and tied him up with the sleeves of his own jacket.

The president's nephew, revolver in hand, shot the padlock on the gate. Charlotte ducked in case the bullet ricocheted. But next came the sounds of cheers and hasty footsteps pounding over the bridge.

Even spoiled, half-drunk young men could be useful from time to time.

"Let's go," said Lord Ingram, "before they decide to lock the gates on the bridge."

The crowd pushed and shoved, but did nothing particularly unruly. Once over the bridge, the more impatient guests ran toward the gate. Charlotte and co. were only halfway there when they heard new shouts.

The front gate, then, must have been locked.

They, too, picked up their paces, not toward the front gate to their south but to the fences in the east.

Mr. Marbleton was up and over the fence in less than a second. Charlotte undid a number of hidden buttons on the skirt of her ball gown so that it wouldn't impede the movement of her limbs. Lord Ingram and Lieutenant Atwood raised her up until she could put her foot on a cross railing near the top.

Lord Ingram climbed up and gave her a hand — or rather, he gave her laden bustle a hand, lifting it clear of the finials. She pivoted around carefully and lowered herself. Mr. Marbleton caught her around the waist and set her down.

The maharani was the next. Mrs. Watson's petticoat caught on a finial, but without any hesitation she tore it loose. Livia waved aside everyone gathered to catch her and leaped off, landing in a perfect crouch position and then bouncing upright.

Now that all the ladies had scaled the obstacle, Lieutenant Atwood climbed over.

Lord Ingram, who could have done so at the same time, did not. "Lady Ingram is at the château. I should remain and make sure she's all right," he said without any inflection to his tone.

"No!" Mrs. Watson and Livia said in unison.

Then everyone, except Lord Ingram, turned toward Charlotte.

"Be careful then, and be quick. We'll see you in the morning," she said quietly.

He nodded and disappeared into the dark.

"How could you let him go?" Livia whispered vehemently.

"What was I to do? Climb back over the

fence and drag him over it? Let's go."

Their carriages were parked near a dirt lane that Mr. Marbleton had discovered on a previous outing. It cut across a large pasture to join a road that led to a village farther west and then the highway to Paris.

Livia, Mr. Marbleton, Mrs. Watson, and the maharani climbed into one carriage.

"Your carriage is closer to the dirt lane. You go first. We'll follow after a bit," Charlotte said as she closed the door for them.

She climbed into the other carriage, Lieutenant Atwood coming in after her. "It's good to put some space between our two carriages," he said.

He did not ask anything about Lord Ingram.

"So how does one disarm multiple opponents at a distance while barely lifting one's fingers?" she said after a while.

Lieutenant Atwood, who'd been glancing out of the window, turned toward her. "I wish I knew enough to tell you."

No questions on how long she planned to wait.

She exhaled. They had better leave. Lord Ingram had been in worse situations than this, she was sure. He would find his way out and back to them.

"Shall we —"

Footsteps, running. Lots of footsteps. Had they been discovered? Why now?

She loosened her mantle, grabbed Lieutenant Atwood by his necktie, and yanked him toward her. "Quick! Pretend you're my paramour!"

He stilled, not so much with shock as with unwillingness — or so it felt. But once he complied, his motion was swift and decisive. With one hand behind her, he maneuvered them so that she lay on the seat with him half above her. She pushed down her décolletage, exposing the top of her corset.

The carriage door yanked open. She shrieked as she sat up. And shrieked again as two burly men shone a bright lantern into her eyes. Pulling up her bodice ineffectually with one hand, while shielding her bosom equally ineffectually with her other hand, she stared at the intruders, gasping.

"Are you my husband's men? Please, please, it's not what you think it is. He — he told me that he can tell me things that will benefit Monsieur de Rochefoucault's business. He did. I'm only here for my husband's sake. You must believe me."

The man in front looked past her still-masked face to stare at her bounteous breasts.

"She's lying!" exclaimed Lieutenant Atwood. "She lured me out here. Please — please don't beat me. I would never have anything to do with a married woman. She told me she was a widow!"

She almost laughed at Lieutenant Atwood's fear and panicked regret.

The other man pulled at his companion. "Enough with these aristocratic degenerates. Let's go."

As they slammed the door closed, Charlotte screamed at Lieutenant Atwood, even as she pulled her mantle back up around herself, "Who are you calling a liar?"

He didn't answer, but she thought she heard muffled laughter.

She waited for her heart to stop pounding — and for the men to be out of sight. "Do you think they are far away enough now that we can go?"

The door was again yanked open.

Her surprised squeal was genuine this time as she threw herself across the carriage into Lieutenant Atwood's arms. "Please, Monsieur, you must save me from my husband. He will lock me in the attic and tell the world I've died."

"And here I thought you didn't even like *Jane Eyre*," said Lord Ingram, closing the door behind himself and taking a seat next to Lieutenant Atwood. He was breathing hard.

She gazed at him. There was a strange sensation in her chest, as if her heart just fell back into place. "It was a terrible plot twist but still a sensational one," she said, returning to her own seat. "Did you find Lady Ingram?"

"No." He knocked against the roof of the carriage, which pulled out of its spot and turned onto the dirt lane. "I came to my senses instead. I don't need to do everything for everyone, and I would do Lady Ingram a bigger favor by looking after her children."

Well, sometimes they do learn.

Charlotte adjusted her mantle — and smiled to herself. "In that case, I think we can term it a productive evening."

NINETEEN

Lieutenant Atwood alit a few streets away from Hôtel Papillon — he would approach on foot and get in from a service entrance. When Charlotte and Lord Ingram reached the house, Livia, Mrs. Watson, the maharani, and Mr. Marbleton were in the foyer, waiting. Mrs. Watson rushed to the door and embraced Lord Ingram. Even Livia, usually a much more reticent person, took him by the hands and told him how glad she was to see his safe return.

His throat moved as he thanked them. Charlotte sighed inwardly. For someone who did so much for others, he was always surprised when anyone returned the care in equal measure.

She asked everyone to go to bed. But when they had done so, she joined Lord Ingram and Lieutenant Atwood, once again back in Forêt's shoes — and clothes — not in the library, which had a number of

439

entrances, but in the much smaller but similarly book-lined study, to sort through the loot.

It didn't take her too long to locate letters from the maharani's son. To be on the safe side, in case Moriarty's subordinates had taken pictures of them, she picked up a few boxes of photographic plates and headed for the portable darkroom that Lieutenant Atwood had set up to develop images taken by Mr. Marbleton's detective camera.

"The pictures, perhaps — perhaps —" Lord Ingram stopped when Charlotte looked up. He took a sip of coffee, which he'd made to help them stay awake. "What am I saying? If there is to be disturbing content, then you should be the one looking through them, since you are the one least likely to be disturbed."

She inclined her head graciously. "I believe you are correct, sir."

He came with her, carrying the rest of the boxes of plates, and put on the safelight for her. The plates weighed at least a stone. She opened the first box and saw that the size of the plates was two and three quarters inches by three and a quarter inches, instead of five and half inches by six and half inches as she'd supposed: they were stored in stacks of ten and four stacks to a box.

There were eight such boxes. She would be looking at more than three hundred images.

Lord Ingram came back then with her coffee. She smiled at him, truly grateful, drank half the cup, and set to work.

About half of the plates portrayed sexual acts. Nothing too outlandish in terms of the acts themselves, so the illicitness would be in the individuals involved in the trysts: There were all sorts of pairings, and groups of up to five people.

Under different circumstances, Charlotte might have spent a little more time working out what all five of the partners were up to. But tonight, since they had nothing to do with the maharani or her son's letters, she set those plates aside after the three seconds she allotted for the study of each image.

The rest of the plates were, on first glance, much less scandalous. Those that did feature people had them fully clothed and not engaged in anything remotely carnal. And some shots had no humans in the frame, only land and buildings.

Charlotte found herself much more intrigued by what she could infer from these photographs. Was this group of men, none of whom she could recognize, but whose countries of origin she could easily deduce, not supposed to be meeting at all? The drays, so extraordinarily heavy, outside what looked to be a nondescript factory — what were they carrying?

Still, she set aside each after three seconds.

Until she came to one with a face she recognized; not one of the central figures meant to be captured, but someone on the periphery, very nearly lost in the crowd.

That one she stared at for an entire ten seconds.

She returned to the study to report that there was nothing related to the maharani in the images, only to see the men both wearing pained expressions, as if the papers before them had turned into a table full of swaying cobras, ready to strike.

"What's the matter?"

Lieutenant Atwood gestured at the documents. "These are state secrets Moriarty has collected."

"Of which states?"

"Britain, Germany, France, Russia, the Austro-Hungarians, the Ottoman Empire, and that's just the top of the stack."

"You are both agents of the British Crown, aren't you?"

Lieutenant Atwood shrugged. "Neither of us ranks high enough for this — and I, frankly, never want to."

"Give them to your superiors then."

"My previous superior *sold* state secrets," said Lord Ingram. "You exposed him, Holmes, if memory serves."

"Not to mention," said Lieutenant Atwood, "if we gave these to anyone, we would be considered privy to the information, even if we didn't glance past a few pages. Not necessarily a good thing for either of us."

"Then buy a safe at Banque de Paris, deposit everything, and deal with it later."

"I don't want to deal with it later either," said Lieutenant Atwood, rubbing the back of his neck. "It's all games that empires play with one another."

Lord Ingram sighed. "I'm beginning to come around to that view."

"Hasn't it always been like this?" asked Charlotte. "Haven't they always been games that empires play with one another?"

"Maybe," answered Lord Ingram. "But it can take a queen-and-country sort like me a while to work that out."

At the resignation in his tone, she felt a pang in her chest. She almost wished he had a few still-intact illusions.

"Is there a safe in this house where we can stow everything for now?"

Lord Ingram nodded.

"Then let's put these away and go to

sleep. This night has been long enough."

When they had done that, Lieutenant At-wood bid them good night and slipped away. Lord Ingram walked her to her room. Before the door, he pulled out a handker-chief bundle from his pocket.

"I don't think you had anything to eat, did you?"

She thought back. They'd had a small sup-per before starting for Château Vaudrieu. And since then, nothing. And suddenly she was very hungry.

He opened the handkerchief to reveal two small puff pastries. "This one has chocolate inside. This one, pâté, in case you are still refraining from sweet things."

"I am," she said, eating the pâté puff in two bites. Then she took the chocolate puff. "But tonight I'll make an exception."

He looked at her, not speaking. He was a man who exerted a pull simply by standing still, a viscerally physical presence. Beneath the black cashmere wool of his evening jacket, and his still-pristine shirt, his chest rose and fell.

She had used to wonder what it would be like to lay her head upon his chest, to feel each expansion of his lungs. At the time she'd had to imagine the texture of his skin and the contours of his musculature. Now she knew how he felt to her fingers and her lips. But she still had never laid her head on his chest.

She lifted her gaze. Their eyes met.

Whenever they'd been in such proximity before, she'd always wanted more — everything that was forbidden to her. Perhaps it was the fatigue at last catching up with her, but this moment she was . . . content to stand close to him, doing nothing but that.

He folded his empty handkerchief and put it back in his pocket. "Good night, Holmes."

"Good night, Ash," she murmured, and watched him walk away.

She entered her room, closed the door, leaned against it, and ate the chocolate puff in the smallest bites possible, thinking, as she did so, not of more and more and more chocolate puffs, but of him.

Of them.

Over a late breakfast, Charlotte read about the gas explosions at Château Vaudrieu. Apparently the guards had first thought they were bombs, which prompted them to prevent the guests from leaving, in an attempt to locate the perpetrators. Once it was clear they were but gas explosions, all was well — or as well as could be with gas explosions.

Some at the château suffered minor injuries. But Herr Albrecht, the owner, was now on hand and all would be well. No mention was made of the château's electrical plant, which obviated most of the need for gas. Or the ball's hosts, Madame Desrosiers and her brother Monsieur Plantier.

Excellent fiction, better than some of the stories Livia had made her read.

Mrs. Watson and the maharani, still veiled, came in and sat down at the breakfast table. Charlotte slid over an envelope. The maharani, through her veil, perused its contents.

"Thank you, ladies." She looked at Charlotte. "Obviously no contingency plan was needed last night, but I'm still curious as to what it would have been."

"The Van Dyck that I saw in Château Vaudrieu on the night of the reception was a forgery." Charlotte took a bite of her plain boiled egg. "The folds of Mary's robe depict a brachistochrone curve, the path of fastest descent of a bead sliding from point A to point B under uniform gravity and with no friction."

"A what?" said Mrs. Watson and the maharani together.

Charlotte took out a pencil and drew a quick diagram to show the ladies what a brachistochrone curve looked like, set

446

against two other lines of descent, one straight, one polygonal. "This is more or less what I saw in the forgery, with three shadowy dots representing the three beads rolling down each line at different speeds."

Mrs. Watson and the maharani glanced at each other, as if Charlotte had spoken in Etruscan.

"Van Dyck died in sixteen forty-one," she explained further. "The brachistochrone curve wasn't developed until more than fifty years after his death. Therefore the painting cannot possibly be authentic. Lord Ingram and I believe that the painting's owner put it up for sale under duress. In that case, it made every sense that the owner would have hired an art forger and given the fake to Château Vaudrieu.

"So our ally called on the owner and asked to have the original by this afternoon — or risk exposure that he tried to sell a forgery at a respectable venue. But of course, given that there is no longer a need for the original, our ally has sent a cable first thing this morning and told the owner that he could keep his heirloom."

"I see," said the maharani, shaking her head a little.

She rose, went to the fireplace, and burned the incriminating letters. When she returned to the breakfast table, she took out an envelope of her own and set it before Mrs. Watson.

Mrs. Watson looked in the envelope and immediately pushed it back toward the maharani. "I said I wouldn't take anything from you."

The maharani wagged a finger. "No, you said we would discuss payments after I had what I want. And now I have it."

"I didn't do this for payment," insisted Mrs. Watson, now looking insulted.

The maharani leaned toward her. "I know that. And I am grateful. But remember what you told me all those years ago? That women should be valued for their work and that women, especially, should not devalue the work of other women. I do not have twenty thousand pounds, but I can still defray your expenses and remunerate everyone for their time."

"But —"

"Set an example for the young lady, Joanna. If you don't let me pay you, I'm sure she won't let you pay her. And everyone's work here, especially hers, should be fairly compensated."

Mrs. Watson, who'd made a point of teaching Charlotte not to let herself be undervalued, could not argue with that. She accepted the envelope.

The maharani turned to Charlotte. She'd set her hands together on the table, her fingers interlaced. Now her fingers flexed, as if she felt a twitch of nerves. "Miss Charlotte, allow me to extend an apology to you. I did not realize it then, but had Sherlock Holmes been able-bodied, I would probably have begged him for help, his lack of experience in robbing French châteaus notwithstanding.

"Whereas even after you revealed that you were responsible for Sherlock Holmes's achievement and reputation, my first, second, and third reaction was still no, I could not entrust this task to a woman.

"I have, I believe, been an excellent ruler of my small realm. So I, of all people, should know better than to deny a woman an opportunity simply because she is a woman. But being a woman of power in the world of men has not always taught me the right lessons. I'm afraid that I'd begun to think that I came to be where I was because I was intrinsically exceptional, different from other women, and not that my particular circumstances afforded me chances that they could not even dream of."

She placed her hands over Charlotte's. "I'm glad you made me see differently. But you shouldn't have needed to. And for that, please accept my sincere regret."

The maharani left first, to catch a steamer leaving Marseille for Bombay. Leighton Atwood would leave last, after he spread the news about the loss of a great many photographic plates in the gas explosions at Château Vaudrieu.

The rest of the company left that evening to cross the channel. The next morning they were in London. There Lord Ingram said good-bye to the ladies and Mr. Marbleton, and continued on to his brother's estate.

A letter awaited him there, a letter he'd been hoping to receive. And when he'd read it, he closed his eyes and breathed a sigh of relief.

He met his brother and sister-in-law. He played with his children and theirs. And when his sister-in-law had gathered all the children for a special tea party, he summoned Miss Yarmouth for a private meeting.

This time she did not tell him not to answer her yet. She understood that he had made up his mind.

"My lord," she murmured as she came into his brother's study, which he'd borrowed for the occasion.

450

She closed the door. He left his seat, walked past her, and reopened it a crack. After all, Holmes considered him a stickler for propriety. He might as well live up to her opinion.

They sat down on two sides of a large mahogany desk, she gingerly, he, with every assurance.

"Miss Yarmouth, I have received a letter from Miss Potter. Miss Potter was my own governess, an excellent and admirable woman, and she has graciously agreed to come work for me and take charge of the children."

"I — I see," stammered Miss Yarmouth.

"I thank you for your proposal, but I do not intend to marry again after my divorce. At least, not in the near term. Therefore I must wish you the very best of luck in Australia. May you find everything there that your heart seeks." He slid an envelope across the table to her. "And you will please allow me to contribute to your dowry, in gratitude for your generosity and kindness to the children."

She touched the envelope and drew back her hand, as if scalded. "But the children — my lord, they will be thrust into the care of a stranger."

"Temporarily, until Miss Potter is no

longer a stranger to them. And I will be there, too, to help them get to know one another."

"Surely —"

"Surely, even if I were intent on matrimony, I must think of myself, too, and not only of my children. I do not believe we shall suit, Miss Yarmouth, and there really isn't anything else to say on the matter. You may return to your duties."

She rose slowly, curtsied, and left, this time holding the envelope tight.

His answer might sting, but the contents of the envelope should go a long way toward soothing any hurt pride.

And now, one less problem in his life.

Mr. Marbleton came with the ladies to Mrs. Watson's house. To celebrate their success, they went out for a sumptuous dinner at Verrey's. Afterward, Charlotte and Mrs. Watson both retired early, leaving the duty of chaperoning Livia entirely to Livia herself.

It was a rare clear night for this time of the year. There were actually stars overhead, small, cold twinkles of light, visible from the window of the afternoon parlor. She and Mr. Marbleton each nursed a finger of whisky, but she didn't need the *eau de vie* in her throat to feel a warmth glowing inside.

She loved summer and he was the most summery man she had ever met.

"I'm leaving in the morning," she said softly, not wanting to face that eventuality herself. "As much as I'd like to remain longer, I simply must go home before my parents realize that I've been gone awhile."

"Will you be all right at home?"

"I think so."

She felt more . . . sturdy. She had not made any particularly crucial contribution to the great endeavor at Château Vaudrieu this past fortnight, but she'd acquitted herself conscientiously. *And* she'd finished her Sherlock Holmes story, possibly the greatest solo undertaking of her life.

Having proved something to herself, she should be able to bear life at home better — at least for a while.

"I must also leave soon," he said. "Remember what I said the other day about having someone inside Moriarty's organization?"

Her stomach tightened at the mention of that name — it was impossible to entirely disregard Charlotte's pronouncements. But she trusted him enough that she was willing to believe he wasn't Moriarty's son — and that if he were, he would have already told her.

"Yes, I remember," she said. "Charlotte thought it might have been Madame Desrosiers."

"Now that Moriarty is back and considers Madame Desrosiers a traitor, our advantage is going to evaporate into thin air. I should find my parents and my sister and tell them what I know firsthand, so that together we can decide what to do next."

She had thought that might be the case, but still, she wished . . .

There was so much she wished for.

"Have you . . . have you ever heard of Andalusia?" he asked, a little hesitantly.

She gazed at him a moment and smiled, her heart as buoyant as a hydrogen balloon. "Andalusia, in the south of Spain, where the Alhambra is? Yes, I've heard of it. Why do you ask?"

That night, Livia dreamed of the Court of the Lions at the Alhambra and of the gardens at the Alcázar in Seville, all balmy and light-drenched. She woke up feeling wistful but not terribly sad. When she descended for breakfast, Mr. Marbleton and Charlotte were already at table, the former staring intently at the paper, the latter

454

finishing up a slice of plain toast with her eggs and looking suitably forlorn about it.

Charlotte rose as Livia sat down. "I'm done. Will you be wanting your usual breakfast?"

"I think so."

"I'll let the kitchen know."

When she'd left, Livia turned her attention to Mr. Marbleton. "Before we say our good-byes, shall we affix some method of communication? Given my parents' current appreciation for the Openshaws, you can probably write to me directly as young Mr. Openshaw. But if there is to be a fallout between the Holmeses and the Openshaws someday, should we have a second system in place?"

He looked up and slowly set aside the paper, his face unusually wan. "I have done something terrible, Miss Olivia."

Her stomach lurched. "Oh?"

"I broke my promise to you: I have already read your Sherlock Holmes story."

This was the last thing she'd expected him to say. "You have?"

Did you — did you like it?

As if he'd heard her question, he said, "You should be enormously proud of yourself. It's absolutely extraordinary. I could read another hundred stories like that and

455

still want more."

She should be floating on clouds. She'd imagined him complimenting her story, but not even in her wildest daydreams had she anticipated such extravagant praise. And yet her gladness was like a bird with broken wings, unable to take flight.

His tone. His tone was all wrong. What had she thought of only last night? That he was the most summery man she'd ever met? But now his tone made her think of abandoned cemeteries and snow-covered ruins.

"Do you really think so?" she said, her voice sounding disembodied to her own ears.

"I have never been more truthful."

Silence fell, a silence with teeth and claws. She knew, didn't she? She knew it would come to this.

"It has been a lovely two weeks," he said, sounding forced.

Under the table, her hands clenched. "Yes, very lovely."

"But I think we both know that we've always been on borrowed time. I cannot give you either safety or stability. I can't even take you away from home except on fraudulent pretenses."

I don't mind, she wanted to say. *I don't want safety or stability with someone else. I'm*

happy with borrowed time and stolen mo-
ments with you.

But all that made it past her rapidly closing throat was a croaked, "I see."

"It would be — I mean, I have already
been selfish enough, taking your time. It
would be unpardonable for me to continue
to do so, knowing that I can offer you nothing of value."

Her nails dug into the center of her palm.
Is laughter something of no value? Is being
seen and heard something of no value? What
of the comfort I feel in my own skin when I am
with you?

"You don't need to explain," she said. "I
understand. I do."

"Do you? Were my circumstances anything
other than what they are, nothing and no
one would have dragged me away from you.
But there are some things I cannot change,
however much I wish and pray otherwise."

Her ears rang. Was this to be the end for
them? So abrupt and so . . . final, when last
night they had been speaking fervently of a
future. A future of stolen moments and
fraudulent pretenses, yes, but surely a future
that included sunny, fragrant Andalusia was
worth fighting for, by whatever means necessary.

"Please look after yourself," she said, her

voice barely audible.

"I will," he said, a bit of the old fervency to his tone. "And I will look for the further adventures of Sherlock Holmes from every last corner in the world."

He rose and bowed. "Forgive me for not writing. It will hurt too much to be reminded that I cannot be near you."

With another bow, he left the breakfast parlor.

Ten minutes after the carriage left, taking Livia and Mrs. Watson to the railway station, Mr. Marbleton was still standing by the window in the dining room, looking out at the direction in which they'd disappeared.

Charlotte watched him for another minute. "I take it something unwelcome happened."

He did not look at her. "There was a message in the papers for me this morning. Moriarty has my parents."

The fall of Madame Desrosiers always portended ill for the Marbletons. But Charlotte had not expected such a rapid development. "How?"

"I don't know, exactly. If Madame Desrosiers didn't have time to take all her secrets with her when she fled Château Vaudrieu, and if she'd left behind something concerning us . . ."

"How do you know it's not a ruse?"

He still stared out the window, his hand on the window frame. "Only the four of us know this particular code. Only the four of us and no one else."

Charlotte left the breakfast parlor. When she returned with a glass of whisky, he was sitting on the floor, his hands covering his face.

Overnight, he had lost everything.

She set down the glass on the table. "What does Moriarty want?"

He expelled a shaky breath. "Me."

"Because you are his son?"

He shuddered. "Because I'm his son."

"Why didn't you tell my sister the truth? I thought you always tell the truth to those who matter."

He laughed bitterly and at last looked up, his eyes bleak. "Nobody can be that honest, Miss Charlotte, especially to those who matter. My parents hid the truth of my parentage. I was the one who found out and confronted them. And then of course I wished I'd never done either. That I'd had the good sense to not question the comforting lies they had told for my sake."

He struggled up from the floor. She remembered his grace and agility, scaling the fence at Château Vaudrieu. Now he moved as if weighted down by shackles.

He picked up the glass of whisky and drained its contents. Staring at the empty glass, he said, as if to himself, "I don't want Miss Livia to know that I'm going to Moriarty. Let her believe that I remain at large, spending my days in little hilltop villages in the Alpes-Maritimes, overlooking the Mediterranean. Let her believe . . . let her believe anything she wants, as long as it's not the truth."

Livia and Mrs. Watson would not have reached the train station yet. Would Livia be weeping in the carriage right now, with Mrs. Watson trying to console her? Or would she clamp down hard and not say anything, not even to Mrs. Watson?

"My sister is a very intelligent woman," said Charlotte, her voice ever so slightly hoarse. "You think she cannot guess the truth?"

Mr. Marbleton wiped the heel of his hand across his eyes. "Then let her guess, but still be able to fool herself. Let her have that one last gift from me."

EPILOGUE

Holmes's letter reached Lord Ingram the next morning just as he was about to leave his brother's estate with his children in tow. For the first time in a long time, she wrote in her own version of shorthand, telling him of Mr. Marbleton's departure.

Of Moriarty's son, forced to return to the fold.

How quickly things changed. One moment Andalusia was within sight; the next it was completely out of reach.

He hadn't planned to stop in London, except to change trains. But now he would break his journey and call on Holmes. He would not wait any longer. She had asked him what he'd thought when Mr. Marbleton brought up Andalusia. And he had given her an answer that was convenient, rather than true.

But this time, when he saw her, he would tell her the truth. Which was that he thought

461

often of Andalusia. That he longed for it. That he would give his eyeteeth for it, if only he had the courage.

Could they still go together this spring, or perhaps sooner?

He settled Lucinda and Carlisle at his town house and started for Mrs. Watson's. He was nervous, far more nervous than he had been before he proposed to or married Lady Ingram. And as his hansom cab approached Mrs. Watson's house, he felt light-headed with both dread and anticipation.

Was this the right choice, after all? He could no longer judge. He never could.

All he knew was that it was the only choice and he would simply have to accept any and all consequences.

He alit before her house, gripping tightly onto his walking stick. Perhaps he should have brought her something. Flowers. Or cake, if she had managed to reverse Maximum Tolerable Chins. But he was empty-handed, with only a burning desire to see her.

Mr. Mears settled him in the afternoon parlor and went off to announce his arrival. His heart thudded. His mouth turned dry.

"Miss Holmes will be here momentarily," Mr. Mears returned to inform him.

The doorbell rang. Had he come on Mrs.

Watson's at-home day when she received her friends? Would he be awkwardly justifying his presence to curious strangers? Mr. Mears excused himself to answer the door.

He caught a woman's voice, speaking low and urgently, and then —

Exactly the outcome he didn't want, two sets of footsteps coming up the stairs.

The new caller was shown into the afternoon parlor. At the sight of her, his dismay turned into a surprised and bemused pleasure. "Mrs. Treadles!"

Alice Treadles was Inspector Treadles's wife. And Inspector Robert Treadles, Lord Ingram's friend, had been heavily involved in some of Holmes's cases. He hadn't known, however, that Mrs. Treadles knew Holmes well enough to visit her not at her office, but on a social call at home.

Mrs. Treadles was equally flabbergasted to see him. "My lord! I hope I'm not imposing dreadfully. Robert told me, confidentially of course, that in a hurry I would more easily find Miss Holmes here, rather than at 18 Upper Baker Street. I did knock on 18 Upper Baker Street as well, but there was no one home and —"

Holmes came in then, lovely, unflappable Holmes, in a dress that was a near literal representation of a Christmas tree. Mrs.

Treadles stared at her, agape.

"Mrs. Treadles to see you, too, Miss," said Mr. Mears, and left.

"Mrs. Treadles, very good to meet you at last," said Holmes. Her gaze turned to him, and lingered for a moment. "My lord, excellent to see you, as always. Do please sit down, everyone."

But Mrs. Treadles did not sit. She rushed over to Holmes, took her by the hands, and said, "Miss Holmes — please, Miss Holmes, you and your brother must help us. Robert — Inspector Treadles — he's been arrested on suspicion of murder!"

ACKNOWLEDGMENTS

Kerry Donovan, for her saintly patience.

Kristin Nelson, for super-agenting day in and day out.

Janine Ballard, for making me write better.

Kate Reading, for bringing the Lady Sherlock books to life in audio.

My poor brain, for having held up for this book.

And you, if you are reading this, thank you. Thank you for everything.

ABOUT THE AUTHOR

USA Today bestselling author **Sherry Thomas** is one of the most acclaimed historical fiction authors writing today, winning the RITA Award two years running and appearing on innumerable "Best of the Year" lists, including those of *Publishers Weekly, Kirkus Reviews, Library Journal,* Dear Author, and All About Romance. Her novels include *A Study in Scarlet Women* and *A Conspiracy in Belgravia,* the first two books in the Lady Sherlock series; *My Beautiful Enemy;* and *The Luckiest Lady in London.*

She lives in Austin, Texas, with her husband and sons.

CONNECT ONLINE
sherrythomas.com